P9-EAY-416

Library Resource Center
Renton Technical College
3000 N.E. 4th St.
Renton, WA 98056

Ready-to-Use

READING PROFICIENCY LESSONS & ACTIVITIES

8th Grade Level

DISCARD

Gary Robert Muschla

JOSSEY-BASS
A Wiley Company
www.josseybass.com

428
.40711
MUSCHLA
2002

Copyright © 2002 by The Center for Applied Research in Education.

Published by Jossey-Bass
A Wiley Imprint
989 Market Street, San Francisco, CA 94103-1741 www.josseybass.com

No part of this publication may be reproduced, stored in a retrieval system, or transmitted in any form or by any means, electronic, mechanical, photocopying, recording, scanning, or otherwise, except as permitted under Section 107 or 108 of the 1976 United States Copyright Act, without either the prior written permission of the Publisher, or authorization through payment of the appropriate per-copy fee to the Copyright Clearance Center, Inc., 222 Rosewood Drive, Danvers, MA 01923, (978) 750-8400, fax (978) 750-4470, or on the web at www.copyright.com. Requests to the Publisher for permission should be addressed to the Permissions Department, John Wiley & Sons, Inc., 111 River Street, Hoboken, NJ 07030, (201) 748-6011, fax (201) 748-6008, e-mail: permcoordinator@wiley.com.

Permission is given for individual classroom teachers to reproduce the student handouts and sample test questions for classroom use. Reproduction of these materials for an entire school system is strictly forbidden.

Many of the illustrations are reproductions from the Dover Clip Art and Dover Pictorial Series, and also *Art Explosion*, Nova Development Corporation.

Jossey-Bass books and products are available through most bookstores. To contact Jossey-Bass directly call our Customer Care Department within the U.S. at (800) 956-7739, outside the U.S. at (317) 572-3993 or fax (317) 572-4002.

Jossey-Bass also publishes its books in a variety of electronic formats. Some content that appears in print may not be available in electronic books.

Library of Congress Cataloging-in-Publication Data:
Muschla, Gary Robert.
Ready-to-use reading proficiency lessons & activities : eighth-grade level / by Gary Robert Muschla.
p. cm. — (TestPrep curriculum activities library)
ISBN 0-13-042446-3
1. Reading (Secondary)—United States. 2. Education, Secondary—Activity programs—United States. 3. Eighth grade (Education)—United States. I. Title. II. Series

LB1632 .M87 2002
428.4'071'2—dc21 2002019363

Printed in the United States of America
FIRST EDITION
HB Printing 10 9 8 7 6 5 4 3 2

For Judy and Erin

About the Author

Gary Robert Muschla received his B.A. and M.A.T. from Trenton State College and taught at Appleby School in Spotswood, New Jersey for more than 25 years. He spent many of his years in the classroom specializing in reading and language arts. In addition to his years as a classroom teacher, Mr. Muschla has been a successful writer, editor, and ghostwriter. He is a member of the Authors Guild and the National Writers Association.

Mr. Muschla has authored several other resources for teachers, including: *Writing Resource Activities Kit* (The Center for Applied Research in Education, 1989), *The Writing Teacher's Book of Lists* (Prentice Hall, 1991), *Writing Workshop Survival Kit* (The Center, 1993), *English Teacher's Great Books Activities Kit* (The Center, 1994), *Reading Workshop Survival Kit* (The Center, 1997), and *Ready-to-Use Reading Proficiency Lessons & Activities, 4th-Grade Level* (The Center, 2002).

With his wife, Judy, he has co-authored *The Math Teacher's Book of Lists* (Prentice Hall, 1995), *Hands-on Math Projects with Real-Life Applications* (The Center, 1996), *Math Starters! 5- to 10-Minute Activities to Make Kids Think, Grades 6–12* (The Center, 1999), *The Geometry Teacher's Activities Kit* (The Center, 2000), and *Math Smart: Ready-to-Use Activities to Motivate and Challenge Students, Grades 6–12* (The Center, 2002).

Mr. Muschla currently writes and works as a consultant in education.

Acknowledgments

My most special thanks go to my wife, Judy, whose support of my work over the years has always made the job of writing easier. I also have her to thank for selecting the art that livens the pages of this book.

Thanks also to my daughter, Erin, who was the first reader of the manuscript and who caught numerous typos and oversights.

I also appreciate the efforts of Michelle Di Giovanni, whose comments and suggestions helped me to polish this book.

Special thanks to Susan Kolwicz, my editor, for her support and encouragement in the writing of yet another book. Her guidance and recommendations helped me to focus and fashion my ideas into a practical resource.

I also wish to thank Diane Turso, my development editor, for her help in putting the manuscript into its finished form. Thanks, too, to Jackie Roulette, my production editor, and Robyn Beckerman, my formatter, who turned this work into a book.

Finally, I would like to thank my colleagues and students, who, over the years, have made teaching and writing a fulfilling and satisfying career.

About Reading and Language Arts Instruction

Reading and language arts are the foundation of literacy. The two subjects are closely intertwined and together encompass all the skills that comprise language. Individuals who cannot read and who have not mastered the skills of spoken and written language suffer a severe handicap in our society.

Mastery of all the other subjects in school starts with a student's ability to read and communicate. Whether it is social studies, science, or the word problems and theorems of mathematics, the ability to read and share ideas in written and spoken form are at the heart of learning.

Because of their importance, reading and language arts, in one form or another, are prominent on virtually all standardized tests. The burden on teachers is clear: Not only must you teach the concepts and skills contained in your reading and language arts curriculums, you must also prepare your students for standardized tests. Thus, proficiency and performance have become dual goals. A solid curriculum, effective teaching, and a focused program of test preparation will undoubtedly enhance both the proficiency and performance of your students.

My best wishes to you in your teaching efforts, as you help your students master the skills of reading and language arts.

Gary Robert Muschla

How to Use This Resource

Ready-to-Use Reading Proficiency Lessons & Activities, 8th-Grade Level is divided into six sections and an appendix. The material in this book is designed to help your students gain proficiency as you prepare them for the reading and language arts portions of the typical eighth-grade standardized test. This resource contains 43 study sheets, 108 worksheets, and 14 practice tests. All are reproducible for easy implementation.

Here is a sample of what you will find in each section:

- **Section 1: Analogies.** This section includes seven worksheets that provide your students with practice in how to solve and complete analogies. Study Sheets 1-A, "Strategies for Solving Analogies," and 1-B, "Common Types of Analogies," help students to recognize the relationships that are crucial to understanding analogies. A practice test is included.
- **Section 2: Vocabulary.** This section contains eight study sheets and 18 worksheets. Topics include base words, prefixes and suffixes, synonyms and antonyms, words with multiple meanings, homographs, homophones, easily confused words, and idioms. Study Sheet 2-H, "Words to Know," is particularly helpful because it contains words that regularly appear on eighth-grade standardized tests. Three practice tests are included in this section.
- **Section 3: Reading Comprehension.** This section includes five study sheets and 30 worksheets. Skills include understanding characterization, inferences and conclusions, main idea and details, sequence, comparison and contrast, cause and effect, predictions, and fact versus opinion. Moreover, examples of specific types of literature are used in the activities. For example, students will work with realistic fiction, persuasive essays, informational articles, a biographical sketch, myths, and poems. This section also includes activities for interpreting a climograph and utilizing data from a table. Three practice tests complete the section.
- **Section 4: Spelling.** This section includes four study sheets and 12 worksheets. The worksheets range from finding misspelled words in groups and phrases to finding misspelled words while proofreading. The study sheets focus on spelling strategies, spelling rules, and, most important, an extensive list of words that regularly appear on the spelling portions of eighth-grade standardized tests. Two practice tests are included.

- **Section 5: Language Mechanics and Word Usage.** This section contains 22 study sheets and 26 worksheets. Just some of the skills covered in this section include recognizing types of sentences; simple subjects and predicates; common, proper, and possessive nouns; verbs; pronouns; agreement; punctuation; capitalization; double negatives; and models of friendly and business letters. The study sheets for this section clarify the various rules that apply to language mechanics and word usage. Three practice tests complete this section.
- **Section 6: Language Expression.** This section includes two study sheets and 15 worksheets. The section focuses on expressing ideas clearly and contains worksheets on topic sentences, details, building sentences, and organizing paragraphs. Two practice tests are included.
- **Appendix.** This section contains information for teachers, parents, and students. It includes reproducible handouts, such as "What Parents Need to Know about Standardized Tests," "Preparing Your Child for Standardized Tests," and "Test-taking Tips for Students." The material of the Appendix can help you create a positive test-taking environment in your classroom.

The material throughout this book reflects the typical eighth-grade reading and language arts curriculum, with emphasis on those skills that appear on standardized tests. Because the skills are curriculum-based, you have much flexibility in how to utilize the study sheets, worksheets, and practice tests. You may use them to introduce new material, as reviews of skills you have already taught, or as a unit of preparation for standardized tests.

The 43 reproducible study sheets offer concise information on specific topics. For example, Study Sheet 2-A, "Common Prefixes," lists prefixes we use all the time and provides their definitions. A thorough understanding of prefixes can help students understand the meanings of words. Most of the study sheets of this book can be distributed and reviewed in one session; a few of the longer ones—for example, Study Sheet 4-C, "Basic Spelling Rules"—are best used over the course of a few sessions to avoid overloading your students with information.

The study sheets are labeled according to section, for example, 1-A, 1-B, 1-C, etc. (The use of letters distinguishes the study sheets from the worksheets.) Titles are clear and practical, stating precisely what the study sheet contains. For example, Study Sheet 5-H, "Rules for Capitalization," focuses on capitalization, while Study Sheet 5-L, "Possessive Nouns," provides information on how to recognize and write possessive nouns.

The 108 reproducible worksheets address numerous eighth-grade reading and language arts skills with the major focus being on those skills that appear on standardized tests. The title of each worksheet indicates the skill that is covered, making it easy to find the worksheets you need in your daily lessons. Thus, the table of contents of this book serves as a skills list. The worksheets of each section are generally sequential, following the development of most eighth-grade curriculums. However, each worksheet also stands alone, giving you the flexibility to use the worksheets that complement your teaching program.

The worksheets are numbered according to section, 1-1, 1-2, 1-3, etc. The first worksheet in Section 1, therefore, is 1-1, "Identifying Relationships." Worksheet 5-17, "Using Who, Whom, Whose, and Who's Correctly," is the seventeenth worksheet of Section 5, while Worksheet 6-6, "Combining Sentences and Expressing Ideas Clearly," is the sixth worksheet of Section 6.

Teaching suggestions for the worksheets are included in each section. The teaching suggestions identify skills to highlight, note study sheets that complement the worksheet, and offer tips on implementation.

Answer keys are included in each section for all of the worksheets. Once your students have completed the worksheets, you should correct their work and explain any questions that your students found confusing. You might collect and correct the worksheets yourself, or you might find it more efficient to simply have students correct their own papers. Whichever way you choose to correct your students' work, be sure to discuss any questions they may have. The material on the worksheets is the kind of material they will likely encounter on standardized tests.

The practice tests that conclude each section are based on the worksheets and cover the skills addressed in the section. The tests are set up in a standardized format with answer sheets. Having your students use the answer sheets will give them practice in completing the answer sheets for standardized tests. Like the worksheets, you should correct the tests and discuss any questions that were confusing to your students.

The Appendix contains useful information for teachers, parents, and students. Several reproducible handouts are included. These handouts are designed to help inform parents about standardized tests—what the tests include and how parents can help prepare their children.

The study sheets, worksheets, and practice tests of this resource can support you in your efforts to help your students become proficient in reading and language arts. They can enhance your students' performance on standardized tests.

Contents

Library Resource Center
Renton Technical College
3000 N.E. 4th St.
Renton, WA 98056

Section 1

Analogies

Analogies test the ability of students to reason with words and recognize relationships between ideas. Solving analogies promotes a student's critical thinking, vocabulary, and ability to identify associations. Analogy tests are found on many standardized tests.

Success on an analogy test is based on two important factors: an understanding of words, and the use of specific strategies that can help uncover the links between the most subtle relationships. To help prepare your students for an analogy test, distribute copies of the study sheets of this section.

Study Sheet 1-A, "Strategies for Solving Analogies," provides steps that your students should take when attempting to solve analogies. Caution your students that these steps are necessary, because some analogies are deceptive.

Discuss the information on the study sheet with your students. Review what an analogy is and how the words that make it up are read. Explain each strategy. The first strategy—reading slowly and concentrating on the words—seems simplistic, yet sometimes the words that make up an analogy are so elementary that students miss the relationship. This can be avoided by diligent exercise of the second strategy: Find the relationship. Encourage your students to seek the connections between the words. Sometimes the relationship will be obvious; for example, the pairs of words may be synonyms. Sometimes, however, the relationships may be hard to identify, being that of purpose or fine degree. (Types of relationships are discussed on Study Sheet 1-B, which follows.) For analogies in which the relationship is not apparent, suggest to your students that they put the pairs of words in logical sentences. Pairing the words in sentences can often reveal relationships. Discuss the example on the study sheet, emphasizing that the sentence that makes the most sense is the best choice to complete an analogy.

Study Sheet 1-B, "Common Types of Analogies," details ten analogous relationships that appear often on analogy tests. Discuss each relationship and example with your students.

Explain that the ideas in an analogy must be related properly, and warn students not to choose an answer in which the order of ideas is incorrect. For example, on Study Sheet 1-B, in the relationship *place and object*, the correct order of ideas is "Arctic : polar bear :: forest : squirrel." The *place* in each pair of words comes first. The reverse, *object and place*, is also true: "polar bear : Arctic :: squirrel : forest." However, the ideas cannot be randomly thrown out of order. "Arctic : polar bear ::

squirrel : forest" is not correct because the order of ideas is not consistent. Misplaced order is a common mistake on analogy tests.

Explain that using the strategies of Study Sheet 1-A will help your students to recognize the relationships that are found on Study Sheet 1-B. Together, these two study sheets can help your students understand analogies.

This section also contains seven worksheets and one practice test of analogies. Although the worksheets generally progress in degree of difficulty, each stands alone and you may assign them in the manner that best meets the needs of your students. To help your students master analogies, consider assigning the worksheets as a unit or over a period of a few weeks prior to testing.

Teaching Suggestions for the Worksheets

1-1: Identifying Relationships

Introduce this worksheet by explaining what analogies are, and that they test the ability to reason with words and recognize relationships between ideas. You may refer your students to Study Sheet 1-A, "Strategies for Solving Analogies," and Study Sheet 1-B, "Common Types of Analogies." Use the study sheets to review the strategies and examples.

Emphasize that the key to solving any analogy is to understand the relationship between the pairs of words. For this worksheet, your students are given analogies and are to describe the relationships between the ideas. Discuss the first analogy together, so that your students understand what they are to do. Upon completion of the worksheet, discuss the answers with the class and point out any relationships your students had trouble identifying.

1-2: Finding Analogies and Relationships

Begin this activity by explaining that analogies show a relationship between ideas. Depending upon the abilities of your students, you may find it helpful to review Study Sheet 1-A, "Strategies for Solving Analogies," and Study Sheet 1-B, "Common Types of Analogies." Go over the instructions on the worksheet and note that students are to complete each analogy and write the relationship. Suggest that they compose logical sentences to "test" for the correct answer. (See Study Sheet 1-A.) When your students have completed the worksheet, discuss any analogies that caused confusion. Have student volunteers model their "test" sentences to clarify any misunderstanding.

1-3: Completing Analogies I

Start this activity by discussing the strategies for finding relationships in analogies. Depending upon the experience your students have with analogies, you may prefer to review Study Sheet 1-A, "Strategies for Solving Analogies," and Study Sheet 1-B, "Common Types of Analogies." Emphasize the importance of recognizing relationships in solving analogies, and encourage your students to write "test" sentences to help them discover the connections between ideas.

Go over the directions on the worksheet with your students. Note that they are to use the words that appear in the Word Bank to complete the analogies, but that not all words will be used. When your students are done, discuss the correct answers with them. Be sure to allow time to answer any questions your students may have.

1-4: Completing Analogies II

Similar to Worksheet 1-3, this activity provides additional practice in completing analogies. Review the instructions with your students and remind them that not all words in the Word Bank will be used. Encourage them to utilize Study Sheet 1-A, "Strategies for Solving Analogies," to complete the worksheet. When your students are finished, discuss any analogies with which they had difficulty.

1-5: Completing Analogies III

This worksheet is similar to Worksheets 1-3 and 1-4, except that your students must find two missing words to complete each analogy. This worksheet will require careful thought and concentration. You may encourage your students to use Study Sheet 1-A, "Strategies for Solving Analogies," as they work.

Review the instructions on the worksheet and note that answers will be found in the Word Bank. Depending upon your class, you may find it helpful to do the first analogy together. Demonstrate how students may have to use "guess and check" to find suitable answers. They should carefully double-check each potential answer before deciding if it is the correct one. When your students are done with the worksheet, discuss the answers and address any questions they may have.

1-6: Solving Analogies I

Begin this activity by discussing the various strategies for solving analogies as detailed on Study Sheet 1-A, "Strategies for Solving Analogies." You may also prefer to review the examples of analogous relationships noted on Study Sheet 1-B, "Common Types of Analogies."

Go over the directions on the worksheet. Explain that students are given a pair of words for which they must identify another pair that share a similar relationship.

You may wish to do the first set of analogies together. Have volunteers offer logical test sentences for *absurd* and *preposterous*. An obvious one is "Absurd is synonymous with preposterous." Now try *accountant* and *lawyer*. "Accountant is synonymous with lawyer." This is not true. Next try *apprehensive* and *anxious*. "Apprehensive is synonymous with anxious." This is reasonable, but warn your students to check the next two possibilities to be certain. (Designers of tests often put seemingly right answers as one of the first choices on multiple-choice tests, anticipating that many students will choose these answers and not bother to check the other possibilities.) "Desirable is synonymous with imaginable." No, this is not valid. "Meager is synonymous with abundance." No. In fact, these words are antonyms. *Apprehensive* and *anxious* is the only choice that can be correct.

Instruct your students to do the rest of the analogies in the same manner. Upon completion, you should discuss the answers with your students, explaining any analogies they found troublesome.

1-7: Solving Analogies II

This activity is similar to Worksheet 1-6. Explain to your students that they are to find a pair of words whose relationship is similar to that of the first pair for each set. You may prefer to do the first one together. Ask for students to compose a logical test sentence for the first pair of words. One example is "Being an amateur is the step before becoming a professional."

Try *minor* and *major*. "Being a minor is the step before becoming a major." This is vague and unclear. Try the next two words. "Being an instructor is the step before becoming a learner." This is backwards, which is the same problem for the following pair. "Being an expert is the step before becoming a novice." Now try *rookie* and *veteran*. "Being a rookie is the step before becoming a veteran." This is a valid statement and is similar to the relationship between *amateur* and *professional*.

Instruct your students to complete the rest of the analogies in the same manner. When they are done with the worksheet, discuss their answers and explain any analogies they found confusing.

Analogies Practice Test

This test contains ten pairs of words for which your students are to find pairs of words that show similar relationships. (The test follows the format of Worksheets 1-6 and 1-7.) Students should mark the letters of their answers on the Answer Sheet, which will give them practice in using standardized answer sheets.

Answer Key for Section 1

1-1. Descriptions of relationships may vary. **2.** The pairs of words are antonyms. **3.** The pairs of words are synonyms. **4.** Spinach is a vegetable; an apple is a fruit. The relationship is that of part to whole. **5.** A dramatist creates a play; a sculptor creates a statue. The relationship is that both dramatists and sculptors create. **6.** The pairs of words are antonyms. **7.** The pairs of words are synonyms. **8.** Today leads to tomorrow; the present leads to the future. The relationship is that of progression. **9.** The solar system contains planets; the universe contains galaxies. The relationship is that of whole to part. **10.** Dogs are domesticated animals; wolves are wild animals. The relationship is that of characteristics.

1-2. Descriptions of relationships may vary. **2.** acknowledge; the pairs of words are antonyms. **3.** dictionary; a word is a part of a dictionary while a tree is a part of a forest. **4.** curtain; an eclipse hides the moon while a curtain hides a stage. **5.** magic; exaggeration is a characteristic of a tall tale while magic is a characteristic of fantasy. **6.** brush; a scalpel is a tool for a surgeon while a brush is a tool for a painter. **7.** past; a historian studies the past while an astronomer studies space. **8.** vertical; latitude lines extend horizontally (east and west) on a map or globe while longitude lines extend vertically (north and south). **9.** perilous; the pairs of words are synonyms. **10.** shortage; the pairs of words are synonyms.

1-3. **1.** television **2.** zoo **3.** pentagon **4.** maturity **5.** materialize **6.** instructor **7.** water **8.** proprietor **9.** ridicule **10.** society **11.** gigantic **12.** import **13.** cabinet **14.** commercial **15.** agility

1-4. **1.** commission **2.** bandage **3.** acquaintance **4.** eternal **5.** flower **6.** demolish **7.** physician **8.** target **9.** warn **10.** tranquillity **11.** wing **12.** order **13.** tactics **14.** solid **15.** sentence

1-5. **1.** galleries, plays **2.** laughter, philanthropist **3.** coffee, candy **4.** climax, beginning *or* beginning, climax **5.** conductor, general **6.** dinosaur, house **7.** soliloquy, candidate **8.** steal, consumer **9.** surety, dubious **10.** circumference, square

1-6. **1.** C **2.** C **3.** A **4.** B **5.** D **6.** A **7.** C **8.** B **9.** A **10.** C **11.** B **12.** D

1-7. **1.** D **2.** B **3.** A **4.** C **5.** B **6.** B **7.** D **8.** A **9.** C **10.** D **11.** B **12.** C

Study Sheet 1-A

Strategies for Solving Analogies

An *analogy* is a way of expressing a relationship between words. *Example:*

student : class :: player : team

The analogy is read:

Student is to class as player is to team.

A student is a member of a class, and a player is a member of a team. The relationship is that of part to a whole.

To solve analogies, do the following:

1. Read the analogy slowly and concentrate on the words.
2. Look for the relationship between the pairs of words. Ask yourself: How are the words similar? How are they different? What is the "connection" between them?
3. Use the words of the analogy in a logical "test" sentence. Example:

attorney : client :: ___________________

A. money : bank

B. forest : squirrel

C. doctor : patient

D. plumber : sink

Here is a possible "test" sentence: An attorney helps a client in legal matters.

Now try the other choices in a similar sentence.

A. money and bank: Money helps a bank. While a bank certainly needs to have money, money does not "help" a bank.

B. forest and squirrel: Forest helps a squirrel. A forest may provide shelter and food for a squirrel, but it does not play an active role like an attorney does for a client.

C. doctor and patient: A doctor helps a patient in medical matters. This is a similar relationship to that of attorney and client, but you must check the last possibility to be sure.

D. plumber and sink: A plumber helps a sink. A plumber may unclog a sink, but a sink is not human as a client or patient.

The best choice is C. Remember, always check *all* possible answers for logic and sense.

© 2002 by John Wiley & Sons, Inc.

Study Sheet 1-B

Common Types of Analogies

- **Synonyms**
  joy : happy :: sad : unhappy

- **Antonyms**
  smile : frown :: light : dark

- **Cause and Effect**
  storm : rain :: clearing : sunshine

- **Purpose**
  camera : photograph :: calculator : computation

- **Characteristics**
  silk : smooth :: cotton : soft

- **Degree**
  surprised : stunned :: upset : hysterical

- **Whole and Part**
  class : student :: team : player

- **Action and Object**
  row : boat :: pedal : bicycle

- **Place and Object**
  Arctic : polar bear :: forest : squirrel

- **Person and Tool**
  carpenter : hammer :: plumber : wrench

© 2002 by John Wiley & Sons, Inc.

Note: The pairs of words of analogies can be reversed, as long as the order of the relationship remains consistent. *Example:*

row : boat :: pedal : bicycle

bicycle : pedal :: boat : row

Name ______________________________ Date ________________

1-1

Identifying Relationships

Directions: Identify the relationship that describes each analogy. The first one is done for you.

1. referee : game :: moderator : debate

   What is the relationship? A referee makes sure that the rules of a game are followed; a moderator makes sure the rules of a debate are followed.

2. reality : illusion :: fact : fantasy

   What is the relationship? ______________________________

3. immortal : eternal :: endless : infinite

   What is the relationship? ______________________________

4. spinach : vegetable :: apple : fruit

   What is the relationship? ______________________________

5. dramatist : play :: sculptor : statue

   What is the relationship? ______________________________

© 2002 by John Wiley & Sons, Inc.

Name ______________________________ Date ____________________

1–1

Identifying Relationships *(continued)*

6. inferior : superior :: passive : advancement

   What is the relationship? ______________________________

   ____

   ____

7. precise : exact :: progress : advancement

   What is the relationship? ______________________________

   ____

   ____

8. today : tomorrow :: present : future

   What is the relationship? ______________________________

   ____

   ____

9. solar system : planet :: universe : galaxy

   What is the relationship? ______________________________

   ____

   ____

10. dogs : domestic :: wolves : wild

    What is the relationship? ______________________________

    ____

    ____

© 2002 by John Wiley & Sons, Inc.

Name ______________________ Date ____________

1-2

Finding Analogies and Relationships

Directions: Write the word that best completes each analogy. Then describe the relationship that creates the analogy. The first one is done for you.

1. whale : ocean :: camel : ___desert___

   water caravan desert herd

   Relationship: A whale lives in the ocean; a camel lives in the desert.

2. ______________ : deny :: accept : reject

   understand assume refuse acknowledge

   Relationship: ______________________

   ____

3. word : ______________ :: tree : forest

   almanac dictionary atlas definition

   Relationship: ______________________

   ____

4. eclipse : moon :: ______________ : stage

   sun curtain illumination night

   Relationship: ______________________

   ____

5. exaggeration : tall tale :: ______________ : fantasy

   unbelievable time travel magic novel

   Relationship: ______________________

   ____

© 2002 by John Wiley & Sons, Inc.

Name ______________________________ Date ________________

1–2

Finding Analogies and Relationships *(continued)*

6. scalpel : surgeon :: ____________________ : painter

   paint brush canvas portrait

   Relationship: ____

   ____

7. historian : ____________________ :: astronomer : space

   epoch archaeology study past

   Relationship: ____

   ____

8. latitude : longitude :: horizontal : ____________________

   parallel vertical straight equator

   Relationship: ____

9. ____________________ : dangerous :: safety : security

   protection guard adventurous perilous

   Relationship: ____

   ____

10. surplus : abundance :: deficit : ____________________

    efficiency amount shortage enough

    Relationship: ____

    ____

© 2002 by John Wiley & Sons, Inc.

Library Resource Center
Renton Technical College
3000 N.E. 4th St.
Renton, WA 98056

Name ______________________________ Date ________________

1-3

Completing Analogies I

Directions: Complete each analogy by writing the correct word in the blank. Choose your answers from the words in the Word Bank. (Not all words in the Word Bank will be used.)

1. listen : radio :: watch : ____________________
2. fish : aquarium :: lion : ____________________
3. quadrilateral : four :: ____________________ : five
4. adolescence : adulthood :: youth : ____________________
5. disappear : vanish :: appear : ____________________
6. class : student :: faculty : ____________________
7. ice : solid :: ____________________ : liquid
8. farmer : farm :: ____________________ : shop
9. disgrace : scandalize :: mock : ____________________
10. pack : wolf :: ____________________ : person
11. miniature : colossal :: minuscule : ____________________
12. domestic : foreign :: ____________________ : export
13. plumber : sink :: carpenter : ____________________
14. anthology : story :: ____________________ : sales pitch
15. strength : power :: ____________________ : grace

Word Bank

concert	water	maturity	school	zoo
materialize	gigantic	jungle	tariff	television
crop	infant	hammer	product	instructor
proprietor	commercial	agility	pentagon	ridicule
import	individual	square	society	cabinet

© 2002 by John Wiley & Sons, Inc.

Name ______________________ Date ______________

1-4

Completing Analogies II

Directions: Complete each analogy by writing the correct word in the blank. Choose your answers from the words in the Word Bank. (Not all words in the Word Bank will be used.)

1. stockholder : dividend :: salesperson : ______________
2. cast : fracture :: ______________ : wound
3. partner : co-worker :: friend : ______________
4. replacement : substitute :: ______________ : permanent
5. dandelion : weed :: tulip : ______________
6. develop : build :: ______________ : tear down
7. court : attorney :: hospital : ______________
8. circle : center :: ______________ : bull's eye
9. patients : patience :: ______________ : worn
10. chaos : disorder :: peace : ______________
11. human : arm :: bird : ______________
12. proposal : suggestion :: ______________ : command
13. strategies : objectives :: ______________ : goals
14. changeable : constant :: liquid : ______________
15. legislator : law :: judge : ______________

© 2002 by John Wiley & Sons, Inc.

Word Bank

selling	plant	warn	court	solid	tranquillity
splint	tactics	physician	flight	eternal	war
relative	commission	flower	acquaintance	nucleus	results
sentence	wing	comment	illness	finite	rust
water	bandage	target	demolish	order	diameter

Name ______________________________ Date ________________

1-5

Completing Analogies III

Directions: Use the words from the Word Bank to find two words to complete each analogy. (Not all words in the Word Bank will be used.)

1. paintings : ____________ :: ____________ : theaters
2. comedian : ____________ :: ____________ : charity
3. caffeine : ____________ :: sugar : ____________
4. ____________ : end :: opening : ____________
5. ____________ : orchestra :: ____________ : army
6. ____________ : skeleton :: ____________ : frame
7. actor : ____________ :: ____________ : speech
8. burglar : ____________ :: ____________ : purchase
9. certainty : ____________ :: doubtful : ____________
10. ____________ : circle :: perimeter : ____________

© 2002 by John Wiley & Sons, Inc.

Word Bank

bones	soliloquy	coffee	square	plays
laughter	steal	house	orphan	climax
sweetness	galleries	consumer	product	dubious
beginning	circumference	general	surety	dinosaur
philanthropist	conductor	candidate	candy	thief

Name ______________________________ Date ________________

1-6

Solving Analogies I

Directions: Write the letter of the pair of words that best expresses a relationship similar to the first pair of words.

1. absurd : preposterous :: _______

   A. accountant : lawyer
   B. desirable : imaginable
   C. apprehensive : anxious
   D. meager : abundance

2. problem : solution :: _______

   A. retaliate : surrender
   B. reject : accept
   C. argument : agreement
   D. stationary : mobile

3. superior : dominant :: _______

   A. inferior : submissive
   B. strong : weak
   C. variety : uniqueness
   D. personal : personable

4. palomino : horse :: _______

   A. bear : grizzly
   B. collie : dog
   C. purring : cat
   D. animal : domestication

5. counterfeit : phony :: _______

   A. fiction : fact
   B. money : finance
   C. data : analysis
   D. authentic : genuine

6. costume : disguise :: _______

   A. seatbelt : safety
   B. leave : embark
   C. mask : face
   D. event : memorable

© 2002 by John Wiley & Sons, Inc.

Name ________________________________ Date ________________

1–6

Solving Analogies I *(continued)*

7. marriage : divorce :: _______

   A. division : union
   B. begin : end
   C. partnership : breakup
   D. hate : love

8. porpoise : sea :: _______

   A. eaglet : nest
   B. hawk : air
   C. vulture : carrion
   D. wolf : prey

9. spectators : participant :: _______

   A. audience : magician
   B. visitors : museum
   C. theater : performance
   D. team : supporters

10. spy : espionage :: _______

    A. computer : programmer
    B. instruction : teacher
    C. doctor : medicine
    D. police officer : thief

11. eccentric : odd :: _______

    A. brilliant : dull
    B. feasible : possible
    C. expansion : contraction
    D. career : work

12. parts : whole :: _______

    A. orchard : apples
    B. synthesis : elements
    C. pots : pans
    D. ingredients : cake

© 2002 by John Wiley & Sons, Inc.

Name ________________________________ Date ________________

1-7

Solving Analogies II

Directions: Write the letter of the pair of words that best expresses a relationship similar to the first pair of words.

1. amateur : professional :: _______

   A. minor : major
   B. instructor : learner
   C. expert : novice
   D. rookie : veteran

2. wicked : sinful :: _______

   A. angelic : pleasant
   B. good : righteous
   C. evil : redemption
   D. hurtful : compassionate

3. apparent : obscure :: _______

   A. synonym : antonym
   B. chaplain : minister
   C. centigram : centipede
   D. dehydration : hunger

4. discussion : argument :: _______

   A. renounce : proclaim
   B. difficult : simple
   C. hill : mountain
   D. river : water

5. illustrator : picture :: _______

   A. doctor : patient
   B. animator : cartoon
   C. lawyer : client
   D. building : architect

6. automobile : road :: _______

   A. saddle : horse
   B. train : track
   C. crust : pie
   D. office : company

© 2002 by John Wiley & Sons, Inc.

Name ________________________________ Date ________________

1–7

Solving Analogies II *(continued)*

7. advance : regress :: _______

   A. behind : ahead

   B. momentum : slow

   C. progress : forward

   D. triumph : defeat

8. joy : ecstasy :: _______

   A. fear : terror

   B. history : past

   C. happiness : enjoyment

   D. belief : faith

9. horses : corral :: _______

   A. bears : wild

   B. elephants : ivory

   C. monkeys : cage

   D. birds : flight

10. ridicule : praise :: _______

    A. scandal : humiliation

    B. shame : tears

    C. sympathy : sincerity

    D. cowardice : valor

11. subconscious : conscious :: _______

    A. submarine : ship

    B. subterranean : surface

    C. subscribe : magazine

    D. dream : nightmare

12. run : stampede :: _______

    A. worry : nervousness

    B. cattle : range

    C. alarm : panic

    D. race : walk

© 2002 by John Wiley & Sons, Inc.

EIGHTH-GRADE LEVEL

Analogies

PRACTICE TEST

© 2002 by John Wiley & Sons, Inc.

Analogies Practice Test

Directions: Choose the pair of words that best expresses a relationship similar to the first pair of words. Use the Answer Sheet to darken the letter of your choice.

1. isolation : loneliness :: ______________

   A. friendship : acquaintance
   B. destination : road
   C. bacteria : disease
   D. lake : forest

2. nose : fragrance :: ______________

   A. touch : skin
   B. ear : melody
   C. food : taste
   D. eye : cornea

3. now : future :: ______________

   A. later : past
   B. today : tomorrow
   C. present : then
   D. night : day

4. meager : scarce :: ______________

   A. surplus : inadequacy
   B. abundance : plenty
   C. need : satisfaction
   D. enough : excess

5. charity : donating :: ______________

   A. humanitarian : society
   B. collect : distribute
   C. philanthropy : giving
   D. kindness : sacrifice

6. approximate : exact :: ______________

   A. about : precise
   B. nearby : vicinity
   C. confusion : clarification
   D. uncertain : sure

© 2002 by John Wiley & Sons, Inc.

Analogies Practice Test *(continued)*

7. Earth : solar system :: ______________

   A. planets : sun
   B. moon : Earth
   C. galaxy : universe
   D. space : stars

8. commotion : tranquillity :: ______________

   A. upheaval : dissension
   B. stormy : turbulent
   C. peaceful : quiet
   D. chaos : calm

9. increase : expand :: ______________

   A. volume : rise
   B. decrease : minimum
   C. decrease : contract
   D. reduce : heighten

10. detective : investigation :: ______________

    A. physician : health
    B. coach : athlete
    C. stewardess : passenger
    D. explorer : discovery

11. heartbeat : pulse :: ______________

    A. headache : pain
    B. water : pump
    C. circulation : transfusion
    D. wail : siren

12. prophecy : prediction :: ______________

    A. storm : rain
    B. clairvoyant : seer
    C. meteorologist : weather
    D. dream : reality

© 2002 by John Wiley & Sons, Inc.

Name ______________________________ Date ______________

Analogies

PRACTICE TEST: ANSWER SHEET

Directions: Darken the circle above the letter that best completes the analogy.

1. ○ A ○ B ○ C ○ D
2. ○ A ○ B ○ C ○ D
3. ○ A ○ B ○ C ○ D
4. ○ A ○ B ○ C ○ D
5. ○ A ○ B ○ C ○ D
6. ○ A ○ B ○ C ○ D
7. ○ A ○ B ○ C ○ D
8. ○ A ○ B ○ C ○ D
9. ○ A ○ B ○ C ○ D
10. ○ A ○ B ○ C ○ D
11. ○ A ○ B ○ C ○ D
12. ○ A ○ B ○ C ○ D

© 2002 by John Wiley & Sons, Inc.

Analogies

KEY TO PRACTICE TEST

	A	B	C	D
1.	○	○	●	○
2.	○	●	○	○
3.	○	●	○	○
4.	○	●	○	○
5.	○	○	●	○
6.	●	○	○	○
7.	○	○	●	○
8.	○	○	○	●
9.	○	○	●	○
10.	○	○	○	●
11.	●	○	○	○
12.	○	●	○	○

© 2002 by John Wiley & Sons, Inc.

Section 2

Vocabulary

Vocabulary is a crucial component of the language portion of any test. Students who possess strong, varied vocabularies invariably achieve higher scores on such tests than students whose vocabularies are limited. Although a variety of factors influence the development of an individual's vocabulary, including background, experiences, and reading habits, there is much you can do to nurture vocabulary development in your students.

One of the most important steps is to make the learning of vocabulary a priority in your classes. Encourage your students to pay attention to new words as they read and study. Suggest that they first attempt to use context clues to figure out the meanings of new words, but also emphasize that they should look up unfamiliar words in a dictionary when necessary. Explain that learning new words will not only help them with the work at hand but also with assignments to come. Stress that once they learn a new word, they should try to use that word in speaking and writing. This will help them to remember the word and make it a part of their vocabulary. Also point out that once they learn a new word, they will understand the various forms of the word. For example, when they learn that *lacerate* means "to rip or cut," they will likely realize that *laceration* means "a rip or cut." This is how a person expands his or her vocabulary.

To encourage the development of your students' vocabulary, distribute copies of this section's study sheets:

- Study Sheet 2-A, "Common Prefixes"
- Study Sheet 2-B, "Common Suffixes"
- Study Sheet 2-C, "Homographs"
- Study Sheet 2-D, "Homophones"
- Study Sheet 2-E, "Easily Confused Words"
- Study Sheet 2-F, "Idioms"
- Study Sheet 2-G, "Ways to Build Your Vocabulary"
- Study Sheet 2-H, "Words to Know"

Most teachers will find that an effective method of utilizing the study sheets is to hand them out to supplement their instruction. For example, a good time to distribute Study Sheet 2-A, "Common Prefixes," is when you are teaching a lesson on prefixes. Likewise, a lesson about suffixes is a good time to hand out Study Sheet 2-B, "Common Suffixes." The other study sheets can be used in the same manner.

Another option for utilizing the study sheets is to hand out the sheets as reviews. In this case you might, for example, hand out Study Sheet 2-C, "Homographs," and Study Sheet 2-D, "Homophones," a few weeks after teaching lessons on homographs and homophones. The study sheets could then serve to reinforce ideas about homographs and homophones that you have previously covered.

A third option is to use the study sheets as the foundations of mini-units. For example, Study Sheet 2-E, "Easily Confused Words," can be the focus of the development of a mini-unit about words that are often used in place of each other. Practice worksheets 2-16 and 2-17, which are included in this section, can supplement the unit.

Although idioms seldom appear on vocabulary tests as items that need to be defined, these phrases often appear in reading selections. Your students need to recognize that idioms are special phrases that over time have assumed specific meanings. Idioms can be particularly troublesome for students for whom English is a second language. While these students may speak standard English well, idioms can be maddening to them. Reviewing the idioms on Study Sheet 2-F can help your students increase their understanding of these phrases.

To further promote the development of vocabulary among your students, hand out copies of Study Sheet 2-G, "Ways to Build Your Vocabulary." Discuss the suggestions on the sheet and encourage your students to work consciously to expand their understanding of words, not just in your class, but in all of their subjects.

The last study sheet of this section, Study Sheet 2-H, "Words to Know," contains words found in the typical eighth-grade curriculum and on eighth-grade standardized tests. Because the list is somewhat extensive, you may find it practical to give 10 to 15 of these words at a time to your students. Start distributing the lists of words well in advance of your testing dates. You may, in fact, begin familiarizing your students with the words as early as September and review them periodically. Encourage your students to define the words, and then go over them in class. Instruct your students to use dictionaries, and suggest that they record the words and their meanings in a Vocabulary Notebook, which they can review periodically. When your students look up words and write their meanings, they are more likely to recall the words and make them a part of their vocabularies.

Along with the study sheets, 18 worksheets and three practice tests are included in this section. Note that the worksheets and tests include many of the words on the study sheets.

Teaching Suggestions for the Worksheets

2-1: Finding Prefixes

Begin this activity by explaining that a prefix is a letter or a group of letters added to the beginning of a word. Some prefixes can greatly change the meaning of the word to which they are added. Offer the example of *illegal* to your students.

While *legal* means "something done within the law," *illegal* means "breaking the law." The prefix *il*, which means "not," has turned the word *legal* into its opposite.

You may find it helpful to distribute copies of Study Sheet 2-A, "Common Prefixes," and review the prefixes, their meanings, and examples with your students. Note how prefixes can alter a word's meaning, especially the prefixes *anti*, *il*, *ir*, and *mal*, which change words from the positive to the negative.

Explain to your students that knowing the meanings of prefixes can help them understand the meanings of new words. Use *malfunction* for an example. If students understand the meaning of *function*—"the proper action or working of something"—and if they understand the meaning of the prefix *mal*—"badly"—they can easily figure out the meaning of *malfunction*, even if the word is unfamiliar. Understanding the meanings of prefixes can be helpful when taking the vocabulary and reading portions of standardized tests.

Review the instructions on the worksheet with your students, noting that this activity contains two parts. For the first ten words, they are to identify the prefixes. For the next ten, they are to identify the meaning of the underlined prefix in each word. When your students have completed the activity, correct their work and discuss any questions they may have.

2-2: Finding Suffixes

Begin this exercise by explaining that a suffix is a letter or a group of letters added to the end of a word. Some suffixes can alter the meaning of a word significantly. Ask your students to consider the word *careless*. *Care*, of course, means "feeling concern or worry." The suffix *less* means "without," changing the meaning of *careless* to "without feeling concern or worry."

To help your students learn about suffixes, you may find it useful to refer to Study Sheet 2-B, "Common Suffixes." Review the suffixes listed on the sheet, their meanings, and the examples. Explain to your students that understanding the meanings of suffixes can help them figure out the meanings of unfamiliar words. Unquestionably, possessing a solid understanding of suffixes can help students expand their overall vocabularies.

Go over the instructions on the worksheet, noting that this activity contains two parts. For the first ten words, students are to identify the suffix of each word. For the next ten words, they are to identify the meaning of the underlined suffix of each word. When your students have completed the worksheet, correct their work and answer any questions they may have.

2-3: Finding Synonyms I

Introduce this activity by explaining that synonyms are words that have similar meanings. Ask for volunteers to offer some examples of synonyms. Students should be able to name several, of which some might include: enormous, gigantic, immense; minuscule, tiny, minute; and potent, mighty, powerful. Remind students that they can find synonyms for words in a thesaurus.

Review the directions on the worksheet and encourage your students to consider all potential answers for each word before making their choice. After your students have completed the activity, correct their work and address any words they found confusing.

2-4: Finding Synonyms II

Start this activity by reviewing the definition of synonyms, which are words similar in meaning. Ask students to volunteer some examples, which might include: common, familiar, customary; imperfect, flawed, deficient; and nonchalant, unconcerned, untroubled.

Go over the instructions on the worksheet and remind your students that not all words in the lists will be used. For those words not used, students should leave the space before them blank. When your students have completed the worksheet, correct their answers and discuss any words they did not understand.

2-5: Finding Antonyms I

Introduce this activity by explaining that antonyms are words that have opposite or nearly opposite meanings. Ask for volunteers to offer some examples of antonyms. Students should be able to name several, of which some might include: enormous, tiny; powerful, weak; and humorous, serious.

Review the directions on the worksheet and encourage your students to consider all potential answers for each word before making their choice. After your students have completed the activity, correct their answers and discuss any words they found confusing.

2-6: Finding Antonyms II

Begin this activity by reviewing the definition of antonyms, which are words that have opposite or nearly opposite meanings. Ask your students to volunteer some examples, which might include: common, extraordinary; perfect, flawed; and deficient, abundant.

Go over the instructions on the worksheet and remind your students that not all words in the lists will be used. Instruct them to leave the space blank before words they do not use. When your students have completed the worksheet, correct their answers and discuss any words they might have found confusing.

2-7: Finding the Correct Word I

Introduce this activity by explaining that we often come across new, unfamiliar words in the materials we read. Although we may not know a word, we can often figure out its meaning from the words around it, the general meaning of the sentence, and the way the word is used in the sentence. We call these hints "context clues."

Write this example on an overhead projector or the board: *The instructions for the project were <u>ambiguous</u>, and the students were not sure what they had to do.* Suppose that *ambiguous* is a new word to your students. Point out that the second part of the sentence, "students were not sure what they had to do," provides a strong clue as to what *ambiguous* means. Since students did not know what to do, the instructions were in some way unclear or incomplete. *Ambiguous* in fact means "unclear, or capable of being understood in various ways."

Go over the directions on the worksheet and encourage your students to use context clues to find the word that best completes each sentence. Upon completion of the activity, correct the worksheets and discuss any sentences that proved to be troublesome.

2-8: Finding the Correct Word II

Begin this exercise by discussing the importance of using context clues to figure out the meanings of unfamiliar words. Emphasize that the meanings of new words can often be inferred from other words in the sentence and the way the new word is used.

Review the instructions on the worksheet, noting that not all words in the Word Bank will be used. Suggest to your students that they use context clues in completing the worksheet. When they are done, correct their answers and discuss any sentences your students found confusing.

2-9: Finding the Correct Word III

Introduce this activity by explaining that context clues are crucial to figuring out the meanings of unfamiliar words. For this activity your students are to read an article and fill in blanks with words that correctly complete sentences.

Review the instructions on the worksheet, and note that each blank is numbered. At the end of the article, four words are offered to fill in each blank. Students should choose the word that best completes each sentence, basing their choice on the context of the sentence. When your students are done, go over the article and clarify any sentences that were unclear.

2-10: Words with Multiple Meanings I

Begin this activity by explaining that English is a marvelously varied and rich language. One of the sources of this richness arises from words that have multiple meanings. Remind students that words with multiple meanings may be pronounced differently, such as *re bel'* and *reb' el.* (Of course, this also leads to confusion and errors on vocabulary tests!)

For this worksheet, your students are given sets of phrases for which they are to find the word that means the same as both phrases. You may want to do the first one together. Explain that *current* means "in the present time," as well as "flowing water." Your students are to complete the rest of the worksheet in the same manner. Caution them to read each set of phrases carefully as some incorrect answer choices may mean the same as one of the phrases but not both.

Emphasize to your students that they should strive to avoid careless mistakes, and remind them that test writers often put seemingly correct answer choices first. Students should always read the entire question and all possible answers before choosing one. When your students finish the worksheet, correct their answers and discuss any questions they may have.

2-11: Words with Multiple Meanings II

Introduce this exercise by explaining that many words in English have multiple meanings. The simple word "do" is not so simple with some 30 meanings. While most multi-meaning words have fewer meanings than that, they can still be confusing and students need to read questions concerning them with great concentration. Remind students that words with multiple meanings may be pronounced differently, such as *con tract'* and *con' tract.*

For this worksheet, your students are given several sets of two sentences. A word is missing in each sentence. Your students are to read the sentences and choose the word that best completes both sentences of the set. Caution your students to read both sentences and the various answer choices. Some of the choices will complete one of the two sentences of the set correctly but not both. When your students are done with the worksheet, correct their answers and discuss any sentences they found difficult to understand.

2-12: Identifying Homographs

Start this exercise by reviewing the meaning of homographs, which are words that are spelled the same but have different meanings and different origins. Most homographs have the same pronunciation. Offer the example of *lumber*, which means "timber or wood," and also "to move heavily." Note that not understanding the different meanings of homographs can lead to misinterpretation of information.

Depending upon the abilities of your students, you may refer them to Study Sheet 2-C, "Homographs." Go over the examples, noting that this sheet contains common homographs; there are many more.

Review the instructions on the worksheet with your students, and remind them that some of the words of the Word Bank will be used more than once while others will not be used at all. When your students are done with the worksheet, correct their answers and discuss any words they found confusing.

2-13: Identifying Homophones I

Begin this exercise by explaining that homophones are words that sound alike but have different spellings and meanings. Failure to use homophones correctly undermines comprehension and leads to mistakes on tests. Offer your students the example of *profit* and *prophet. Profit* means "to gain or benefit"; a *prophet* is a "person who speaks the will of a god." Because the words sound alike, they are easily used in place of each other.

You may find it helpful to refer your students to Study Sheet 2-D, "Homophones." Go over the examples and note that these are some of the most common homophones. These words are frequently misused.

Review the instructions on the worksheet, cautioning your students to pay close attention to the answer choices. It is easy to make errors with homophones. Upon completion of the activity, correct the work of your students and answer any questions they may have.

2-14: Identifying Homophones II

This worksheet is similar to Worksheet 2-13. Start this activity by reviewing the definition of homophones, which are words that sound the same but have different spellings and meanings. Emphasize that it is easy to make mistakes with homophones, even though students may understand the meanings of the words they are misusing. As an example, ask your students how many of them have ever written *write* when they meant to use *right.* Or how many have written *role* when they meant *roll.* With homophones, our eyes can see one word but our minds think of the other. To avoid mistakes with homophones, encourage your students to concentrate on words and focus on their meanings.

You may find it worthwhile to refer your students to Study Sheet 2-D, "Homophones." Encourage them to become familiar with the words on the study sheet, as this will help them to avoid using homophones incorrectly.

Review the instructions on the worksheet. Note that there are three choices to complete each sentence, and students should consider each word before choosing their answer. When your students are done, go over the worksheets and clarify any confusion.

2-15: Identifying Homophones III

Begin this exercise with a review, noting that homophones are words that sound the same but have different spellings and meanings. Emphasize that it is easy to make mistakes with homophones and that only through concentration can errors be avoided.

This worksheet requires students to match homophones with their meanings. Remind them to pay close attention to their answers. When they are done, correct the worksheets and answer any questions they may have.

2-16: Easily Confused Words I

Homographs and homophones are not the only words in English that can cause confusion. Many words are so similar in spelling and pronunciation that, even though they may have very different meanings, they are often used in place of each other. Offer the example of *bizarre,* which means "odd," and *bazaar,* which means "a market or fair," and note how easy it is to confuse the two.

You may wish to have students refer to Study Sheet 2-E, "Easily Confused Words," to help them with this activity. Review the words on the list and encourage your students to concentrate on their meanings. Suggest that whenever they encounter any of the words on this list, they pause and think of what the word means. This will help them to remember the word and its definition.

Go over the instructions on the worksheet, stressing that your students should consider each potential answer choice carefully. Upon completion of the worksheets, correct their answers and discuss any words that caused confusion.

2-17: Easily Confused Words II

This worksheet is similar to Worksheet 2-16. Begin this activity by explaining that many words in English are similar in spelling and pronunciation but have vastly different meanings. Because of their similarities, such words are often confused with each other. You may refer students to Study Sheet 2-E, "Easily Confused Words." Go over the study sheet and note the many instances of words that are often used incorrectly in place of each other.

Review the instructions on the worksheet and caution your students to consider each potential answer carefully. When they are done with the exercise, correct the worksheets and discuss any words that gave them trouble.

2-18: Interpreting Idioms

Introduce this activity by explaining that idioms are phrases that over time have assumed special meanings. An idiom is not to be taken literally. For example, in the sentence "It is raining cats and dogs," cats and dogs are not falling from the sky. The phrase "raining cats and dogs" means that it is raining hard. For students who lack an understanding of idiomatic phrases, particularly students for whom English is a second language, idioms can offer serious challenges to comprehension.

Depending upon the abilities of your students, you may refer them to Study Sheet 2-F, "Idioms." Discuss the idioms on the sheet, noting that these are examples of some of the most common idioms. There are many more. Encourage your students to volunteer others, which you should write on an overhead projector or the board.

Go over the instructions on the worksheet, and remind your students that they are to write the meaning of each idiom they identify on the line after the sentence. Upon completion of the worksheet, correct their answers and discuss any idioms that were confusing.

Vocabulary Practice Tests I, II, and III

This section contains three tests for vocabulary. The first test focuses on identifying and determining the meanings of prefixes and suffixes. The second test centers on identifying synonyms, antonyms, and words with multiple meanings. The third test is comprised of activities in which students must identify the word that correctly completes sentences.

Answer Key for Section 2

2-1. **Part 1. 1.** inter **2.** dis **3.** im **4.** ir **5.** non **6.** pre **7.** in **8.** trans **9.** un **10.** bi **Part 2. 1.** below **2.** against **3.** without **4.** not **5.** bad **6.** one **7.** across **8.** before **9.** badly **10.** above

2-2. **Part 1. 1.** ance **2.** ment **3.** y **4.** ness **5.** ence **6.** ist **7.** ent **8.** ic **9.** ism **10.** or **Part 2. 1.** capable of **2.** condition of **3.** act of **4.** one who **5.** like **6.** practice of **7.** able to **8.** one who does **9.** moving toward **10.** practice of

2-3. **1.** thick **2.** investigator **3.** threatening **4.** incident **5.** change **6.** disastrous **7.** astounding **8.** usual **9.** undivided **10.** distrustful **11.** main **12.** valuable **13.** judge **14.** restriction **15.** substantial

2-4. **(first column)** 9, 15, 6, 8, —, 11, 14, 5 **(second column)** 18, 1, 2, 7, —, 20, 16, 4 **(third column)** —, 10, 3, —, 12, 19, 13, 17

2-5. **1.** public **2.** duplicate **3.** domestic **4.** simple **5.** boring **6.** typical **7.** support **8.** serious **9.** disregard **10.** lazy **11.** permanent **12.** peaceful **13.** small **14.** solution **15.** cheap

2-6. **(first column)** —, 17, 8, 9, 12, 16, 3, 2 **(second column)** 14, 11, 15, —, 6, —, 7, 18 **(third column)** 1, 20, 5, 10, 19, 4, —, 13

2-7. **1.** agility **2.** confession **3.** prosperity **4.** absurd **5.** extensions **6.** performance **7.** sufficient **8.** unconstitutional **9.** bilingual **10.** antiseptic **11.** elated **12.** frugal

2-8. **1.** miserable **2.** populous **3.** prosecutor **4.** renovate **5.** tedious **6.** suspense **7.** intermittent **8.** conclusion **9.** catastrophe **10.** reliable **11.** abrupt **12.** restored

2-9. **2.** occupied **3.** economy **4.** principal **5.** ruins **6.** developed **7.** recorded **8.** devised **9.** decline **10.** disaster

2-10. **1.** current **2.** cast **3.** reflect **4.** suspect **5.** article **6.** rebel **7.** contract **8.** project **9.** perfect **10.** issue **11.** coordinate **12.** advocate

2-11. **1.** cycle **2.** conduct **3.** route **4.** balance **5.** convert **6.** reform **7.** determined **8.** plot **9.** engage **10.** regret

2-12. **1.** hamper **2.** flat **3.** pitcher **4.** tire **5.** kind **6.** fresh **7.** close **8.** hamper **9.** grave **10.** fresh **11.** flat **12.** angle **13.** pitcher **14.** jar **15.** grave **16.** kind **17.** jar **18.** close **19.** angle **20.** tire

2-13. **1.** band **2.** cereal **3.** Fourth **4.** council **5.** patience **6.** complimented **7.** its **8.** whether **9.** Whose **10.** straight **11.** stationery **12.** your **13.** team **14.** principal **15.** lesson

2-14. **1.** vane **2.** They're **3.** heal **4.** flu **5.** site **6.** wear **7.** reign **8.** so **9.** right **10.** cent

2-15. **1.** serial **2.** bough **3.** peal **4.** lessen **5.** cheap **6.** patience **7.** hoarse **8.** lesson **9.** horse **10.** bow **11.** dual **12.** patients **13.** cheep **14.** duel **15.** symbol **16.** peel **17.** urn **18.** cereal **19.** earn **20.** cymbal

2-16. **1.** breathe **2.** confident **3.** dessert **4.** proceed **5.** angle **6.** descent **7.** casual **8.** later **9.** lightning **10.** farther **11.** lose **12.** imminent

2-17. **1.** medal **2.** emigrated **3.** morale **4.** passed **5.** lie **6.** country **7.** between **8.** contagious **9.** illusion **10.** quiet **11.** ally **12.** adapt

2-18. Interpretations of the idioms may vary somewhat; possible answers are included. **1.** in the same boat—in the same situation **2.** call it a day—quit, stop working **3.** put their heads together—work together **4.** throw in the towel—quit, give up **5.** get the show on the road—start on their trip **6.** face the music—receive punishment **7.** stopped dead in her tracks—stopped suddenly **8.** still up in the air—unsettled **9.** out of sight, out of mind—forgotten **10.** go all out—try their best **11.** a ball of fire—had a lot of energy **12.** in the bag—a certainty

Study Sheet 2-A

Common Prefixes

A *prefix* is a letter or group of letters added to the beginning of a word to change its meaning. Understanding the meanings of prefixes can help you to understand the meanings of new words. Following are common prefixes with their meanings and examples.

Prefix	Meaning	Examples
• anti	against	antifreeze, antisocial
• bi	two, double	bicycle, biweekly
• dis	not, opposite of, absence of	dislike, dishonest
• ex	out of or from	exchange, exclaim
• il, im, in, ir	not, without	illegal, irregular, impossible, incomplete
• inter	between or among	international, interlace
• mal	bad, wrong, ill	malfunction, maltreat
• mis	badly, wrong	misjudge, mistreat
• non, un	not, opposite of	nonsense, unpleasant
• pre	before	pretest, prehistoric
• post	after, later	postscript, postdate
• re	again, back	rewrite, reenact
• sub	beneath, below	submarine, subconscious
• super	above, greater	superhero, superstar
• trans	across	transform, transplant
• uni	one	unicycle, unilateral

© 2002 by John Wiley & Sons, Inc.

Study Sheet 2-B

Common Suffixes

A *suffix* is a letter or group of letters added to the end of a word to change its meaning. Understanding the meanings of suffixes can help you to understand the meanings of new words. Following are common suffixes with their meanings and examples.

Suffix	Meaning	Examples
• able, ible	able to, capable of	comfortable, visible
• ance	act of	performance, continuance
• ant, ent, er, or	one who	occupant, respondent, teacher, inventor
• ful	full of	restful, thoughtful
• ic	of, like	angelic, volcanic
• ion	act or condition of	correction, communion
• ism	practice of	patriotism, favoritism
• ist	one who does	artist, violinist
• ive	having the nature of	active, massive
• less	without, does not	heartless, careless
• ly	like in nature	proudly, royally
• ment	act, or state of	agreement, payment
• ness	quality, state of	kindness, sadness
• ous	full of	dangerous, glorious
• ship	art or skill of	friendship, kingship
• ward	moving toward	backward, southward
• y	full of, like	fruity, willowy

© 2002 by John Wiley & Sons, Inc.

Study Sheet 2-C

Homographs

Homographs are words that are spelled alike but have different meanings and origins. Most, but not all, homographs are even pronounced the same way. Following are common homographs.

angle – to fish with line and hook
angle – a geometric figure

arms – limbs extending from the shoulders to the hand
arms – weapons

ball – a round object
ball – a formal dance

bank – a building where money is kept
bank – the edge of a river
bank – a long mound; a snow "bank"

base – bottom
base – morally low

bass (bās) – a low-pitched voice
bass (bas) – a type of fish

bear – to carry
bear – a large animal

blaze – fire
blaze – mark or set a trail

boil – to heat water to 212° Fahrenheit or 100° Celsius
boil – a sore on the skin

buck – a male deer
buck – slang for a dollar

clip – cut
clip – fasten

close (klōz) – to shut
close (klōs) – nearby

compound – having more than one part
compound – an enclosed yard or area

content (kon tent') – pleased, satisfied
content (kon' tent) – that which is contained

count – a title of nobility
count – to number

cue – a signal
cue – a long, tapering stick used in a game of pool

date – time of an event
date – a sweet fruit of the Eastern date palm tree

duck – to dip quickly
duck – a water bird with webbed feet

fair – beautiful
fair – honest; just
fair – a carnival; a bazaar

fan – a machine that produces currents of air
fan – a follower or supporter

flat – level
flat – a small apartment

© 2002 by John Wiley & Sons, Inc.

Study Sheet 2-C

Homographs *(continued)*

fresh – new
fresh – disrespectful

grave – very important
grave – a place of burial

hamper – a large covered container or basket
hamper – to hinder, or slow, the movement of

incense (in sens') – to enrage
incense (in' sens) – substance that has a rich smell when burned

invalid (in' va lid) – a bedridden person
invalid (in val' id) – not valid

jar – a glass container
jar – to bump or bounce

kind – friendly, considerate
kind – a group with similar traits

lark – a small bird
lark – to play or frolic

like – similar
like – to be pleased with

pitcher – a container for pouring liquids
pitcher – a baseball player

pupil – a student
pupil – part of the eye

quack – the sound made by a duck
quack – one who pretends to be a doctor

rash – quick, in a hasty manner
rash – a skin infection

ray – a narrow beam of light
ray – a flat fish

saw – past tense of *see*
saw – a tool for cutting

school – a place for learning
school – a group of fish

sock – a short stocking
sock – to hit

spell – a period of time
spell – an enchantment
spell – to say or write the letters of a word

stable – a building in which horses stay
stable – unchanging

tear (tir) – a drop of fluid from the eye
tear (ter) – to rip

temple – a building for worship
temple – side of head near the eye

tire – to become weary or fatigued
tire – the rubber part of a wheel

wind – moving air
wind (wīnd) – to turn or twist

yard – three feet in length
yard – the area surrounding a building

© 2002 by John Wiley & Sons, Inc.

Study Sheet 2-D

Homophones

Homophones are words that sound alike but are spelled differently and have different meanings. Because they sound the same, it is easy to confuse them. Here are common homophones.

ad – short form for *advertisement*
add – to find the sum

air – the atmosphere
heir – a successor to property or rank

aisle – path
I'll – contraction for *I will*
isle – island

allowed – to be able to do something; permitted
aloud – in a loud voice

altar – a raised structure for worship
alter – to change

assistance – help
assistants – helpers

ate – past tense of *eat*
eight – the number after seven

attendance – being present
attendants – escorts

ball – a round object
bawl – to cry

band – a group of musicians
banned – not allowed

bare – having no cover
bear – a big animal

base – bottom of an object
bass – a low-pitched voice

be – to exist
bee – an insect

blew – past tense of *blow*
blue – color of a clear sky in the daytime

board – long wooden plank
bored – not interested

bough – a limb of a tree
bow – to bend forward from the waist

brake – a device to slow or stop a moving vehicle
break – to shatter or ruin

buy – to purchase
by – near or close
bye – short for *goodbye*

canvas – cloth
canvass – to survey

capital – money that is available for investment
capitol – the building in which a state government meets

cell – the basic unit of life
sell – to trade for money

cent – a penny
scent – a smell or odor
sent – past tense of *send*

cereal – breakfast food made from grains
serial – a story written in parts or installments

cheap – not expensive
cheep – sound made by a bird

chews – to bite and crush with teeth
choose – to pick

chord – a combination of musical tones played together
cord – a thick string or thin rope

© 2002 by John Wiley & Sons, Inc.

Study Sheet 2-D

Homophones *(continued)*

cite – to show as proof
sight – act of "seeing" with the eyes
site – a place

coarse – rough
course – a path or way

colonel – military rank
kernal – grain of corn

complement – a complete set
compliment – praise

council – an assembly
counsel – to give advice

dear – a term of affection
deer – an animal

die – to stop living
dye – a substance used to color things

doe – a female deer
dough – a moist mixture of flour used in baking

dual – two
duel – combat between two people

earn – to gain something through work
urn – a container

fir – type of evergreen tree
fur – hair of some animals

flea – a tiny insect
flee – to run away

flew – past tense of *fly*
flu – a viral infection with severe cold symptoms
flue – the tube in a chimney through which smoke rises

forth – forward in time or place
fourth – next after third

foul – filthy, dirty
fowl – a domesticated bird such as a chicken

hair – fine, threadlike structure that grows from skin
hare – a rabbit

hangar – a building for storing airplanes
hanger – a device from which to hang something

heal – to bring back to health
heel – back part of bottom of the foot
he'll – contraction for *he will*

hear – to sense with the ear
here – in this spot

heard – past tense of *hear*
herd – a group of animals

hi – a greeting
high – tall, far up

hoarse – low, scratchy, or husky sounding
horse – a large animal

hole – an opening
whole – an entire amount

hour – sixty minutes
our – belonging to *us*

instance – an example
instants – short periods of time

its – a pronoun that means belonging *to it*
it's – contraction for *it is*

knew – past tense of *know*
new – fresh, not having existed before

knight – a soldier of the Middle Ages
night – the time between daylight and sunset

© 2002 by John Wiley & Sons, Inc.

Study Sheet 2-D

Homophones *(continued)*

know – to be aware of
no – a negative reply

lead – a heavy metal
led – past tense of *lead*, means "to guide"

lessen – to decrease
lesson – something to be learned

loan – to lend
lone – single, by oneself

made – past tense of *make*
maid – a female servant

main – most important
mane – long hair on the neck of an animal

meat – food that comes from animals
meet – to encounter

medal – an award
meddle – to interfere

might – strength, power
mite – a small insect

knot – a tying of a rope or string
not – in no way

oar – a wooden pole with a flat end used to row a boat
or – a word used before an alternative
ore – a mineral deposit

one – the first number after zero
won – past tense of *win*

pail – a bucket
pale – faint, light in color

patience – the ability to wait calmly
patients – people who are treated for health problems

peace – calmness
piece – a part

peal – to ring
peel – to remove a covering

peer – an equal, such as a classmate
pier – a dock

plain – flat land
plane – short for *airplane*

pray – to worship
prey – an animal hunted for food

principal – most important in rank
principle – a fundamental law or truth

profit – benefit
prophet – one who speaks the will of a god

rain – liquid moisture that falls from the sky
reign – the time a king or queen rules
rein – strap to control a horse

read – past tense of *read*
red – the color of blood

right – correct, proper
rite – a religious practice
write – to put into letters and words on paper

road – a street or way for travelers
rode – past tense of *ride*

role – a part played by an actor
roll – to turn over and over

root – part of a plant that grows underground
route – a course, path, or way

sail – a sheet of canvas used to catch wind to move a boat
sale – to sell things for money

© 2002 by John Wiley & Sons, Inc.

Study Sheet 2-D

Homophones *(continued)*

sane – having a sound mind
seine – an open net used for fishing

sea – a part of an ocean
see – to observe with the eyes

sew – to stitch together with needle and thread
so – in such manner
sow – to plant

slay – to kill
sleigh – a large sled pulled by horses

soar – to fly high
sore – painful

sole – flat bottom part of the foot
soul – the spiritual part of a person

some – a part of
sum – total

son – a boy in relation to his father
sun – the star around which the Earth revolves

stake – a sharpened stick
steak – a slice of beef

stationary – stable, not moving
stationery – writing paper

steal – to rob
steel – a strong metal

straight – going in a direct line between two points
strait – a narrow channel of water

symbol – something that represents something else
cymbal – a musical instrument

tail – a flexible extension of an animal's spine
tale – a story

team – a group of people working together
teem – to be stocked to overflowing

their – pronoun meaning *of them*
there – in a certain place
they're – contraction for *they are*

to – word expressing motion toward something
too – also
two – the sum of one and one

vain – conceited; thinking very highly of oneself
vane – device that shows the direction of the wind
vein – a blood vessel

waist – middle part of the body
waste – to use foolishly

wait – to stay
weight – amount of heaviness

ware – something you can buy
wear – to carry clothing on one's body
where – at what place

weak – feeble; not strong
week – seven days in a row

weather – the condition of the atmosphere
whether – if

which – who or what one
witch – a woman who practices magic

whose – pronoun meaning *of whom*
who's – contraction for *who is*

your – pronoun meaning belonging *to you*
you're – contraction for *you are*

© 2002 by John Wiley & Sons, Inc.

Study Sheet 2-E

Easily Confused Words

Many words in English sound a lot like others. These words are easily confused. Here are some of the most common easily confused words and their meanings.

accept – to receive
except – to leave out

access – a way of approach
excess – that which surpasses a limit

advice – an offered opinion
advise – to give advice

affect – to act upon
effect – a result

alley – a passageway between buildings
alloy – a mixture of two or more metals
ally – a partner in an alliance

allot – to divide according to shares
a lot – many

all ready – everything is set
already – before this

all together – everything or everyone in one place
altogether – entirely

angel – a heavenly spirit
angle – a geometric figure

annual – yearly
annul – to make void

appraise – to place a value on
apprise – to inform

bazaar – a market, a fair
bizarre – odd

beside – at the side of
besides – in addition

between – in the middle of two
among – mixed with

biannual – happening twice a year
biennial – happening every other year

breath – air taken into the lungs
breathe – to inhale and exhale

casual – a relaxed, easy manner
causal – relating to a cause

cease – to end
seize – to grasp

close – to shut
clothes – garments a person wears

coma – a deep sleep caused by sickness or injury to the brain
comma – a punctuation mark

command – an order
commend – praise

confidant – a person in whom one can confide
confident – self-assured

conscience – knowledge or sense of right and wrong
conscious – being aware of one's surroundings

cooperate – working together
corporation – a major company

country – a nation
county – a part of a state

decent – proper in attitude and action
descent – the act of coming down

desert – a dry wasteland
dessert – a tasty food served at the end of a meal

© 2002 by John Wiley & Sons, Inc.

Study Sheet 2-E

Easily Confused Words *(continued)*

device – something built for a specific plan
devise – to invent or scheme

disburse – to pay out
disperse – to scatter

elicit – to draw out
illicit – unlawful

elusive – hard to catch
illusive – misleading

emerge – to rise out of
immerse – to plunge into

emigrate – to leave one's country to settle in another
immigrate – to come into another country to settle

eminent – high in rank
imminent – threatening to occur soon

envelop – to surround
envelope – the cover of a letter

farther – to a greater distance
further – in addition to

fewer – smaller in number
less – not as much

finale – the end
finally – at the end

formally – in a conventional manner
formerly – earlier in time

human – a person
humane – kind, decent

illusion – an unreal image
allusion – an indirect hint or suggestion

later – coming afterward
latter – the second of two

lay – to place or put
lie – to be in a reclined position

lightening – to make less heavy; to make bright
lightning – a flash of static electricity in the sky

loose – not tight
lose – to misplace

medal – an award
metal – a mineral; for example, iron

moral – ethical, virtuous
morale – strong spirit in the face of emergency

passed – having gone beyond
past – an earlier time

perpetrate – to commit
perpetuate – to make enduring

persecute – to annoy or injure
prosecute – to try to bring about punishment for a crime

personal – pertaining to a particular individual
personnel – people employed by a business or organization

precede – to go before
proceed – to move onward

quiet – without noise
quit – to give up
quite – completely

respectively – in the order indicated
respectfully – in a manner showing high regard

than – a word showing a comparison
then – at that time

through – going from beginning to end
thorough – complete

veracious – truthful
voracious – greedy

© 2002 by John Wiley & Sons, Inc.

Study Sheet 2-F

Idioms

Idioms are phrases that have special meanings. For example, the idiom "raining cats and dogs" does not mean that cats and dogs are falling from the sky. It means that it is raining very hard. Here are some more common idioms and their meanings.

1. **a ball of fire** — having a lot of energy
2. **bark up the wrong tree** — make a mistake
3. **blow off steam** — let go of anger
4. **by the skin of your teeth** — just barely
5. **call it a day** — stop doing whatever you are doing
6. **face the music** — accept responsibility; be punished
7. **feeling his (or her) oats** — having a lot of energy
8. **get the show on the road** — begin; start
9. **go all out** — try your hardest
10. **got a tiger by the tail** — having a big problem
11. **hold your horses** — stop; wait
12. **in a jam** — in trouble
13. **in the bag** — a certainty; a sure thing
14. **in the same boat** — sharing the same thing, usually a problem
15. **let the cat out of the bag** — reveal a secret
16. **out of sight, out of mind** — a person (or thing) who (that) is not present is not remembered
17. **over the hill** — too old for a particular job or task
18. **pulling my leg** — tricking or kidding someone
19. **put their heads together** — work together to solve a problem
20. **spur of the moment** — do something spontaneously without thinking about it
21. **start the ball rolling** — begin; start
22. **stop dead in his (or her) tracks** — stop or end something abruptly
23. **still up in the air** — not settled yet
24. **throw in the towel** — give up
25. **up the creek** — lost; in trouble

© 2002 by John Wiley & Sons, Inc.

Study Sheet 2-G

Ways to Build Your Vocabulary

Use the following steps to improve your vocabulary.

1. Read as much as you can. Read a variety of different materials, including novels, nonfiction books, short stories, magazines, and newspapers.
2. Look for context clues to help you understand the meanings of new words. Practice figuring out the meanings of unfamiliar words from the way they are used in a sentence.
3. When you cannot figure out the meanings of words from context clues, look them up in a dictionary. Keep a notebook of new words.
4. Pay close attention to words that have multiple meanings.
5. Learn the meanings of prefixes, suffixes, and the roots of words.
6. Use new words in your speaking and writing.
7. Learn to pronounce and spell words correctly.
8. Use a thesaurus to vary your word usage when writing.
9. Make the learning of new words a goal in every subject. Use the glossaries of your textbooks to find the meanings of words.
10. Do crossword puzzles and other word puzzles to have fun and to build your vocabulary.

© 2002 by John Wiley & Sons, Inc.

Study Sheet 2-H

Words to Know

abandon
abnormal
abolish
abrupt
absence
absolute
abstract
absurd
abundant
acceptance
accomplice
accuse
acquiescent
acquittal
adapt
adept
adequate
adjacent
admonish
adversary
aerial
aggressive
agility
aisle
allegiance
allergy
allusion
almanac
amateur
ambiguous
ambitious
amnesia

amnesty
analysis
anniversary
annoyance
anthropology
antique
antiseptic
anxiety
apparatus
applicant
appreciate
appropriate
approximate
archaeology
archipelago
architect
ardent
arrival
artificial
aspire
astound
atrocious
authoritarian
auxiliary
aviation
balmy
belligerent
biannual
bimonthly
boycott
brevity
campaign

candidate
capital
capitol
captivating
carnivorous
catastrophe
cautious
certified
character
chronic
circumference
circuit
civilization
clarity
clemency
coalition
cohesive
coincidence
collapse
commercial
commodity
commotion
complete
compromise
compulsory
conduct
confidential
confusion
conscience
conscious
consistent
conspicuous

conspiracy
constrain
consume
contagious
contemplate
contemporary
contempt
continuous
contradict
control
controversy
convert
convince
coordinate
corrupt
counterfeit
credible
crisis
cunning
curiosity
curtail
custody
customary
cyclical
deem
deficiency
degrade
dejection
deliberate
delicate
denounce
depression

© 2002 by John Wiley & Sons, Inc.

Study Sheet 2-H

Words to Know *(continued)*

descendant
desolation
despair
detour
detract
disaster
discipline
disguise
evidence
evolve
exhaustion
exile
exodus
exorbitant
expensive
expertise
expire
expulsion
extraordinary
exult
fantasized
feasible
feign
ferocity
fidelity
finite
flamboyant
flaw
forfeit
fragrance
frugal
furious

gadget
genuine
glisten
grandeur
guise
harassment
humane
humanitarian
humanity
humility
humorous
hygiene
hysterical
identical
identify
idyllic
ignite
ignorance
illiterate
illogical
illusion
imagery
imitate
immediate
immerse
immigrant
immortal
impact
impartial
impeccable
impede
imperfect

implication
impressive
improper
impudent
impulse
inclusive
inconsiderate
inconspicuous
inconvenient
incredible
incredulous
indecision
indelible
independent
indestructible
ineligible
inflammable
ingredient
inhabitant
injection
inquisitive
innocent
innocuous
innuendo
intellect
interact
intercept
interference
interlude
intermediate
intermittent
intersperse

intricate
intrigue
inundate
invaluable
invincible
involvement
irresistible
irresponsible
irreversible
isthmus
judicial
jurisdiction
justice
knoll
lacerate
laudable
liaison
limitation
literacy
literature
lively
loathe
magistrate
malign
meager
memoir
menace
miraculous
misfortune
miserable
modify
momentum

© 2002 by John Wiley & Sons, Inc.

Study Sheet 2-H

Words to Know *(continued)*

monotonous
morale
musical
nausea
negligence
negotiate
nucleus
obligation
obscure
occasional
ominous
oppress
optimistic
ordinary
pageantry
participant
particular
partition
patience
patients
perception
performance
permanence
permissible
persist
personal
personnel
persuasion
phenomena
philanthropy
pilgrimage
placate
posterity
preceding
precious
precipice
precise
preclude
prejudice
preliminary
premature
preoccupy
prescribe
pretense
prevail
prevention
principal
principle
prior
privilege
projection
prophecy
proprietor
prosecution
prosperity
provision
saturate
scandalous
scarcity
scholar
scrutiny
secrecy
self-conscious
sensible
separate
significance
simulation
slender
slogan
solemn
sophisticated
spacious
specialize
specific
spectacle
speculate
squander
stampede
strategic
strenuous
strew
stringent
stubbornness
stunning
submarine
subtle
suffice
sufficient
sumptuous
supersede
supplement
surplus
surveillance
suspect
suspicious
symbol
synthesis
tangible
technique
tedious
temperament
tenacious
tolerant
torrid
tortuous
tranquil
transformation
transparent
tributary
triumph
trophy
turbulence
ultimately
unanimous
unique
urgent
versatile
vigilance
waive
wrath

© 2002 by John Wiley & Sons, Inc.

Name ______________________ Date ______________

2-1

Finding Prefixes

Part 1. Directions: Circle the prefix of each word.

1. international: nation al in inter
2. dishonest: di dis est honest
3. improbable: im imp impro able
4. irreversible: ir irr reverse ible
5. nonprofit: no non pro profit
6. prehistorical: preh pre hist al
7. inactive: inact act ive in
8. transparent: al tra trans parent
9. uninterested: uni unin interest un
10. biannual: bia annual bi al

Part 2. Directions: Circle the word or phrase that means the same or about the same as the underlined prefix.

1. submarine: without before below after
2. antifreeze: bad double against back
3. immortal: without before after above
4. inconsiderate: bad not before wrong
5. misfortune: bad not later opposite of
6. unicycle: across beneath one badly
7. transcontinental: greater across wrong not
8. preview: before after again between
9. malfunction: not badly among absence of
10. superstar: against between again above

© 2002 by John Wiley & Sons, Inc.

Name ______________________________ Date ________________

2-2

Finding Suffixes

Part 1. Directions: Circle the suffix of each word.

1. performance: per form ance ce
2. retirement: ment re tire nt
3. showy: show owy wy y
4. eagerness: e eager ness es
5. existence: tence ence ex exist
6. artist: tist art st ist
7. respondent: re dent ent respond
8. acidic: ic ac acid aci
9. patriotism: tism ism patriot pat
10. creator: ator create tor or

Part 2. Directions: Circle the word or phrase that means the same or about the same as the underlined suffix.

1. reversible: without capable of like state of
2. correction: condition of does not art of like
3. disappearance: one who full of act of does not
4. assistant: one who state of like without
5. volcanic: does not act of one who like
6. favoritism: able to not practice of badly
7. visible: badly full of without able to
8. violinist: like without one who does act of
9. backward: act of moving toward not full of
10. carnivorous: full of practice of like not

© 2002 by John Wiley & Sons, Inc.

Name ________________________________ Date ____________________

2-3

Finding Synonyms I

Directions: Circle the word that means the same or about the same as the underlined word in each phrase.

1. **a <u>dense</u> fog**

   chilly   thick   damp   thin

2. **an experienced <u>detective</u>**

   police officer   lawyer   investigator   analyst

3. **<u>ominous</u> clouds before a storm**

   threatening   high   fearful   insidious

4. **a strange <u>occurrence</u> that no one could explain**

   evening   tragedy   surprise   incident

5. **<u>modify</u> the schedule for the assembly**

   distribute   change   follow   ignore

6. **<u>catastrophic</u> hurricane**

   flooding   phenomenal   impending   disastrous

7. **<u>amazing</u> news that caused excitement throughout the town**

   awful   astounding   confusing   trivial

8. **another <u>ordinary</u> day**

   unique   stupendous   usual   astonishing

© 2002 by John Wiley & Sons, Inc.

Name ______________________________ Date ________________

2-3

Finding Synonyms I *(continued)*

9. **<u>unanimous</u> decision by the committee**

   undivided split disputed wrong

10. **a <u>suspicious</u> nature**

    trusting complex unstable distrustful

11. **the <u>primary</u> objective**

    only substantial noteworthy main

12. **<u>precious</u> diamonds**

    imitation valuable inexpensive dazzling

13. **decision of the <u>magistrate</u>**

    mayor judge senator president

14. **a severe <u>limitation</u>**

    law announcement proclamation restriction

15. **a <u>generous</u> contribution**

    substantial thoughtful satisfying stingy

© 2002 by John Wiley & Sons, Inc.

Name ______________________________ Date ________________

2-4

Finding Synonyms II

Directions: Write the number of the word in the box on the space before its synonym in the lists below. (Not all words in the lists will be used.)

1. consumer	6. fury	11. permanent	16. exalt
2. reject	7. booklet	12. irresponsible	17. impolite
3. flaw	8. illusion	13. fundamental	18. exceptional
4. barrier	9. festival	14. contemplate	19. pity
5. enormous	10. imply	15. vacant	20. unique

© 2002 by John Wiley & Sons, Inc.

_____ celebration

_____ empty

_____ anger

_____ hallucination

_____ accuse

_____ enduring

_____ ponder

_____ colossal

_____ unusual

_____ shopper

_____ refuse

_____ pamphlet

_____ illuminate

_____ singular

_____ glorify

_____ obstacle

_____ contempt

_____ suggest

_____ defect

_____ avid

_____ untrustworthy

_____ compassion

_____ basic

_____ rude

Name ________________________________ Date ________________

2-5

Finding Antonyms I

Directions: Circle the word that means the opposite of the underlined word in each phrase.

1. **a <u>confidential</u> report**

   secret public private detailed

2. **the <u>original</u> document**

   authentic handwritten duplicate unique

3. **<u>foreign</u> products**

   overseas international expensive domestic

4. **a <u>difficult</u> situation**

   complicated simple confusing extraordinary

5. **an <u>interesting</u> movie**

   boring enjoyable scary complex

6. **an <u>incredible</u> day**

   unusual typical shocking frightening

7. **<u>oppose</u> the reformers**

   fight undermine dispute support

8. **<u>mild</u> reaction to a bee sting**

   uncomfortable itchy serious minor

© 2002 by John Wiley & Sons, Inc.

Name ______________________ Date ______________

2-5

Finding Antonyms I *(continued)*

9. **<u>follow</u> the orders**

disregard accept question receive

10. **a very <u>energetic</u> person**

adventurous cautious nervous lazy

11. **a <u>temporary</u> solution to the problem**

incomplete permanent quick tedious

12. **<u>violent</u> change in society**

rapid destructive peaceful expected

13. **a <u>spacious</u> room**

small huge empty open

14. **a difficult <u>problem</u>**

question dilemma solution undertaking

15. **a very <u>expensive</u> ring**

valuable imitation phony cheap

© 2002 by John Wiley & Sons, Inc.

Name ______________________________ Date ________________

2-6

Finding Antonyms II

Directions: Write the number of the word in the box on the space before its antonym in the lists below. (Not all words in the lists will be used.)

1. success	6. artificial	11. modern	16. ambitious
2. expand	7. specific	12. majority	17. finite
3. interesting	8. innocence	13. precious	18. accept
4. squander	9. omitted	14. ignite	19. dazzling
5. closing	10. enormous	15. forget	20. miserable

_____ shriek

_____ unlimited

_____ guilt

_____ included

_____ minority

_____ lazy

_____ boring

_____ contract

_____ extinguish

_____ primitive

_____ remember

_____ linear

_____ genuine

_____ difference

_____ general

_____ reject

_____ failure

_____ contented

_____ opening

_____ tiny

_____ dull

_____ conserve

_____ fascinate

_____ valueless

© 2002 by John Wiley & Sons, Inc.

Name ______________________________ Date ________________

2-7

Finding the Correct Word I

Directions: Circle the word that best completes each sentence.

1. The dancers showed grace and __________.

   advantage   exercise   agility   melody

2. The suspect admitted his part in the crime and gave a full __________ to the police.

   persuasion   defense   morale   confession

3. The strong economy brought _________ to the country.

   prosperity   poverty   recreation   relaxation

4. Tom does not believe in UFOs and found the story of the flying saucer to be __________.

   true   absurd   plausible   possible

5. The teacher warned that there would be no __________ to the due date for the report.

   standards   expressions   interlude   extensions

6. The school band's __________ at the winter recital was excellent.

   song   performance   arrival   orchestra

7. The colonists hoped they had __________ supplies for the winter.

   meager   efficient   sufficient   inadequate

© 2002 by John Wiley & Sons, Inc.

Name ______________________________ Date ________________

2-7

Finding the Correct Word I *(continued)*

8. Senator Harkins spoke out against the proposed law because he felt it was __________.

   needed　　constitutional　　appropriate　　unconstitutional

9. Maria is __________ and can speak English and Spanish.

   biannual　　bifocal　　bilingual　　bicyclist

10. Tanya put a(n) __________ cream on her cut to prevent infection.

    antibody　　antiseptic　　cohesive　　dubious

11. Seth had worked hard on his report and was __________ when he received an "A."

    dissatisfied　　dynamic　　elated　　exasperated

12. She was a __________ person, who always looked for ways to save money.

    frugal　　industrious　　weary　　grateful

© 2002 by John Wiley & Sons, Inc.

Name ______________________________ Date ________________

2-8

Finding the Correct Word II

Directions: Complete each sentence by filling in the correct word from the Word Bank. (Not all words in the Word Bank will be used.)

1. Sara felt ____________________ because of her cold.
2. China is the most ____________________ country in the world with over 1.2 billion people.
3. The ____________________ provided a strong case against the defendant.
4. The Smiths decided to ________________ their house and add a family room.
5. Double-checking all of the data for the science experiment was a ____________ task and took two class periods.
6. The movie was a great mystery and kept the audience in ________________.
7. Although it did not rain hard, the day was overcast with ______________ drizzle.
8. Jillian forgot to write the ____________________ for her story, leaving the mystery unsolved.
9. The powerful winds, heavy rain, and flooding caused by the hurricane were a ____________________ for the small town.
10. Unlike his brother, who always did what he said he would, Tom was not very ____________________.
11. The fire drill came near the end of the period and brought an ________________ finish to the class.
12. Although the drought had been severe, a series of storms __________________ reservoirs throughout the state.

© 2002 by John Wiley & Sons, Inc.

Word Bank

tedious	energetic	proportion	populous	renovate
intermittent	suspense	conclusion	catastrophe	reliable
immature	restored	prosecutor	terror	subject
abrupt	irresponsible	prosper	miserable	develop

Name ______________________________ Date ______________

2-9

Finding the Correct Word III

Directions: Read the article. Complete the paragraph by filling in each numbered blank with the best word from the choices in the box. The first one is done for you.

Of the various native American peoples, it was the Mayans of Mexico who in many respects developed the most advanced pre-European (1) civilization in the Americas. From about 1500 B.C. to 900 A.D., the Mayans (2) ______________ much of southern Mexico and nearby lands.

Farming was the basis of the Mayan (3) ______________. Their (4) ______________ crop was maize, although cotton, beans, squash, and cacao were also widely grown.

The Mayans built a magnificent civilization. Stone (5) ______________ of several cities still stand throughout the region. Mayan scholars (6) ______________ a form of hieroglyphic, or picture, writing with which they (7) ______________ their mythology, history, and religious practices. Astronomers (8) ______________ a calendar that was the most accurate of its day, craftsmen produced fine pottery, and metalworkers created ornaments and jewelry of gold and silver.

Around 900 A.D. something happened and the Mayans began a rapid (9) ______________. Cities fell and crops were abandoned. No one knows whether war, massive crop failures, disease, or some other (10) ______________ brought the end to this wonderful civilization.

1.	authority	invasion	civilization	chronology
2.	occupied	comprised	convened	generated
3.	fertility	economy	cities	religion
4.	tasty	expensive	festival	principal
5.	ruins	monuments	artifacts	monoliths
6.	found	imagined	developed	rejected
7.	discovered	recorded	invented	remembered
8.	sought	built	discussed	devised
9.	decline	disappearance	revolution	expansion
10.	surprise	shock	disaster	unexpected

© 2002 by John Wiley & Sons, Inc.

Name ________________________________ Date ____________________

2-10

Words with Multiple Meanings I

Directions: Circle the word that has the same meaning as the two phrases.

1. in the present time
   a steady flow of water

   now   river   current   movement

2. actors and actresses in a play
   to throw a fishing line into the water

   cast   caste   troupe   production

3. thinking seriously on an idea or issue
   bending or throwing back light from a surface

   ponder   refract   consider   reflect

4. to believe something is true or likely
   a person believed to have committed a crime

   assailant   criminal   suspect   perpetrator

5. an item
   a nonfiction essay or composition

   particle   article   abstract   letter

6. to fight against authority
   a person who fights against authority

   accomplice   chancellor   agitator   rebel

7. a written agreement
   to draw together; shrink

   arrangement   contract   collapse   formation

© 2002 by John Wiley & Sons, Inc.

Name ______________________________ Date ________________

2-10

Words with Multiple Meanings I *(continued)*

8. to thrust forward or outward
   a plan or major undertaking

   project vocation development ordinance

9. in a state of excellence
   bringing to completion

   finish accomplish perfect solution

10. a subject of concern or discussion
    a single copy of a magazine

    controversy discourse topic issue

11. to apply efforts together working toward a common goal
    one of two numbers that locates a point on a grid

    contemplate coordinate designate vertex

12. speaking in favor of something
    a person who supports a cause

    ardent eccentric advocate visionary

© 2002 by John Wiley & Sons, Inc.

Name ______________________________ Date ______________

2-11

Words with Multiple Meanings II

Directions: Circle the word that best completes both sentences.

1. They decided to __________ to the beach on their bikes.
   The life __________ of a butterfly includes four stages: egg, larva (caterpillar), pupa (cocoon), and adult.

   span travel cycle marathon

2. The child has a pleasant personality and her __________ is always admirable.
   In Lynn's absence it was Tom's responsibility to __________ the meeting.

   conduct behavior attitude manage

3. The __________ to their next stop was direct.
   Gil made sure to __________ the packages of supplies to the proper offices.

   send road forward route

4. The first time Mira went ice skating, she had trouble keeping her __________.
   In science class students used a __________ to compare the weights of various objects.

   balance scale equilibrium footing

5. Under normal conditions, freezing temperatures __________ water to ice.
   Since arriving in our country, Inez has become a __________ to our way of life.

   transfer supporter convert turn

6. The __________ movements throughout our nation's history have improved the lives of countless people.
   In response to the student government's inability to manage problems, Alex started a committee to help __________ the organization.

   administer democratic reform legislative

© 2002 by John Wiley & Sons, Inc.

Name ______________________________ Date ________________

2-11

Words with Multiple Meanings II *(continued)*

7. Becoming lost while camping, Josh __________ the direction of north and was able to find his way back to camp.

   Trevor was __________ to do well on his report card.

   determined   guessed   discovered   decided

8. The __________ of the story was confusing, making the story difficult to understand.

   The thieves thought they had a foolproof __________ to steal money from the bank, but the police quickly figured out their plan.

   scheme   method   procedure   plot

9. A naturally talkative individual, Juan was always ready to __________ people in conversation.

   Carla knew that once she went to high school, studying would __________ most of her time.

   accept   engage   immerse   persuade

10. Will wrote a note of apology, expressing his __________ at missing the family reunion.

    Kim knew she would __________ having forgotten to study for the math test.

    disappointment   failure   regret   mistake

© 2002 by John Wiley & Sons, Inc.

Name ______________________ Date ______________

2-12

Identifying Homographs

Directions: Write the homograph after its definition. Use the words from the Word Bank to find your answers. (Most of the words in the Word Bank will be used more than once. Some words will not be used at all.)

1. to slow the movement of someone or something: ____________
2. a small apartment: ____________
3. a baseball player: ____________
4. rubber exterior covering for a wheel: ____________
5. considerate, thoughtful: ____________
6. new, novel: ____________
7. to shut: ____________
8. a large, covered basket: ____________
9. place of burial: ____________
10. behavior showing lack of respect: ____________
11. level: ____________
12. a geometric figure composed of two rays: ____________
13. container for pouring liquids: ____________
14. a glass container holding jam: ____________
15. an extremely serious condition: ____________

© 2002 by John Wiley & Sons, Inc.

Name ______________________________ Date ________________

2-12

Identifying Homographs *(continued)*

16. a group that shares like traits: ____________

17. to bounce or jolt: ____________

18. nearby: ____________

19. to fish: ____________

20. to become exhausted or weary: ____________

Word Bank

wind	tire	tear	duck	contract	bear
principal	hamper	grave	angle	sock	school
close	kind	buck	spell	pitcher	flat
fresh	bank	jar	count	yard	pupil

© 2002 by John Wiley & Sons, Inc.

Name ______________________________ Date ________________

2-13

Identifying Homophones I

Directions: Circle the correct homophone to complete each sentence.

1. Marie's favorite __________ was scheduled to play at the benefit concert.

   band   banned

2. Christina has __________ for breakfast each morning.

   cereal   serial

3. __________ period was canceled because of the pep rally.

   Forth   Fourth

4. The town __________ met last night to discuss building a new park.

   council   counsel

5. The little girl had no __________ and kept fidgeting as she waited at the bus stop with her mother.

   patients   patience

6. Eddie smiled when his mother __________ him for cleaning his room.

   complemented   complimented

7. The kitten batted the ball of yarn with __________ paw.

   it's   its

8. After she chose her topic for the science project, Heather wondered __________ she had made the right choice.

   whether   weather

© 2002 by John Wiley & Sons, Inc.

Name ______________________________ Date ________________

2-13

Identifying Homophones I *(continued)*

9. __________ books are on the table?

   Who's   Whose

10. The shortest distance between two points is a __________ line.

    straight   strait

11. Elena wrote the thank-you note on __________ she had designed herself.

    stationery   stationary

12. Watch __________ step on the stairs.

    you're   your

13. The football __________ practices until dusk each day.

    teem   team

14. Mr. Williams is the __________ of our school.

    principle   principal

15. Marsha's piano __________ was canceled because of the bad storm.

    lesson   lessen

© 2002 by John Wiley & Sons, Inc.

Name ______________________________ Date ________________

2-14

Identifying Homophones II

Directions: Circle the correct homophone to complete each sentence.

1. After the storm passed, the weather _________ showed the wind coming from the west.

   vain vane vein

2. _________ going to the movies tonight at seven.

   There Their They're

3. Jason's broken ankle required several months to _________ completely.

   heal he'll heel

4. Conor missed a week of school because of the _________.

   flew flue flu

5. It was hot, dry, and dusty at the archaeological _________ of the ancient city.

   cite site sight

6. Despite a closet full of clothes, Ricky could not find anything to _________ to the fall dance.

   ware wear where

7. The _________ of Queen Elizabeth I of England lasted 44 years.

   reign rein rain

8. Alana arranged her schedule _________ that she would have time to study for the upcoming exams.

   sew sow so

9. Eddie was relieved when he got his quiz back, because he had nine _________ answers out of ten questions.

   rite right write

10. Mandy's grandfather remembered when postcards cost only a _________.

    scent sent cent

© 2002 by John Wiley & Sons, Inc.

Name ________________________________ Date ________________

2-15

Identifying Homophones III

Directions: Read each definition. Then write the correct homophone from the Word Bank on the line.

1. a story published in installments: ________________
2. a tree limb: ________________
3. to ring: ________________
4. to decrease: ________________
5. inexpensive: ________________
6. ability to wait calmly: ________________
7. low, scratchy voice: ________________
8. something to be learned: ________________
9. a large animal typically used for riding: ________________
10. to bend forward: ________________
11. two: ________________
12. people treated by a doctor: ________________
13. the chirping of a bird: ________________
14. combat between two people: ________________
15. an idea that represents something else: ________________
16. removing a covering, for example of fruit: ________________
17. a container: ________________
18. a breakfast food: ________________
19. to gain money by working: ________________
20. a musical instrument: ________________

Word Bank

bow	bough	horse	earn	lesson
cymbal	lessen	patience	cheep	peal
cheap	peel	duel	hoarse	patients
serial	dual	cereal	urn	symbol

© 2002 by John Wiley & Sons, Inc.

Name ______________________________ Date ________________

2-16

Easily Confused Words I

Directions: Circle the correct word to complete each sentence.

1. The wind blew the smoke from the forest fire into town, making it hard for people to _________.

   breath breathe

2. Felipe had studied and was _________ that he would do well on the math test.

   confident confidant

3. Ruth always looked forward to _________ after dinner.

   desert dessert

4. During the fire drill students were to _________ to the front door and exit the school.

   precede proceed

5. While doing his geometry homework, Billy carefully measured the _________ with his protractor.

   angle angel

6. Despite the thunderstorms their plane had to fly through en route to the airport, their _________ and landing were smooth.

   decent descent

7. Kara is well liked because of her _________ and easy-going manner.

   casual causal

© 2002 by John Wiley & Sons, Inc.

Name ______________________________ Date ________________

2-16

Easily Confused Words I *(continued)*

8. Because of the bad weather, the computer club meeting was canceled and rescheduled for __________ in the week.

   later latter

9. The __________ flashed brilliantly across the night sky.

   lightening lightning

10. From our home, Philadelphia is __________ than New York.

    further farther

11. Having lost her keys once, Mindy was careful not to __________ them again.

    loose lose

12. Hearing the thunder in the distance, Todd knew a storm was __________.

    imminent eminent

© 2002 by John Wiley & Sons, Inc.

Name ______________________________ Date ________________

2-17

Easily Confused Words II

Directions: Circle the correct word to complete each sentence.

1. Dan received a _________ for his brave actions during the fire.

   metal   medal

2. Dieter's family _________ from Germany.

   emigrated   immigrated

3. Despite the destruction the tornado caused to their town, the _________ of the people was high as they began the clean-up.

   moral   morale

4. Sara liked studying history and learning about times that had _________.

   passed   past

5. Jay's ideal way to relax was to _________ in a hammock in his backyard.

   lie   lay

6. Canada is a big _________ with abundant natural resources.

   county   country

7. Tom sits in the third row _________ Mike and Julie.

   between   among

8. The virus that causes influenza is very _________.

   contiguous   contagious

© 2002 by John Wiley & Sons, Inc.

Name ________________________________ Date ____________________

2-17

Easily Confused Words II *(continued)*

9. Watching what appeared to be a strange object in the sky, Tyrel later convinced himself it was an __________ caused by the moonlight reflecting on the clouds.

   allusion illusion

10. The teacher reminded the class to be __________ in the library.

    quiet quit quite

11. During World War II, Great Britain was an __________ of the United States.

    alley ally alloy

12. In order to survive, all creatures must __________ to their environment.

    adept adopt adapt

© 2002 by John Wiley & Sons, Inc.

Name ______________________________ Date ________________

2-18

Interpreting Idioms

Directions: Read the sentences and underline the idioms. Then write the meaning of each idiom.

1. Having not completed the history project on time, Renee and Amanda were in the same boat.

   ____

2. After studying for three hours after dinner, Cal decided to call it a day.

   ____

3. The school's social committee put their heads together to plan the spring events.

   ____

4. Frustrated that he could not understand his math homework, Jimmy was ready to throw in the towel.

   ____

5. On the day his family was to leave for Walt Disney World, Santo woke up early, ready to get the show on the road.

   ____

6. Once his parents saw his report card, Zak knew that he would have to face the music.

   ____

7. Upon reaching the front steps of the school, Lil stopped dead in her tracks—she had forgotten her science report!

   ____

© 2002 by John Wiley & Sons, Inc.

Name ______________________________ Date ________________

2-18

Interpreting Idioms *(continued)*

8. Although they had been trying to settle their argument all day, the problem between Angie and Elena was still up in the air.

____

9. The moment Ryan came home, school was out of sight, out of mind.

____

10. The coach urged the players to go all out during the soccer game.

____

11. After waking up from a restful sleep, Sean was a ball of fire.

____

12. Even though he had not studied much, Taylor knew the material for his math test and figured a good grade was in the bag.

____

© 2002 by John Wiley & Sons, Inc.

EIGHTH-GRADE LEVEL

Vocabulary

PRACTICE TESTS

© 2002 by John Wiley & Sons, Inc.

Vocabulary Practice Test I

Part 1. Directions: Use the Answer Sheet to darken the letter of the prefix for each of the following words.

1. bicentennial:

   A. al B. bic C. bi D. bicen

2. irregular:

   A. irr B. ir C. lar D. ar

3. exclamation:

   A. ex B. exc C. ion D. tion

4. impossible:

   A. ble B. imp C. ible D. im

5. preoccupation:

   A. preoc B. pre C. tion D. ion

6. uniformity:

   A. un B. ty C. uni D. ty

© 2002 by John Wiley & Sons, Inc.

Part 2. Directions: Use the Answer Sheet to darken the suffix for each of the following words.

1. inventor:

   A. in B. or C. tor D. vent

2. disagreement:

   A. dis B. agree C. ment D. ent

3. performance:

   A. per B. mance C. ance D. form

4. glorious:

   A. ious B. glory C. glo D. ous

5. violinist:

    A. vio B. ist C. violin D. nist

6. capitalism:

    A. ism B. lism C. capital D. cap

Part 3. Directions: Use the Answer Sheet to darken the meaning of each underlined prefix and suffix.

1. visible:

    A. full of B. state of C. like D. able to

2. international:

    A. before B. again C. across D. between

3. willowy:

    A. like B. without C. state of D. act of

4. dangerous:

    A. skill of B. act of C. full of D. without

5. malnutrition:

    A. after B. bad C. against D. opposite of

6. nonsensical:

    A. wrong B. badly C. against D. not

7. occupant:

    A. one who B. state of C. like D. without

8. reprocess:

    A. after B. again C. not D. among

© 2002 by John Wiley & Sons, Inc.

Vocabulary Practice Test II

Part 1. Directions: Use the Answer Sheet to darken the letter of the word that has the same or almost the same meaning as the underlined word.

1. a strange incident

   A. era B. occurrence C. discussion D. confession

2. the delicate flower

   A. fragile B. hardy C. colorful D. magnificent

3. the sensible decision

   A. foolish B. impractical C. complex D. reasonable

4. threatening clouds

   A. puffy B. wispy C. ominous D. obscure

5. the miraculous recovery from the accident

   A. unsuccessful B. extraordinary C. torturous D. incomplete

© 2002 by John Wiley & Sons, Inc.

Part 2. Directions: Use the Answer Sheet to darken the letter of the word that has the opposite meaning of the underlined word.

1. precise calculations

   A. exact B. inaccurate C. positive D. summarized

2. the preceding announcement

   A. important B. serious C. following D. imminent

3. the prudent course of action

   A. foolish B. sensible C. delightful D. unhealthy

4. possessing a trusting nature

   A. careful B. honest C. mature D. suspicious

5. the <u>ambitious</u> individual

   A. headstrong B. lazy C. commanding D. informed

Part 3. Directions: Use the Answer Sheet to darken the letter of the word that has the same meaning as the two phrases.

1. a phony appearance
   to conceal one's true identity

   A. outfit B. change C. costume D. disguise

2. a steady improvement
   to advance and move forward

   A. grow B. progress C. accomplish D. result

3. the nature of an individual
   a ghost

   A. wraith B. emotion C. spirit D. personality

4. a series of steps in the production of something
   to make ready

   A. process B. instructions C. construct D. create

5. an identical copy of an original
   to make a copy

   A. forgery B. duplicate C. genuine D. repeat

6. capable of being changed in form
   a type of car

   A. altered B. sedan C. vehicle D. convertible

7. to recognize the quality of a thing
   to increase in value

   A. appreciate B. grow C. appropriate D. inflate

© 2002 by John Wiley & Sons, Inc.

Vocabulary Practice Test II *(continued)*

8. a person's signature
   to write your name on an object

   A. sign B. handwriting C. autograph D. pen name

9. dishonest, immoral
   to ruin

   A. criminal B. destroy C. vicious D. corrupt

10. the most important region or part of a thing
    the positively charged central part of an atom

    A. middle B. essential C. nucleus D. proton

© 2002 by John Wiley & Sons, Inc.

Vocabulary Practice Test III

Part 1. Directions: Use the Answer Sheet to darken the letter of the word that best completes each sentence.

1. Even though the traffic accident in front of the school was minor, it caused a lot of __________.

   A. bewildering B. fury C. commotion D. demolish

2. Kerrie's little sister tried to __________ Kerrie's actions and expressions.

   A. mimic B. imagine C. murmur D. placate

3. The __________ leaves of the garden's plants showed the effects of the severe drought.

   A. colorful B. withered C. effusive D. abundant

4. Before the discovery of vaccines, many serious diseases were __________ throughout the country.

   A. available B. contagious C. severe D. prevalent

5. Students __________ a petition expressing their dissatisfaction with the lunches served in the school cafeteria.

   A. demonstrated B. circulated C. comprised D. injected

6. The plot of the mystery was __________, and Melissa guessed who had committed the crime long before the climax.

   A. suspenseful B. boring C. predictable D. confusing

7. Knowing she had a lot of homework, Shawna's decision not to go to the basketball game until she was finished was a __________ one.

   A. moral B. hasty C. mistaken D. sensible

© 2002 by John Wiley & Sons, Inc.

Vocabulary Practice Test III *(continued)*

Part 2. Directions: Use the Answer Sheet to darken the letter of the word that best completes both sentences.

1. Tina had to __________ her two younger brothers before their argument over the toy turned into a fight.
   Raymond kept his aggressive fish in a __________ tank to prevent them from eating his other fish.

   A. stop B. scold C. separate D. special

2. After the long week of soccer practice, Eddie was sure his team would __________ in their upcoming playoff game.
   The football team's win over their arch rival was a great __________.

   A. victory B. triumph C. prevail D. success

3. The tool set came with a lifetime __________.
   The salesman told us he would personally __________ the stereo system.

   A. warranty B. promise C. validate D. guarantee

4. Hallie's father __________ the services of a contractor to manage the renovation on their home.
   Santos likes to talk and is always __________ in conversation.

   A. hired B. engaged C. involved D. sought

5. The brave knight offered a __________ to the false king to meet him in combat.
   Scaling the side of the mountain would be a great __________.

   A. challenge B. summons C. calling D. dilemma

6. The neighborhood's __________ of a local gas station for its price-gouging during the gasoline shortage was successful, and the station owner lowered his prices.
   Students decided to __________ the school store because of the high prices of its school supplies.

   A. disgust B. demonstrate C. boycott D. avoid

© 2002 by John Wiley & Sons, Inc.

Vocabulary Practice Test III *(continued)*

7. While giving her speech, Tania tried to __________ her voice so that everyone could hear her.

   Anthony's history __________ included essays, a slide show, and special activities for the class.

   A. presentation B. project C. direct D. extend

Part 3. Directions: Read the paragraph and use the Answer Sheet to darken the letter of the word that best completes each sentence.

Most Americans have heard about Meriwether Lewis and William Clark, who were (1) ___________ by President Thomas Jefferson to explore the Louisiana Purchase. Most, however, do not know much about Sacagawea, a Shoshoni Indian woman who played a major role in the success of the (2) ___________. Sacagawea is believed to have been born in Idaho about 1786. After being captured by another Indian tribe, she was sold to a Canadian trapper, Toussaint Charbonneau, who made her his wife in 1804. When Lewis and Clark hired Charbonneau in 1805 as a guide and interpreter on their way to the Pacific Coast, Sacagawea came too. With her (3) ___________ of the western lands, she was able to lead the explorers through the (4) ___________, identify (5) ___________ plants that the explorers added to their diets, and communicate with the Indian tribes they met. Sacagawea proved to be (6) ___________ to the success of the journey.

1.	A. adapted	B. commissioned	C. denounced	D. interacted
2.	A. interlude	B. delegation	C. expedition	D. alliance
3.	A. knowledge	B. history	C. progress	D. jurisdiction
4.	A. crisis	B. precipice	C. junction	D. wilderness
5.	A. interesting	B. edible	C. familiar	D. protein
6.	A. responsible	B. minor	C. invaluable	D. melodramatic

© 2002 by John Wiley & Sons, Inc.

Name ______________________ Date ______________

Vocabulary

PRACTICE TEST I: ANSWER SHEET

Directions: Darken the circle above the letter of the correct answer.

Part 1

1. ○ A ○ B ○ C ○ D

2. ○ A ○ B ○ C ○ D

3. ○ A ○ B ○ C ○ D

4. ○ A ○ B ○ C ○ D

5. ○ A ○ B ○ C ○ D

6. ○ A ○ B ○ C ○ D

Part 2

1. ○ A ○ B ○ C ○ D

2. ○ A ○ B ○ C ○ D

3. ○ A ○ B ○ C ○ D

4. ○ A ○ B ○ C ○ D

5. ○ A ○ B ○ C ○ D

6. ○ A ○ B ○ C ○ D

Part 3

1. ○ A ○ B ○ C ○ D

2. ○ A ○ B ○ C ○ D

3. ○ A ○ B ○ C ○ D

4. ○ A ○ B ○ C ○ D

5. ○ A ○ B ○ C ○ D

6. ○ A ○ B ○ C ○ D

7. ○ A ○ B ○ C ○ D

8. ○ A ○ B ○ C ○ D

© 2002 by John Wiley & Sons, Inc.

Name ______________________________ Date ______________

Vocabulary

PRACTICE TEST II: ANSWER SHEET

Directions: Darken the circle above the letter of the correct answer.

Part 1

1. ○ A ○ B ○ C ○ D
2. ○ A ○ B ○ C ○ D
3. ○ A ○ B ○ C ○ D
4. ○ A ○ B ○ C ○ D
5. ○ A ○ B ○ C ○ D

Part 2

1. ○ A ○ B ○ C ○ D
2. ○ A ○ B ○ C ○ D
3. ○ A ○ B ○ C ○ D
4. ○ A ○ B ○ C ○ D
5. ○ A ○ B ○ C ○ D

Part 3

1. ○ A ○ B ○ C ○ D
2. ○ A ○ B ○ C ○ D
3. ○ A ○ B ○ C ○ D
4. ○ A ○ B ○ C ○ D
5. ○ A ○ B ○ C ○ D
6. ○ A ○ B ○ C ○ D
7. ○ A ○ B ○ C ○ D
8. ○ A ○ B ○ C ○ D
9. ○ A ○ B ○ C ○ D
10. ○ A ○ B ○ C ○ D

© 2002 by John Wiley & Sons, Inc.

Name ______________________________ Date ________________

Vocabulary

PRACTICE TEST III: ANSWER SHEET

Directions: Darken the circle above the letter of the correct answer.

Part 1

1. ○ A ○ B ○ C ○ D
2. ○ A ○ B ○ C ○ D
3. ○ A ○ B ○ C ○ D
4. ○ A ○ B ○ C ○ D
5. ○ A ○ B ○ C ○ D
6. ○ A ○ B ○ C ○ D
7. ○ A ○ B ○ C ○ D

Part 2

1. ○ A ○ B ○ C ○ D
2. ○ A ○ B ○ C ○ D
3. ○ A ○ B ○ C ○ D
4. ○ A ○ B ○ C ○ D
5. ○ A ○ B ○ C ○ D
6. ○ A ○ B ○ C ○ D
7. ○ A ○ B ○ C ○ D

Part 3

1. ○ A ○ B ○ C ○ D
2. ○ A ○ B ○ C ○ D
3. ○ A ○ B ○ C ○ D
4. ○ A ○ B ○ C ○ D
5. ○ A ○ B ○ C ○ D
6. ○ A ○ B ○ C ○ D

© 2002 by John Wiley & Sons, Inc.

Vocabulary

KEY TO PRACTICE TEST I

Part 1

	A	B	C	D
1.	○	○	●	○
2.	○	●	○	○
3.	●	○	○	○
4.	○	○	○	●
5.	○	●	○	○
6.	○	○	●	○

Part 2

	A	B	C	D
1.	○	●	○	○
2.	○	○	●	○
3.	○	○	●	○
4.	○	○	○	●
5.	○	●	○	○
6.	●	○	○	○

Part 3

	A	B	C	D
1.	○	○	○	●
2.	○	○	○	●
3.	●	○	○	○
4.	○	○	●	○
5.	○	●	○	○
6.	○	○	○	●
7.	●	○	○	○
8.	○	●	○	○

© 2002 by John Wiley & Sons, Inc.

Vocabulary

KEY TO PRACTICE TEST II

Part 1

1. ○ A ● B ○ C ○ D
2. ● A ○ B ○ C ○ D
3. ○ A ○ B ○ C ● D
4. ○ A ○ B ● C ○ D
5. ○ A ● B ○ C ○ D

Part 2

1. ○ A ● B ○ C ○ D
2. ○ A ○ B ● C ○ D
3. ● A ○ B ○ C ○ D
4. ○ A ○ B ○ C ● D
5. ○ A ● B ○ C ○ D

Part 3

1. ○ A ○ B ○ C ● D
2. ○ A ● B ○ C ○ D
3. ○ A ○ B ● C ○ D
4. ● A ○ B ○ C ○ D
5. ○ A ● B ○ C ○ D
6. ○ A ○ B ○ C ● D
7. ● A ○ B ○ C ○ D
8. ○ A ○ B ● C ○ D
9. ○ A ○ B ○ C ● D
10. ○ A ○ B ● C ○ D

© 2002 by John Wiley & Sons, Inc.

Vocabulary

KEY TO PRACTICE TEST III

Part 1

	A	B	C	D
1.	○	○	●	○
2.	●	○	○	○
3.	○	●	○	○
4.	○	○	○	●
5.	○	●	○	○
6.	○	○	●	○
7.	○	○	○	●

Part 2

	A	B	C	D
1.	○	○	●	○
2.	○	●	○	○
3.	○	○	○	●
4.	○	●	○	○
5.	●	○	○	○
6.	○	○	●	○
7.	○	●	○	○

Part 3

	A	B	C	D
1.	○	●	○	○
2.	○	○	●	○
3.	●	○	○	○
4.	○	○	○	●
5.	○	●	○	○
6.	○	○	●	○

© 2002 by John Wiley & Sons, Inc.

Section 3

Reading Comprehension

The ability to read is crucial for success in our information-driven society, a fact underscored by the prominence of reading on standardized tests. Virtually every standardized test has a "Reading Comprehension" or "Verbal Section" that focuses largely on reading skills. Not only is a student's ability to read clearly indicated on the reading portions of tests, it is also indirectly shown on all of the other tests. The student who cannot read with proficiency is unlikely to excel on any of the verbal tests, understand questions on science tests, or be able to solve word problems on math tests. When a student lacks reading skills, his or her scores on other tests will be undermined.

You can do much to promote reading in your classes. Most important:

- Provide time for reading in school. If time is not provided in class, some students, because of their schedules outside of school, will not have time to read.
- Make various reading materials available to your students: short stories, novels, nonfiction books, biographies, autobiographies, magazines, newspapers, and poetry.
- Provide materials that are appropriate for the abilities of your students. Eighth-grade students of low reading ability are unlikely to be able to handle materials good readers can. Likewise, good readers will be bored with the materials geared for students who have weak reading skills. Matching interesting materials with reading abilities is essential for a successful reading class.
- While making an effort to match materials with abilities, keep in mind the value of providing challenging reading that pulls students forward to the next level of skills.
- Show your own pleasure of reading by sharing your thoughts on material you are reading. The times that your students are reading in class are times you can be reading, too. Model reading for your students whenever you can.
- Promote reading through special programs, events, and displays. Simple things like a display showing the "Book of the Month" or the "Student Pick of the Month" can elevate awareness of the importance and value of reading.

To further help your students develop their reading skills, distribute copies of this section's study sheets:

- Study Sheet 3-A, "Traits of Good Readers"
- Study Sheet 3-B, "The SQ3R System for Reading"
- Study Sheet 3-C, "Guidelines for Reading Logs"
- Study Sheet 3-D, "Story Elements"
- Study Sheet 3-E, "Breaking Down a Story into Parts"

Use the study sheets in a manner that best supports your reading program. While you can hand out the study sheets at any time during the school year, many teachers find that the most effective time to distribute them is soon after the beginning of the year as they are starting their reading programs.

When you hand out Study Sheet 3-A, "Traits of Good Readers," explain that a trait is a characteristic of a person. A trait helps to describe that person. Many people who enjoy similar activities share some of the same traits. This is true of good readers. Note that while not all good readers share all of the traits listed on the study sheet, all good readers possess many of them. Discuss the various traits and emphasize that good readers are not born; people become good readers through reading. As your students read more, they will acquire more of the traits on the study sheet.

You might also like to distribute Study Sheet 3-B, "The SQ3R System for Reading." Developed in 1941 by Francis Robinson, the SQ3R System remains one of the most popular and effective reading methods.

Introduce the study sheet by explaining to your students that the SQ3R System is a plan, or method, that can help them improve their reading. The best way to ensure that your students understand the system is to review the study sheet with them and then demonstrate the system by applying it to a short story, an article, or even a section of a textbook. Go through the steps together and note that mastering the system takes time and practice. The more your students use it, the more proficient they will become. Emphasize that the SQ3R System helps most people who use it read with better comprehension, and encourage your students to utilize the system for all of their reading assignments.

Reading logs are yet another way to foster the reading skills of your students. Study Sheet 3-C, "Guidelines for Reading Logs," offers the basics for maintaining a reading log. Reading logs, which are also called reading journals, reading response journals, literary journals, or summary logs, serve as a place for students to record their reactions to reading. Logs are the place where students may write about their feelings or opinions regarding what they read, make notes, answer questions posed by their teacher, or write down questions of their own. Reading logs can become the repository of all of a student's responses to reading.

While spiral notebooks are perhaps the best choice for reading logs, notepads, sections of three-ring binders, or even composition paper stapled together can be used for logs. Require that your students make all of their entries in their logs, because entries made elsewhere frequently become lost and the continuity of the log is disrupted.

While you may use reading logs primarily as a vehicle in which students record their reactions to reading, you can maximize the potential benefit of logs by presenting students with specific questions that require them to delve deeply into their reading. Following are examples of questions you might consider having your students answer in their logs. Note that they are open-ended, requiring explanations.

- What do you think the author's purpose was in writing this story (or article)?
- How do the characters change in this story? How are they different at the end of the story from the way they were at the beginning?
- Which character do you like the most? Why? Which character do you like the least? Why?
- How does the author make the characters seem like real people?
- What three words would you use to describe the lead characters? Give examples of how these words describe the character.
- If you were confronted with the same situations as (character's name), what would you have done? Why?
- What was the major conflict of this story?
- What suggestions do you have for the characters to solve their problem?
- Describe the climax of the story. Did you find the climax satisfying? Why or why not?
- What did you learn from this story (or article)?
- What questions would you like to ask the author about this story (or article)?
- Has the author changed your mind about the topic? If the author has, how? If the author has not, why not?

Study Sheet 3-D, "Story Elements," details the major parts of a story. Discuss the study sheet with your students and ask volunteers to identify the various parts of a story the class is currently reading or has recently read. Explain to your students that when they understand the parts of a story, they are more likely to understand the story as a whole.

Study Sheet 3-E, "Breaking Down a Story into Parts," can be used at any time of the year with any story. The sheet can be used over and over again. Answering the questions on the study sheet will help your students focus on the various parts of stories, thereby enhancing their comprehension.

Along with the five study sheets, this section has 30 worksheets and three practice tests. Worksheets 3-1 through 3-14 focus on specific reading skills, which are indicated in the title of the worksheet. Worksheets 3-15 through 3-30 present various types of literature and include questions on literal, interpretive, and applied comprehension skills. The skills covered in the first set of worksheets are reinforced in the second set.

The study sheets, worksheets, and practice tests of this section cover reading skills that are regularly found on eighth-grade standardized tests. You should utilize the materials of this section in ways that best satisfy the needs of your students.

Teaching Suggestions for the Worksheets

3-1: Understanding Characterization

Introduce this activity by explaining to your students that characterization is the method through which an author shows what the characters in a story are like. Explain that characterization includes emotional and physical traits. A character may be short or tall, courageous or cowardly, crafty or naïve. A character may be self-assured or self-conscious. He or she may have dark hair and eyes, be blonde and have blue eyes, or possess any variety of features that reflect real people. Of course, characters in fantasy, horror, or science fiction stories may not possess any human traits at all. Through characterization, an author makes his or her characters come alive for the reader.

Instruct your students to read the story and pay close attention to the traits of the characters. After they have completed the questions, discuss the story, go over their work, and answer any questions about characterization that they may have.

3-2: Making Inferences and Conclusions

Begin this activity by explaining that an inference is the process of making a conclusion based upon facts or premises. When dark clouds approach on a hot, humid day, you can infer that a storm is probably coming, and your conclusion is that it is going to rain.

For this worksheet, your students are to read the story and answer the questions that follow. When they are finished, discuss the story and the answers. In particular, emphasize the evidence at the end of the story that led students to conclude a tornado was approaching.

3-3: Finding Main Ideas and Details

Begin this exercise by explaining that well-written paragraphs are built around main ideas, supported with details. The main idea is the focus of the paragraph, and the details explain the main idea. Mention that the main idea is often contained in the first sentence of a paragraph, but caution your students that this is not always true. The sentence that contains the main idea may appear in the middle or even the end of a paragraph. Sometimes, the main idea is not contained in a single sentence, but is sprinkled throughout the paragraph.

This worksheet consists of four paragraphs. Your students are to read each paragraph and identify the main idea and supporting details. When your students are finished with the worksheet, read and discuss the paragraphs together. Make sure everyone understands how to find the main idea and details of the paragraphs.

3-4: Sequencing

Start this exercise by explaining that sequence refers to the logical order of the ideas or events in a story or article. Most stories and articles are organized chronologically. In chronological organization, what happens first in time comes first in a story, what happens second comes second, and so on. The events of the story are a part of a sequence.

For this worksheet, your students are to read the story. Then they are to number the statements that follow in the order in which they happened in the story by writing a number from 1 to 10 on the blanks before the statements. Upon completion of the worksheet, go over the sequence with your students and answer any questions they may have.

3-5: Understanding Context Clues

Begin this activity by explaining to your students that they can improve their comprehension through the use of context clues. When they understand some words of a sentence and what the sentence is generally about, they will often be able to figure out the meanings of unfamiliar words from the way they are used in the sentence. This will in turn help them to better understand the overall meaning of the sentence.

For this worksheet, your students are to read each sentence and find the meaning of the underlined word. Then they are to circle the clue in the sentence that helped them figure out the meaning of the underlined word.

Once your students have completed the worksheet, go over the sentences and discuss the clues that your students used to find the meanings of the underlined words. In question one, for example, the meaning of "vivacious" is "lively," which is implied in the first sentence, ". . . Aunt Trish was always happy and full of energy." Discussing the various clues will help to ensure that your students recognize the use and value of context clues to comprehension.

3-6: Understanding Comparison and Contrast

Introduce this activity by explaining the meanings of comparing and contrasting. To compare things means to identify similarities, and to contrast things means to identify differences. Being able to compare and contrast ideas is essential to comprehension, for it enables the reader to understand how things are alike and unlike.

Instruct your students to read the selection about the McAllister twins and answer the questions that follow. (You might want to mention that the McAllister girls are fraternal twins and not identical twins. Identical twins tend to share many more characteristics than fraternal twins.) After your students have finished the worksheet, discuss the selection and go over the questions and their answers.

3-7: Understanding Cause and Effect

Introduce this exercise by explaining that actions and events demonstrate cause and effect. Everything in our observable world is caused by something. An action, which is a cause, leads to an event, which is the effect. Ask your students to volunteer some examples of cause and effect. It is likely that they will be able to name several. One example close to home is the student who *does not* complete his homework **(cause)** and receives detention **(effect).**

Mention that sometimes a cause can result in several effects, and that an effect may be the result of multiple causes. Causes and effects may also be a part of a pattern. A cause results in an effect, which then becomes a cause and leads to another effect, and so on. Offer this example: A powerful storm **(cause)** results in flooding **(effect)**; the flooding **(now a cause)** results in people losing their homes **(effect)**.

For this worksheet, your students are to read the story and answer the questions. When they are done, discuss the material and address any confusion they may have about cause and effect.

3-8: Making Predictions

Begin this activity by explaining that good readers become actively engaged in their reading. They often ask themselves questions about the material they are reading, and make predictions of what they think will happen next. To foster active reading on the parts of your students, you may wish to review Study Sheet 3-B, "The SQ3R System for Reading," with the class.

For this worksheet, your students are to read three selections and, based upon the material, predict what will happen next for each. Upon completion of the worksheet, go over the material with your students and answer any questions they may have.

3-9: Understanding Fact and Opinion

Introduce this exercise by discussing with your students the difference between a fact and opinion. At their most basic, a fact is a statement that can be proven, and an opinion is a view that stems from a person's feelings about a subject or issue. You might wish to mention that major issues in life are seldom a case of straightforward facts or opinions, but often are a complex mix of both. This is one of the reasons why controversies are so hard to resolve. It is most difficult to sort the reality from fantasy when fact and opinion become interwoven and opinion obscures fact.

Instruct your students to read the article about hurricanes and decide whether the statements that follow are facts or opinions. When your students are done, go over the worksheet and discuss any statements your students did not identify correctly.

3-10: Determining Summaries

Begin this activity by explaining that a summary is a statement that tells what an article or story is about. A summary of a short piece may be a single sentence and a summary of a longer work may be a few sentences. All summaries, however, are brief, generally focusing on the main idea of the material.

For this worksheet, your students are given three selections to summarize. Caution them to read each selection carefully and choose the best summary. When they are done, read the selections together and discuss the answers.

3-11: Understanding an Author's Purpose

Start this activity by discussing the importance of being able to recognize an author's purpose for writing, which might be to inform, influence, or simply entertain readers. This is especially true in a democratic society where it is incumbent upon citizens to understand the issues of the day. While most editorials and persuasive essays are clear in their intention to influence the reader, some authors who wish to influence readers employ subtle methods. A good example of such writing is propaganda, in which opinions are presented as facts in an effort to mold the public's perception of an issue. Recognizing an author's purpose can help individuals understand and respond to what they are reading.

This worksheet contains two selections that address a proposal for building an ice-skating rink. Although both writers discuss the same rink, their opinions and purposes are quite different. After your students have completed the worksheet, discuss the selections and point out the differences in the arguments the two writers present. Be sure to answer any questions your students may have regarding an author's purpose.

3-12: Identifying Story Elements

Begin this exercise by explaining that all stories share common elements. The most important of these elements include: characters, setting, conflict, mood, plot, climax, and theme.

Depending upon the abilities of your students, you may need to discuss each element in detail. If you haven't already distributed it, hand out copies of Study Sheet 3-D, "Story Elements," and review the information with your students.

For this worksheet, your students are to read the story and answer the questions that follow. When they are done, discuss the story and review the various story elements. Be sure to answer any questions your students may have.

3-13: Identifying Figurative Language

Begin this exercise by explaining that figurative language is a written (or spoken) expression that creates strong images in the minds of the readers (or listeners). Figures of speech such as similes, metaphors, and personification are often at the heart of figurative expressions.

Offer your students this example:

The sun was bright overhead.

The sun, a golden ball, blazed overhead.

In the first sentence, the idea of the bright sun is straightforward. The sentence is quite literal.

In the second, however, the sun, through use of the metaphor, is described as a blazing golden ball. Of course, the sun is not a ball, but the reference creates a clear, striking image in the mind of the reader. Ask your students to volunteer some examples of figurative language.

For this worksheet, your students are given pairs of sentences. One sentence in each pair is an example of figurative language. Your students are to identify this sentence, then explain why it is an example of figurative language. When they are done, go over the worksheet and discuss their answers, particularly the reasons for their choices.

3-14: Determining Which Reference Source to Use

Introduce this activity by explaining that we have so many resources for finding information that sometimes the most difficult part of research is to identify the best ones. Being able to determine the best sources of information is a valuable skill.

You might like to mention that while most people still think of reference sources in the forms of books, many references are also found in electronic databases and can easily be accessed via computers. An advantage to researching a topic in an online encyclopedia, for example, is the search feature. Merely by entering the topic, you will be provided information on it. Moreover, many online references are linked to related sites on the Internet and are regularly updated with current information. Finding useful information is often just a few clicks away.

As you go over the instructions of the worksheet with your students, note that some questions may have more than one answer. When your students are done, discuss the worksheet and their answers.

3-15: This Isn't Goodbye (Realistic Fiction)

Begin this activity by explaining that the story students are about to read is an example of realistic fiction. It is a story in which the events *could* happen.

For the worksheet, students are to read the story and answer the questions that follow. Note that there are two parts to the questions, Part A and Part B, and that students are to complete both parts. When your students are finished with the worksheet, discuss the story and answers to the questions.

3-16: The Changing of the Earth (Persuasive Essay)

Introduce this activity by explaining that the selection is an example of a persuasive essay, an article in which the author discusses a subject and attempts to influence the reader's opinion. Persuasive essays are also referred to as *editorials* and *opinion pieces.* Note that such articles are most frequently found in the editorial section or "Letters to the Editor" page of newspapers and magazines.

This article addresses the issue of how human beings are changing the Earth. As the human population increases, so does the demand for natural resources. Utilizing natural resources inevitably stresses the environment, causes pollution, and destroys ecosystems. The Earth changes. For example, the housing development that is built on land that once was a forest results in a radical change to the natural habitat, affecting countless plants and animals. Once the forest is gone, the environment is substantially altered. While the author admits that progress is unstoppable, he argues that the effect on nature must also be considered.

Go over the instructions on the worksheet with your students and note that the questions are divided into two parts, A and B. Upon completion of the worksheet, discuss the article, focusing on why it is an example of a persuasive essay.

3-17: Is Your Computer Protected Against Viruses? (Informational Article)

Begin this activity by explaining that the selection is an example of an informational article. The purpose of an informational article is to inform the reader about a specific topic. In this case, the article provides information about computer viruses, their causes, and how to prevent them.

For this worksheet, your students are to read the article and answer the questions that follow. Note that there are two parts to the questions, A and B. When your students are done with the worksheet, discuss the article and answer any questions they may have.

3-18: Strange Lights Over Sumner's Cove (Newspaper Article)

Begin this exercise by asking your students how many of them read a newspaper regularly—even if it's only the sports, comics, or TV listings. Hopefully, most of your students will respond that they read at least part of a newspaper each day.

Explain that newspapers provide information on daily events. While many newspapers report on world, national, and local news, others are specialized and focus on specific subjects. For example, some local newspapers concentrate only on local stories; the *New York Times* covers national and international news; and the *Wall Street Journal* focuses on national and international business, finance, and related topics.

You might also mention that a well-written newspaper article reports facts without the reporter's opinions. Opinions are reserved for the editorial pages.

Explain to your students that articles in the typical newspaper are organized around what are known as the five W's—Who, What, When, Where, Why—and *How*. By answering these questions, reporters are able to provide the most important information about an event. Moreover, the most important information is usually provided in the first few paragraphs.

Instruct your students to read the article on the worksheet and then answer the questions that follow. Note that there are two sets of questions, A and B. When your students are done, discuss the article and their answers.

3-19: Maggie Draper Walker (Biographical Sketch)

Introduce this activity by explaining that the selection is an example of a biographical sketch, which is a short biography that focuses on the accomplishments or major events in the life of the subject. This article, for example, focuses on Maggie Draper Walker's success in the Richmond, Virginia insurance and banking industry.

Go over the instructions with your students, and point out that this activity has two sets of questions, A and B. When your students are done with the worksheet, discuss the selection and answer any questions they may have.

3-20: Penguins: Birds of the Ice (Science Article)

Begin this exercise by explaining that this selection is an example of a science article. Depending upon the abilities and prior knowledge of your students, you may find it helpful to provide some background information. Although there are several species of penguins, they share many of the same traits. Most live on Antarctica, on the islands nearby, and in the waters around the continent. Show students where Antarctica is located on a map or globe, and note that much of the continent is covered with a permanent ice cap.

Instruct your students to read the article and complete the statements that follow. When they are done, discuss the article and answer any questions they may have.

3-21: Thunder and Lightning (Myth)

Introduce this selection as an example of a myth. Discuss how a myth is a story, created by primitive people, to explain something in nature or some mystery of life. This myth was originally told in Nigeria. You might wish to point out Nigeria on a world map or globe.

For this activity, your students are to read the myth and answer the questions. Note that there are two sets of questions, A and B. When your students are done with the worksheet, discuss the myth and explain the answers to any questions your students found confusing.

3-22: A Retelling of Pecos Bill and the Cyclone (Tall Tale)

Begin this activity by explaining that a tall tale is a story in which exaggeration is a major element. You might mention that the line between tall tales and folk tales is vague, and that tall tales and their heroes are often considered to be folk tales as well. You might also mention that the heroes of tall tales (and also folk tales) are often loosely based on real people or a group of people. Edward O'Reilly, for example, was the creator of Pecos Bill. O'Reilly combined parts of various folklore stories told by people of the Old West and cast Pecos Bill as the star. The first stories of Pecos Bill began appearing in magazines in the early 1920s.

For this worksheet, your students are to read the story and answer the questions that follow. Note that there are two sets of questions, A and B. After your students have completed the worksheet, discuss the tall tale and answer any questions they may have.

3-23: How to Bake Carrot Cake (Recipe)

Introduce this article by explaining that the selection is a recipe. (Incidentally, the recipe on the worksheet is an actual recipe, which results in a delightful carrot cake.) Ask your students how many of them have ever cooked or baked something for which they needed to follow a recipe. Note that a recipe is a list of instructions detailing how to prepare a particular food. Also note that the directions of a recipe must be followed closely, or the finished food may be disappointing if not outright inedible. (Emphasize to your students that they should not attempt cooking any food without the approval or guidance of their parents or guardians.)

For this worksheet, instruct your students to read the recipe and answer the questions that follow. Note that there are two sets of questions, A and B. When your students have finished the worksheet, go over the recipe and the answers to the questions. Clarify any misunderstanding your students may have.

3-24: Songfest (A Review)

Begin this exercise by asking your students if they have ever read a review of a movie, play, book, or perhaps of a computer game or CD. It is likely that many of them have read some type of review. Explain that a review is an article about a performance, event, book, or work of art that describes the subject, usually offering both highlights and weaknesses.

This worksheet includes a review of a musical (which is fictitious). Your students are to read the review and answer the two sets of questions that follow. Upon completion of the worksheet, discuss the review and answer any questions your students may have.

3-25: Charity Drive at Local Firehouse (ANNOUNCEMENT)

Start this activity by explaining that announcements are a practical form of written communication. PTA flyers for parents and handouts informing students of the next school dance are common examples of announcements.

For this worksheet, your students are to read the announcement and answer the questions. When they are finished with the worksheet, review the announcement and answer any questions they may have.

3-26: "Still Here" by Langston Hughes (POEM)

Introduce this poem and explain that Langston Hughes (1902–1967) is considered to be one of America's most popular African-American poets. You might ask your students if they have read any of his poems in the past. You might also mention that they are likely to encounter some of his poetry in the future.

Instruct your students to read the poem, noting the style, use of language, and message. They are to then answer the two sets of questions. When your students are done with the worksheet, read the poem aloud and discuss the answers to the questions.

3-27: Verse by Walt Whitman (POEM)

Begin this exercise by explaining that Walt Whitman (1819–1892) is one of America's most famous poets, known for poetry that celebrates the worth of the individual and the common bonds among humans.

For this worksheet, your students are to read the excerpt of his poem "Song of the Open Road" and answer the questions that follow. Note that there are two sets of questions, A and B. Upon completion of the worksheet, read and discuss the excerpt together, noting the theme of individuality.

3-28: Following Directions (READING DIRECTIONS)

Start this activity by explaining that being able to read and follow directions is among the most important reading skills. Ask your students if they have ever had to read instructions in order to play a game, assemble a product, or find a place while on vacation. How well they were able to understand the directions probably determined how easy (or how difficult) it was to accomplish their task. A key to understanding directions is to scan or read through the directions quickly the first time, then go back and read them more slowly and carefully the second time. Of course, some directions may require several readings before they become clear.

For this worksheet, your students are to read the directions that a girl must follow to visit her friend at her friend's new home. Caution your students to read the directions carefully. Upon completion of the worksheet, review the directions together and go over the answers to the questions. Clarify any confusion your students may have.

3-29: Interpreting a Climograph (Graph)

Introduce this activity by explaining that a climograph is a special graph that shows both the temperature and precipitation of a place on the same grid. It is, essentially, a double graph. While this provides much information about a place's weather, climographs can also be tricky to read.

Before having your students start the worksheet, review the graph with them, noting that temperature in degrees Fahrenheit is marked along the left side of the grid and that precipitation in inches is marked along the right. Emphasize that the same lines of the grid are used for both, but that the lines assume different values for temperature and precipitation. You might also mention that precipitation includes all forms of moisture that fall from the sky: rain, snow, sleet, and hail.

Instruct your students to study the climograph for Chicago and answer the questions that follow. Note that there are two sets of questions, A and B. When your students have completed the worksheet, review the graph once more and discuss any questions they may have.

3-30: Fast-Food Facts (Reading a Table)

Begin this activity by asking your students how many of them enjoy fast food such as hamburgers, cheeseburgers, pizza, and tacos. If your class is like most, just about every student will raise his or her hand. Explain that fast food is "fast," popular, but not very healthy. The caloric and fat content of most fast foods is high.

For this worksheet, your students will get a chance to compare the fat and caloric content of typical fast foods. They are to use the information on the chart for answering the questions of Parts A and B. When they are done, review the chart and discuss any questions they may have found confusing.

Reading Comprehension Practice Tests I, II, and III

You may assign any or all of these practice tests. Along with the skills covered previously in this section, the tests include questions for literal, interpretive, and applied comprehension. Test I includes a story, a myth, and a persuasive essay. Test II includes an informational article, a selection on reading directions, and a poem. Test III includes a biographical sketch, review, and climograph. Your students should use the Answer Sheet with these tests, which will give them practice marking their answers on the answer sheets of standardized tests.

Answer Key for Section 3

3-1. **1.** Todd is tall, rugged, and has blue eyes. He is a good athlete, but is easily frustrated with school work. **2.** Maria has dark curly hair, has a positive outlook, and believes in herself. **3.** He feels that math is difficult. **4.** Todd's feelings are negative; Maria's feelings are positive. **5.** Todd gives up easily; Maria works hard and keeps trying. **6.** Accept reasonable answers.

3-2. **1.** She was e-mailing her cousin Erin. **2.** California; earthquake **3.** She is afraid. She shudders at the thought of a tornado. **4.** A possible answer is that she hears thunder in the distance. **5.** A tornado would occur. A tornado watch had been upgraded to a warning, Rachel had never seen such threatening clouds, and at the window her eyes grew big with sudden fear.

3-3. **1.** *Main Idea:* Tornadoes are among the most violent, destructive storms on Earth. *Details:* powerful vortex of spinning air; wind speeds as high as 300 mph; tornadoes can destroy entire towns, uproot massive trees, rip houses apart, and toss cars and trucks through the air **2.** *Main Idea:* Jorge was conducting research for his history report. *Details:* Jorge was looking at a website for the War of 1812; books and notes were spread across the desk; he had already looked through five books and had three more books and several websites to go **3.** *Main Idea:* Mongooses are tough, bold snake hunters. *Details:* gray mongooses are not afraid to hunt poisonous snakes; mongooses have no natural immunity to snake venom; mongooses rely on courage, speed, and an uncanny ability to avoid being bitten when facing a snake **4.** *Main Idea:* Sheryl was bored with the science review. *Details:* Sheryl looked at her watch and frowned; Sheryl thought the review would be done by 3:00; Sheryl had an "A" average in science; as the teacher conducted the review, Sheryl jotted down ideas for a story she planned to write

3-4. 6, 3, 7, 2, 8, 1, 10, 4, 9, 5

3-5. **1.** lively; Aunt Trish was always happy and full of energy **2.** mild; she didn't like the cold and missed the agreeable climate of California **3.** tasty; meat-flavored treat **4.** climb; to the mountain's summit **5.** fair; to be a good peer mediator **6.** careful; she almost always caught every mistake and oversight **7.** outraged; poorly chosen words were insulting **8.** disgusting; she nearly screamed **9.** overjoyed; jumped out of their seats and congratulated each other **10.** wealth; a house that had six bedrooms, five baths, three-car garage, swimming pool, and tennis court **11.** outgoing; ready to talk with anyone anywhere **12.** dull; disappointed at its dark appearance

3-6. **1.** Tara is taller than her sister. She has green eyes and blonde hair. She is active, a good student, likes math and in-line skating, plays basketball, and likes horror movies. **2.** Megan has green eyes and brown hair. She has outstanding musical talent, plays the piano and flute, likes to read, ice skate, and dance. **3.** The girls have green eyes, they are active, good students who consider each other to be best friends. They enjoy watching movies. **4.** They are not the same height; Tara has blonde hair and Megan has brown hair; they like different types of movies; Tara likes in-line skating, and Megan likes ice skating. Tara enjoys basketball while Megan has musical talent. **5.** Accept reasonable answers.

3-7. **Part A.** **1.** Her reaction was disappointment. **2.** Her mother told her to be sure that the decision Bekka makes is the right one. **3.** Bekka agreed with her mother, but kept thinking about the party. **4.** She wanted to see if Mrs. Jensen

could make other arrangements. **5.** Mrs. Jensen was disappointed and surprised, but she said that she would try. **6.** Bekka told Mrs. Jensen that she would be happy to watch Danny. **7.** She enjoyed watching Danny.
Part B. 1. C **2.** E **3.** C, E **4.** E **5.** E

3-8. Accept any reasonable answers.

3-9. **1.** F **2.** O **3.** O **4.** F **5.** O **6.** F **7.** O **8.** F **9.** O **10.** F **11.** F **12.** F

3-10. **1.** B **2.** C **3.** B

3-11. **A. 1.** favors **2.** The rink will provide a place for people to skate, and it will produce revenue. **3.** Accept reasonable answers. **4.** To influence people to favor the building of the proposed rink **B. 1.** opposes **2.** There is competition from the new rink in Cedar Hill, the rink will serve a small number of residents, the rink may not be profitable, and the rink will result in traffic congestion. **3.** Accept reasonable answers. **4.** To influence people to oppose the building of the proposed rink **C.** Accept reasonable answers.

3-12. **1.** Derek, Alex, and Bernie **2.** In darkness the boys are standing in front of an old house that is supposed to be haunted. The house was dark and gray, wild weeds and bushes like the gnarled hands of demons can be seen through the pale moonlight. **3.** Bernie had dared Derek and Alex to stay the night inside the "supposed" haunted house. **4.** Accept reasonable answers, which might include *frightening*, *suspenseful*, and *creepy*. **5.** Bernie dared Derek and Alex to stay in the house, but Derek and Alex are afraid. Alex turns the dare back onto Bernie by saying he and Derek will stay in the house if Bernie stays, too. Like them, Bernie is afraid and the boys all manage to save face by agreeing they aren't afraid but none stay in the house. **6.** Bernie backs down from his dare. **7.** Accept reasonable answers. One theme is: Avoid daring others to do what you yourself wouldn't do. Another is: Don't accept any dare.

3-13. **Part A. 1.** B—The alligator is compared to a submarine, its eyes like a periscope. **2.** A—The sound of the wind is compared to the howl of a wolf. **3.** A—The girl's eyes are compared to bright moons. **4.** B—The traffic is compared to a long snake. **5.** A—Spring is said to have a gentle kiss. **6.** B—The kitten is compared to a fox. **7.** A—The stars are compared to tiny diamonds. **8.** A—The turtle's shell is compared to an impregnable fortress. **9.** B—The tennis ball is compared to a rocket. **10.** A—Winter is said to have a cold sword. **11.** B—The sun is compared to a friend. **12.** B—The dishes are said to be a mountain in the sink. **Part B.** Accept reasonable sentences.

3-14. **1.** E **2.** C, D, E **3.** A **4.** D, E **5.** B **6.** E **7.** C, D, E **8.** D, E **9.** C **10.** A, E **11.** C, D **12.** C

3-15. **Part A. 1.** D **2.** B **3.** A **4.** C **Part B. 1.** Tess Willis belonged to a popular group of students. **2.** Accept reasonable answers. **3.** Accept reasonable answers.

3-16. **Part A. 1.** D **2.** A **Part B. 1.** Accept reasonable answers. **2.** No, because he says that human advancement must go on, but that people should also consider the consequences. **3.** Accept reasonable answers. **4.** Accept reasonable answers.

3-17. **Part A. 1.** B **2.** A **3.** C **Part B. 1.** human illness; accept reasonable answers. **2.** Accept reasonable answers.

3-18. **Part A. 1.** C **2.** A **3.** B **4.** D **Part B.** Accept reasonable answers.

3-19. **Part A. 1.** A **2.** C **3.** D **4.** B **Part B.** Accept reasonable answers.

3-20. **1.** C **2.** C **3.** D **4.** B **5.** A

3-21. **Part A. 1.** B **2.** D **3.** C **4.** B **5.** A **6.** D **Part B.** Accept reasonable answers.

3-22. **Part A. 1.** D **2.** B **3.** C **4.** A **Part B. 1.** lassoing water from the Rio Grande River and Gulf of Mexico; horses and cows drying up and blowing away; Bill riding a twister and squeezing rain out of a tornado; so much rain falling that land sank and created Death Valley **2.** Accept reasonable answers.

3-23. **Part A. 1.** B **2.** A **3.** B **Part B.** Accept reasonable answers.

3-24. **Part A. 1.** C **2.** A **3.** C **4.** D **5.** B **Part B. 1.** Accept reasonable answers. **2.** Accept reasonable answers.

3-25. **1.** D **2.** C **3.** C **4.** B **5.** C

3-26. **Part A. 1.** C **2.** B **Part B. 1.** He says, "I don't care! I'm still here!" **2.** He uses the first person narration, which gives the impression he is speaking directly to the reader. **3.** Accept reasonable answers.

3-27. **Part A. 1.** D **2.** B **3.** C **Part B. 1.** Accept reasonable answers. **2.** Accept reasonable answers.

3-28. **Part A. 1.** D **2.** D **3.** B **4.** A **5.** D **Part B.** Accept reasonable answers.

3-29. **Part A. 1.** C **2.** D **3.** B **4.** A **5.** B **Part B. 1.** It shows both average monthly temperature and precipitation. **2.** The fact that two scales are used on the same graph can be confusing.

3-30. **Part A. 1.** D **2.** A **3.** A **Part B.** Accept reasonable answers.

Study Sheet 3-A

Traits of Good Readers

Good readers share many of the following traits:

1. Most good readers read many different kinds of stories, articles, and poems. They read books, magazines, and newspapers.
2. Most good readers read every day.
3. Most good readers enjoy reading material that challenges them.
4. Most good readers ask themselves questions about the material they are reading. They try to find the answers to their questions as they read.
5. Most good readers reflect on what they read. They compare new information with what they already know and then draw conclusions.
6. Most good readers use context clues to figure out the meaning of new words.
7. Most good readers look at three, four, or more words at once when they read. They do not look at one word at a time.
8. Most good readers enjoy discussing books and articles with their friends.
9. Most good readers have favorite authors.
10. Most good readers look for books in libraries and bookstores. Many even search the Internet for hard-to-find books they have heard about.

© 2002 by John Wiley & Sons, Inc.

Study Sheet 3-B

The SQ3R System for Reading

The SQ3R System can help you improve your reading. SQ3R means:

S: Survey

Survey, or preview, the material you are about to read. You should note titles, subtitles, illustrations, photographs, tables, or charts. Try to get an idea about the material *before you start reading.*

Q: Question

As you are surveying, think of *questions* you have about the material. Consider what you already know about the material and what you would like to learn. Write down your questions. If your teacher has given you questions, think about how you might answer them.

© 2002 by John Wiley & Sons, Inc.

3R: Read, Recite, Review

The first R in the SQ3R System stands for *read.* As you read the material, try to find the answers to your questions.

The second R stands for *recite.* When you find the answer to a question, pause and repeat the answer to yourself. You may also write it down. This will help you to remember the answer.

The third R stands for *review.* After you are done reading, go over the material once more. Look for answers to any questions you still have and double-check facts. Reviewing will help you to remember what you read.

Study Sheet 3-C

Guidelines for Reading Logs

A reading log is a place you can write down your thoughts about reading. Here are some guidelines.

1. Use a standard spiral notebook for your reading log. Write your name and class on it.
2. Bring your reading log to class each day.
3. Use your reading log only for reading. Do not use it for any other subjects.
4. Use your reading log in school and at home to record your thoughts and opinions about what you read.
5. Start each entry on a new page.
6. Always include a title and date when you write in your log. For example: November 15, 2002, The Outsiders, Chapter 2.
7. Be sure to answer assigned questions in your log, but also be willing to share your ideas.
8. Always use facts from the reading to support your ideas. Include examples and cite page numbers.
9. Be aware that your teacher will read your log periodically. If your teacher reads something in your log that he or she feels endangers you or someone else, he or she must report it.
10. Review your log from time to time and revisit your ideas about your reading.

© 2002 by John Wiley & Sons, Inc.

Study Sheet 3-D

Story Elements

All stories can be broken down into several elements, or parts.

- **Characters:** Characters are the people who take part in a story. In science fiction and fantasy, characters may not be human and may instead be aliens, trolls, demons, or whatever the writer can imagine. In some stories, animals are leading characters.
- **Setting:** The setting is the location of the events in a story. Most stories, especially novels, have many settings. A setting may be a suburban neighborhood, a city, a submarine deep below the surface of the ocean, or even a human colony on Mars.
- **Plot:** The events that make up a story are its plot. The plot is the action plan of a story. In a typical plot, the lead character, or characters, face a problem that they must solve. As the characters try to solve the problem, they run into circumstances, called *complications*, that stop them from solving the problem. Eventually, they either solve or fail to solve the problem.
- **Conflict:** Conflict arises from the problems characters face in stories. As they try to solve their problems, characters may come into conflict with other characters, nature, the supernatural, or themselves. Conflict, which may be physical or emotional, usually leads to the characters taking some action.
- **Climax:** The climax of the story is the moment the lead characters either solve their problem or fail.
- **Theme:** The theme of a story is the author's message or insight about the world that is interwoven throughout the story. *Good triumphs over evil* is a common theme.

© 2002 by John Wiley & Sons, Inc.

Library Resource Center
Renton Technical College
3000 N.E. 4th St.
Renton, WA 98056

Study Sheet 3-E

Breaking Down a Story into Parts

Understanding the parts, or elements, of stories can help you to better understand the overall story. Answer the following questions about the story you are reading on a separate sheet of paper.

1. Who are the main characters in the story?
2. Describe the lead characters.
3. Who is your favorite character? Why?
4. Who is your least favorite character? Why?
5. Describe the setting of the story.
6. Give examples of how the author makes the setting realistic. What kinds of imagery words does he or she use?
7. What is the plot of the story?
8. What is the central conflict of the story? Give at least three examples of how this conflict is shown.
9. Describe the climax of the story.
10. What is the theme of the story? If the story has more than one theme, what are they?

© 2002 by John Wiley & Sons, Inc.

Name ______________________________ Date ________________

3-1

Understanding Characterization

Directions: Read the story and answer the questions.

"No." Maria shook her head, her dark curls bouncing on her shoulders. She tried to keep frustration out of her voice. "You have to divide there."

Todd put his pencil down and leaned back against the chair. It was nearly 5 P.M. and they were the only students remaining in the school library.

"I can't understand this stuff," he said.

"You can, but you have to try," Maria said.

For the past month Maria had been tutoring Todd, one of her best friends, in math. She looked at him, certain that he could be a successful student if he only believed in himself. She felt awful to see the tall, rugged Todd look so dejected, his usual smile replaced with a frown and his blue eyes filled with failure.

"If I can't get at least a C on my report card, I won't be able to play basketball this season," he said. "And things will only get worse from there."

"You can do this," Maria said. "You just have to convince yourself that you can."

"That's easy for you to say," Todd said. "Math has always been easy for you."

"Not always," said Maria. "I have to study." She looked gently at her friend. "I'm not going to let you fail."

"It's not going to do any good," said Todd hopelessly. "There are things in life you can't do. So why try?"

Maria picked up his pencil and handed it to him.

"Let's get started," she said.

1. Describe Todd. ______________________________

____

____

2. Describe Maria. ______________________________

____

____

© 2002 by John Wiley & Sons, Inc.

Name ________________________________ Date ________________

3-1

Understanding Characterization *(continued)*

3. How does Todd feel about his ability to do math? ______________________

____

____

____

4. How is Todd's feeling about math different from Maria's? ________________

____

____

____

5. What do their attitudes toward learning tell you about Todd and Maria? ______

____

____

____

6. If Maria needed help in a subject, do you think Todd would have been able to help her? Why or why not? ______________________________

____

____

____

© 2002 by John Wiley & Sons, Inc.

Name ______________________________ Date ________________

3-2

Making Inferences and Conclusions

Directions: Read the story and answer the questions that follow.

Rachel finished reading the e-mail message from her cousin Erin in California. Erin was telling her about the minor earthquake that had occurred in her town that morning.

Rachel was glad no one was hurt. She couldn't imagine what an earthquake was like. It was bad enough living here in eastern Oklahoma where she had to worry about tornadoes. Just the thought made her shudder.

With her fingers flying over the keyboard, Rachel informed Erin that the weather forecast called for severe thunderstorms with the possibility of tornadoes. Already a tornado watch was in effect.

A little while later Rachel heard thunder in the distance and wrote to Erin that she had to shut down her computer. The thunder was getting louder, and Rachel did not like to use electricity when lightning was near.

When Rachel went to the window, she saw dark, ominous clouds approaching from the southwest. She had never seen such threatening clouds.

Just then her mother called to her from the kitchen.

"The weather service has issued a tornado warning," she said.

Rachel looked back out the window. Her eyes grew big with sudden fear . . .

© 2002 by John Wiley & Sons, Inc.

1. What was Rachel doing before the storm? ______________________________

____

____

2. Where does Erin live? ____________________ What had happened in the morning there? ______________________________

____

____

____

____

Name ______________________________ Date ______________

3-2

Making Inferences and Conclusions *(continued)*

3. How does Rachel feel about tornadoes? ______________________________

____

How do you know? ______________________________

____

____

4. Why did Rachel stop e-mailing Erin and shut down her computer? ______________

____

____

____

____

5. What was likely going to happen at the end of the story? ______________

____

How do you know? ______________________________

____

____

____

____

____

© 2002 by John Wiley & Sons, Inc.

Name ______________________ Date ______________

3-3

Finding Main Ideas and Details

Directions: Read each paragraph. Then write the main idea and details.

1. Tornadoes are among the most violent, destructive storms on Earth. A powerful vortex of spinning air with wind speeds as high as 300 miles per hour, tornadoes can destroy entire towns. Even a small tornado can uproot massive trees, rip houses apart, and toss cars and trucks through the air like toys. While some tornadoes may be only a few feet wide and be limited in the destruction they cause, tornadoes as wide as a mile have been recorded. Such monster storms destroy everything in their path.

Main Idea: ______________________

____

Details: ______________________

____

____

____

© 2002 by John Wiley & Sons, Inc.

2. Jorge sat before his computer and looked at a website for the War of 1812. That was the topic of his history report, which was due next week. He glanced at the books and notes spread across his nearby desk. He sighed. He had already looked through five books and had three more books and several websites to go. He clicked on a link to learn more about the causes of the war.

Main Idea: ______________________

____

Details: ______________________

____

____

____

Name ______________________________ Date ________________

3-3

Finding Main Ideas and Details *(continued)*

3. Although mongooses are only about two feet long, they are tough, bold snake-hunters. The gray mongoose of India, made famous by Rikki-tikki-tavi in Rudyard Kipling's *Jungle Book*, is not afraid to hunt poisonous snakes, even though it has no natural immunity to counteract the snake's venom. When facing a snake, the mongoose relies on courage, speed, and an uncanny ability to avoid being bitten.

Main Idea: ______________________________

____

Details: ______________________________

____

____

____

4. Sheryl looked at her watch and frowned. It was 3:30 and the after-school review for the upcoming science test was still going on. When she had agreed to come with her friend Deidre, Sheryl thought that the review would be done by 3:00. She told herself miserably that she shouldn't have come. Although Deidre needed the extra help, Sheryl had an "A" average in science. As the teacher talked about life cycles and ecosystems, Sheryl began jotting down ideas for a story she planned to write. Just as Sheryl was writing down ideas for the climax of her story, Deidre poked her arm. The review was finished.

Main Idea: ______________________________

____

Details: ______________________________

____

____

____

© 2002 by John Wiley & Sons, Inc.

Name ______________________________ Date ________________

3-4

Sequencing

Directions: Read the story. Then number the statements from 1 to 10 showing the order in which the events occurred.

Traci explained the final details of the plan to Jason and Keri. The kids had invited Larissa, their friend, to Traci's house this afternoon where they hoped to surprise her with a birthday party.

"We don't have much time," Traci said to Jason and Keri as she led them into the family room. "Larissa will be here soon. I told her we were going to a movie."

"Larissa's always early," said Keri. "We'd better hurry."

Traci nodded. "Start by putting up the streamers," she said.

As Jason and Keri began hanging up decorations, Traci put the cake she had gotten on the table.

© 2002 by John Wiley & Sons, Inc.

"I bet she'll be surprised," said Keri, looking at the cake with white icing and *Happy Birthday* written across the top.

"I'm sure she will," agreed Traci. She handed Keri paper plates and napkins. "Here, set the table."

As Keri arranged the plates and napkins on the table, Traci and Jason selected CDs of Larissa's favorite groups.

When they were done, Traci showed Jason and Keri the card she had gotten. "Sign it on the bottom," she said.

Just then, they heard the doorbell.

"Quick," Traci said to Jason. "Answer the door, but don't let her come in here until Keri and I have a chance to wrap her present."

"How do I do that?" said Jason. "She'll just come right in."

"Make up a story," said Keri. "Tell her you got an A on your math test."

Jason laughed. "She'll know that's not true."

"That's why she'll listen," said Keri. "She'll be curious."

As Jason hurried to answer the door, Traci and Keri started wrapping a picture album the three friends had filled with photographs of the many fun times they had shared with Larissa.

Name ________________________________ Date __________________

3-4

Sequencing *(continued)*

When Jason led Larissa into the room, everything was ready and Larissa's three friends yelled, "Happy Birthday!"

Larissa was surprised and grateful.

_____ Traci, Keri, and Jason signed the birthday card.

_____ Traci put the cake on the table.

_____ The kids heard the doorbell.

_____ Jason and Keri started decorating the room.

_____ Jason went to answer the doorbell.

_____ Traci explained the plan to Keri and Jason.

_____ Larissa was surprised and grateful.

_____ Keri set the table with paper plates and napkins.

_____ Traci and Keri wrapped the gift.

_____ Traci and Jason selected CDs of Larissa's favorite groups.

© 2002 by John Wiley & Sons, Inc.

Name ______________________________ Date ________________

3-5

Understanding Context Clues

Directions: Read the sentences. Use context clues to figure out the meaning of the underlined word. Circle the correct meaning from the four choices, then circle the clue you used.

1. Jess's Aunt Trish was always happy and full of energy. She was the most <u>vivacious</u> person Jess knew.

   pretty   intelligent   lively   willful

2. When Melanie's family first moved to Michigan, she looked forward to snow in the coming winter. But she soon realized she didn't like the cold and missed the agreeable, <u>benign</u> climate of Southern California.

   hot   mild   changeable   rugged

3. The meat-flavored treat was a <u>savory</u> snack for Daria's puppy.

   good   nutritious   necessary   tasty

4. Because of the storm, their <u>ascent</u> to the mountain's summit took longer than they had anticipated.

   walk   exploration   adventure   climb

5. Ally knew that to be a good peer mediator, she had to be <u>impartial.</u> But her best friend was one of the people involved in the problem she had to help solve.

   certain   fair   dynamic   attentive

6. Roseann was <u>meticulous</u> when she proofread her writing. She almost always caught every mistake and oversight.

   overbearing   careful   fast   perfect

© 2002 by John Wiley & Sons, Inc.

Name ______________________ Date ______________

3-5

Understanding Context Clues *(continued)*

7. The candidate's poorly chosen words were insulting and many of his listeners were affronted.

   outraged pleased confused gratified

8. Sara considered spiders to be loathsome creatures. When she saw one scampering across her desk, she nearly screamed.

   disgusting interesting unique curious

9. Peter's group was jubilant when it was announced that their science project was awarded the top prize at the science fair. They jumped out of their seats and congratulated each other.

   satisfied overjoyed pleased humble

10. When Jacob went to Eric's house for the first time, he quickly realized the affluence of his new friend's family. Jacob had never seen a house that had six bedrooms, five baths, a three-car garage, swimming pool, and tennis court.

    arrogance wastefulness wealth importance

11. Uncle George was a gregarious fellow. People said that he was always ready to talk with anyone anywhere.

    outgoing happy shy deceitful

12. After her room was painted, Kera was disappointed at its dark, lackluster appearance.

    vivid brilliant bright dull

© 2002 by John Wiley & Sons, Inc.

Name ______________________ Date ______________

3-6

Understanding Comparison and Contrast

Directions: Read the story and answer the questions.

Unless he or she knew them, a person would never guess that Tara and Megan McAllister are twins. Although the girls both have green eyes, possess a lot of energy, and are good students, the similarities end there.

Tara is the taller of the two. She is also the only McAllister who has blonde hair. Her favorite subject is math, she loves in-line skating, and she plays basketball in the town's recreation league.

Megan has brown hair like her parents and their brother Kyle. Megan has outstanding musical talent, and plays the piano and flute. She likes to read, ice skate, and dance.

The girls consider each other to be their best friend, and enjoy being together. One of their favorite pastimes is watching movies, even though Tara likes horror flicks and Megan likes comedies.

The girls believe that the main reason they get along so well is because they are different. They never get bored with each other.

© 2002 by John Wiley & Sons, Inc.

1. Describe Tara. ______________________________

____

____

____

2. Describe Megan. ______________________________

____

____

____

Name ________________________ Date ____________

3-6

Understanding Comparison and Contrast *(continued)*

3. What do the sisters have in common? ________________________

4. How are the sisters different? ________________________

5. There is an old saying that “opposites attract.” How might this phrase apply to Tara and Megan? ________________________

© 2002 by John Wiley & Sons, Inc.

Name ______________________________ Date ________________

3-7

Understanding Cause and Effect

Part A. Directions: Read the story and answer the questions.

When Bekka heard that Ali's party had been moved to this coming Saturday night, disappointment fell on her like a heavy weight. That was the night she had agreed to watch Danny Jensen, the little boy who lived next door, while his parents went to a dinner sponsored by Mr. Jensen's employer.

Bekka liked Danny, and Danny liked her, but Ali's party would be the best one of the entire year. All of Bekka's friends would be there.

When Bekka got home from school that day, she told her mother about the problem.

"Do you think the Jensens can get someone else to watch Danny?" her mother asked as Bekka helped her prepare dinner.

"I doubt it," said Bekka. "All of the other kids will be at the party. Besides, Danny knows I'm staying with him, and he'll be disappointed if I don't show up."

Her mother seemed thoughtful for a moment. "Well, whatever you decide to do, you must make sure that it's the right thing," she finally said.

Bekka nodded, but she kept thinking of the party and how much she wanted to go.

That night she called Mrs. Jensen, told her about Ali's party, and asked her if she might be able to find a different sitter.

Mrs. Jensen sounded a little surprised, but said that she would try.

Afterward Bekka felt awful for having called.

On Saturday afternoon, Mrs. Jensen called and told Bekka that she and her husband would cancel their plans.

"Oh, no," Bekka said, feeling terrible that the Jensens were willing to stay home just so she could go to a party. "I'm happy to watch Danny."

That evening, even though she was missing Ali's party, Bekka enjoyed baby-sitting Danny. She knew she had made the right decision.

1. What was Bekka's reaction to the news that Ali's party had been changed to this Saturday night? ____

   ____

2. What advice did Bekka's mother give her? ______________________

   ____

   ____

© 2002 by John Wiley & Sons, Inc.

Name ______________________________ Date ________________

3-7

Understanding Cause and Effect *(continued)*

3. How did Bekka react to this advice? ______________________________

____

____

4. Why did Bekka call Mrs. Jensen on Friday night? ______________________________

____

____

5. How did Mrs. Jensen react to the call? ______________________________

____

____

6. When Mrs. Jensen called Bekka on Saturday, telling Bekka that she and her husband would cancel their plans for the evening, what did Bekka do? ______________

____

____

7. On Saturday night, while she was watching Danny, how did Bekka feel? __________

____

____

Part B. Directions: Write **C** if the statement is a *cause* in the story, or **E** if it is an *effect*. If a statement is both a cause and effect, write **CE.**

1. _____ Ali's party had been moved to this Saturday night.
2. _____ Bekka felt disappointed that the party was moved.
3. _____ Bekka told her mother about the problem.
4. _____ Bekka's mother offered her advice.
5. _____ Bekka watched Danny and felt she had done the right thing.

© 2002 by John Wiley & Sons, Inc.

Name ______________________________ Date ____________________

3-8

Making Predictions

Directions: Read each selection and predict what is likely to happen next.

A. Roger stood before the display of the stereo system and read the card that listed its many advanced features.

"This is everything I need," he said to his best friend Jared.

Roger had asked Jared to accompany him to the store. Jared was knowledgeable about stereos, but that wasn't the only reason Roger had asked him to come. Roger's biggest fault was buying on impulse without really thinking about what he was buying.

"It's more than what you need," said Jared, "and it costs more than what you want to pay. Remember, you told me not to let you spend more than $300. That way you'd have money left over to buy new CDs."

Roger frowned. Jared was right. But, after all, it was his money which he had earned doing chores around the neighborhood.

© 2002 by John Wiley & Sons, Inc.

1. What will Roger do? ______________________________

____

2. Why do you think he will do this? ______________________________

____

____

____

3. If you were Roger, what would you do and why? ______________________________

____

____

____

Name ______________________ Date ______________

3-8

Making Predictions *(continued)*

B. Christy needed a good grade on her science quiz this afternoon, or she would be grounded for a month.

That was why Matt, one of her friends, sat next to her at lunch and offered to show her the answers to the quiz.

"Where did you get that?" Christy asked, looking at the paper in his hand but not looking at the answers.

"Somebody from the morning class who owed me a favor."

"How do you know they're the right answers?" Christy asked.

"Mr. Grimes never changes the quizzes," said Matt. "I know you need the grade. I'm only trying to help."

Christy had never cheated on her work. She prided herself on always being able to manage on her own.

"Well?" said Matt. "I did this for you."

Christy needed a good grade, but . . .

1. What will Christy do? ______________________

____

2. Why do you think she will do this? ______________________

____

____

____

3. If you were Christy, what would you do and why? ______________________

____

____

____

C. Stacy couldn't believe her eyes when she saw Jimmy, the boyfriend of her best friend, Elena, with Ariel at her locker after school. Stopping, Stacy ducked in a nearby doorway. What she heard was even more shocking. Jimmy asked Ariel to go to the movies with him on Friday night.

"What about Elena?" asked Ariel.

© 2002 by John Wiley & Sons, Inc.

Name ______________________________ Date ____________

3-8

Making Predictions *(continued)*

"Oh, she's baby-sitting again," said Jimmy. "Besides, she won't mind. We have an understanding."

Stacy's hand flew to her mouth to keep from speaking out. Elena had told her that she and Jimmy were having some trouble, but she hadn't said anything about an *understanding*.

Stacy decided that she would call Elena as soon as she got home, but then she paused. What she had to say would hurt Elena, and she didn't want to do that. Still, she thought, Elena should know . . .

1. What will Stacy do? ______________________________

____

2. Why do you think she will do this? ______________________________

____

____

____

3. If you were Stacy, what would you do and why? ______________________________

____

____

____

____

____

© 2002 by John Wiley & Sons, Inc.

Name ______________________________ Date ________________

3-9

Understanding Fact and Opinion

Directions: Read the article. Then decide if the statements that follow are facts or opinions. If the statement is a fact, write an **F** on the blank. If the statement is an opinion, write an **O** on the blank.

Hurricanes are the most devastating storms on Earth. With wind speeds that can reach up to 200 miles per hour, rain and storm surges that can cause massive flooding, and powerful waves that can wash away coastlines, hurricanes can result in widespread destruction and billions of dollars in damage.

The Atlantic hurricane season begins June 1 and ends November 30, with the highest number of storms occurring from mid August through October. (In the Pacific Ocean, hurricanes are called typhoons.) Most Atlantic hurricanes originate within the doldrums, a narrow stretch of water that extends east–west just north of the equator. The doldrums are characterized by light, variable winds and fair weather, which hardly seem to be the necessary conditions for spawning such fearsome storms.

Hurricanes usually start off as a small storm that, given the right atmospheric conditions, begins to spin in a counterclockwise direction. As the storm gathers strength, wind speed and rainfall increase. When wind speeds reach 74 miles per hour, the storm achieves hurricane status. The winds swirl around the hurricane's center, which is called the eye. Despite the violence around it, the weather in the eye is sunny and calm, making the eye of any hurricane its most remarkable feature.

Hurricanes are categorized 1 to 5 on the Saffir–Simpson Scale. Category 1 storms are minimal hurricanes with wind speeds between 74 and 95 miles per hour. At the high end of the scale is the Category 5 storm with wind speeds greater than 155 miles per hour. Although any hurricane can cause great damage, Category 5 storms are monsters and cause unimaginable destruction. Nothing is more terrifying than being caught in a major hurricane.

© 2002 by John Wiley & Sons, Inc.

Name ______________________________ Date ______________

3-9

Understanding Fact and Opinion *(continued)*

1. _____ When the wind speed of an Atlantic storm reaches 74 miles per hour, it becomes a hurricane.

2. _____ The eye of a hurricane is the storm's most remarkable feature.

3. _____ Hurricanes are the most devastating storms on Earth.

4. _____ The Atlantic hurricane season begins June 1 and ends November 30.

5. _____ Nothing is more terrifying than being caught in a major hurricane.

6. _____ Most Atlantic hurricanes begin in the doldrums.

7. _____ Category 5 storms are monsters that cause unimaginable destruction.

8. _____ Calm, sunny conditions are found in the eye of a hurricane.

9. _____ The doldrums hardly seem to have the necessary conditions for spawning such fearsome storms.

10. _____ Pacific hurricanes are called typhoons.

11. _____ Hurricanes spin in a counterclockwise direction.

12. _____ The powerful waves of hurricanes can wash away coastlines.

© 2002 by John Wiley & Sons, Inc.

Name ________________________________ Date ________________

3-10

Determining Summaries

Directions: Read each selection. Then place a check on the blank before the best summary.

1. Snowflakes are made of ice crystals. The crystals form around dust or other small particles in the air when water vapor condenses at temperatures below freezing. When partially melted crystals cling together, snowflakes are formed. Snowflakes are hexagonal, meaning that they are six-sided, but the actual shape of each snowflake is dependent upon the precise weather conditions in which it was formed. Since the amount of water vapor and temperature are always varying slightly, even in the same cloud, every snowflake is unique in shape.

A. ____ Snowflakes are one of nature's greatest marvels.

B. ____ Snowflakes are created when water vapor freezes around dust or other small particles in the air, forming hexagonal ice crystals.

C. ____ Snowflakes are ice crystals in clouds that fall to Earth as snow when the weather at the ground is near the freezing point or below.

D. ____ Snowflakes are ice crystals that fall to the ground in the winter.

© 2002 by John Wiley & Sons, Inc.

2. The relationship between humans and dogs stretches back into prehistory. Ancient cave paintings show the importance of dogs for hunting in some of the earliest human cultures. Many historians believe that dogs, which descended from wolves, were the first animal to be domesticated by humans. It is probable that primitive people recognized the wolf's exceptional hunting skills. At some point a forward-looking individual captured and raised wolf cubs, which then remained with him. Over the years, selective breeding by humans and adaptation to varying environments have resulted in the development of the many breeds of dogs we have today.

A. ____ Primitive people recognized the wolf's exceptional hunting skills.

B. ____ People have liked dogs since prehistoric times when they drew pictures of dogs on caves.

C. ____ Dogs, which were the descendants of wolves, were probably the first animal to be domesticated in prehistoric times.

D. ____ Selective breeding by people since prehistoric times has led to the development of the many different breeds of dogs today.

Name ______________________ Date ____________

3-10

Determining Summaries *(continued)*

3. Starfish are unusual creatures. Scientifically known as echinoderms, their skeleton is made up of many plates that move like flexible joints. Several limbs, or arms, extend outward from the animal's center, giving it a star-like appearance. Unlike fish that have scales, starfish possess a spiny skin. Perhaps the most remarkable feature of a starfish, though, is its ability to regenerate. If a starfish is injured and loses a limb, the limb will grow back. If a starfish is cut in half, two individual starfish will regenerate. Scientists study starfish in an attempt to understand this extraordinary ability.

A. ____ Starfish are echinoderms that are unusual.

B. ____ Starfish are unusual creatures that possess the ability to regenerate.

C. ____ The body of a starfish is made up of plates that move like flexible joints.

D. ____ If a starfish loses a limb, another will grow in its place.

© 2002 by John Wiley & Sons, Inc.

Name ______________________________ Date ________________

3-11

Understanding an Author's Purpose

Directions: Read the two articles about a proposed ice-skating rink in Circle City. Then answer the questions.

A. The proposed ice-skating rink for Circle City is a good idea. Along with providing a place for people who like to skate, it will produce revenue, which the town can use to pay for additional recreational activities.

The rink can be open from early morning to late at night and offer a host of activities. Beginning, intermediate, and advanced skating lessons, youth and adult hockey leagues, and open ice-time for the community will ensure that the needs of all community skaters are met.

While the town will need to provide the initial funding for construction, the rink is expected to become profitable within the first year and pay off any debts associated with construction within ten years.

Clearly the proposed ice-skating rink is right for Circle City.

1. Does the author favor or oppose the construction of an ice-skating rink in Circle City? ______________________________

2. What evidence does the author offer to support this view? ______________________________

3. Do you find the author's points to be valid? Why or why not? ______________________________

© 2002 by John Wiley & Sons, Inc.

Name ______________________ Date ______________

3-11

Understanding an Author's Purpose *(continued)*

4. What was the author's purpose in writing this? ______________________

____

____

____

B. Building an ice-skating rink in Circle City is a mistake. The proposed rink will at best serve a small number of area residents, be expensive to maintain, and cause traffic congestion.

The proposed site is only 12 miles away from the new rink in Cedar Hill. Having two rinks so near to each other will only result in competition that will limit the number of skaters at both rinks.

There is also the issue of cost. Why should the town pay for something it doesn't need? As to speculation that the proposed rink will become profitable within the first year and pay off any construction debt within ten years—this is only speculation. No one can guarantee that the rink will even be profitable. What if the rink isn't profitable? Will the people of Circle City have to pay to maintain it?

And what about the increased traffic congestion? The proposed site for the rink is near one of the busiest intersections in town. No plans to control the increase in traffic that the rink will cause have been discussed.

Circle City does not need an ice-skating rink. The costs and potential problems outweigh any benefits.

1. Does the author favor or oppose the construction of an ice-skating rink in Circle City? ______________________

2. What evidence does the author offer to support this view? ______________________

____

____

____

____

© 2002 by John Wiley & Sons, Inc.

Name ______________________________ Date ________________

3-11

Understanding an Author's Purpose *(continued)*

3. Do you find the author's points to be valid? Why or why not? ________________

4. What was the author's purpose in writing this? ________________

C. Having read the two articles, which one do you feel is more convincing? Why?

© 2002 by John Wiley & Sons, Inc.

Name ______________________________ Date ________________

3-12

Identifying Story Elements

Directions: Read the story and answer the questions.

"We must be crazy," said Derek to his friend Alex.

In the darkness they stood in front of the old Turner house that was supposed to be haunted. Having accepted a dare from Bernie Carter that they would stay in the house overnight, they had no choice but to go inside. Bernie was one of the most popular kids in the eighth grade, and if they backed out they would be humiliated before all of their friends.

"You were the one who said we'd do this," said Alex.

"Only after you said you weren't afraid to stay here," Derek shot back.

They continued looking at the house. It was dark and gray, the pale moonlight offering glimpses of wild weeds and bushes that seemed like the gnarled hands of demons laying claim to the property. The place had been deserted for years since its owner had mysteriously died there one night. Some people were convinced he had been murdered and that his ghost wandered from room to room.

"If something goes wrong, our folks won't even know we're in there," said Alex. Each of the boys had told his parents that he was staying over the other's house tonight.

"Nothing will go wrong," said Derek, "I hope."

The sudden sound behind them startled the boys and they spun around to face four other boys, led by Bernie.

"You guys seem a little jumpy," Bernie said. "Not planning to chicken out, are you?"

"No way," said Derek.

"Good," said Bernie, "because some of us will be outside here watching all night."

Derek and Alex both inhaled deeply to steady their pounding hearts.

Derek turned to his friend. "Ready?"

"No," said Alex. "Not until Bernie agrees to go with us."

"That wasn't the deal," said Bernie quickly. "You guys are afraid."

"Not any more than you are," said Derek. "If you're not afraid, then come on. Show everybody."

Bernie didn't speak for a long moment. "I'm not scared," he finally said. "But I don't have to prove it to you."

"Then we don't have to prove it to you either," said Alex.

"That's fine with me," said Bernie. "But I'm not afraid to go in there."

"Neither are we," said Derek.

After a few more denials of their fear, all of the boys left for home.

On the way back to Derek's house, Alex said, "I really wasn't afraid to go in there."

"Why should you be?" said Derek. "We all know there's no such thing as ghosts."

© 2002 by John Wiley & Sons, Inc.

Name ______________________________ Date ________________

3-12

Identifying Story Elements *(continued)*

1. Who are the main characters of this story? ______________________________

____

2. Describe the setting. ______________________________

____

____

3. Explain the major conflict in the story. ______________________________

____

____

4. Describe the mood of the story. ______________________________

____

How does the author achieve this mood? ______________________________

____

____

5. Describe the plot. ______________________________

____

____

____

6. Describe the climax. ______________________________

____

____

7. Explain the theme of the story. ______________________________

____

____

© 2002 by John Wiley & Sons, Inc.

Name ________________________________ Date ________________

3-13

Identifying Figurative Language

Part A. Directions: Read each pair of sentences. Place a check before the one that is an example of figurative language. On the line that follows, explain why your choice is an example of figurative language.

1. ____ A. The alligator swam toward the unsuspecting duck that paddled leisurely on the river.

   ____ B. Like a submarine, its eyes like periscopes, the alligator swam silently toward the unsuspecting duck.

   ____

2. ____ A. The winter wind howled across the field like a wolf.

   ____ B. The powerful winter wind blew across the field.

   ____

3. ____ A. The little girl's eyes widened into bright moons as she unwrapped the gift and saw the big doll.

   ____ B. The little girl was happy as she unwrapped the gift and saw the doll.

   ____

4. ____ A. The accident caused traffic to back up four miles along the highway through the valley.

   ____ B. The accident caused the traffic to back up like a long snake through the valley.

   ____

5. ____ A. Spring, with its gentle kiss of warmth on the land, awakened the world to new growth.

   ____ B. Spring, with its warm temperatures after the cold winter, is the time of year plants begin to grow again.

   ____

© 2002 by John Wiley & Sons, Inc.

Name ________________________________ Date ____________________

3-13

Identifying Figurative Language *(continued)*

6. ____ A. The kitten crept stealthily up on the ball of yarn.

   ____ B. The kitten crept like a fox up to the ball of yarn.

   ____

7. ____ A. The stars filled the night sky, a million tiny diamonds set against a black tapestry.

   ____ B. The stars shined brightly in the night sky.

   ____

8. ____ A. The turtle's shell, an impregnable fortress, protects it from predators.

   ____ B. The turtle's hard shell protects it from predators.

   ____

9. ____ A. Mandy served the tennis ball hard and fast over the net.

   ____ B. Mandy served the tennis ball, now a rocket streaking over the net.

   ____

10. ____ A. Gianna disliked winter, which always depressed her with its cold sword that brought death and desolation to the land.

    ____ B. Gianna disliked winter, which always depressed her because of the cold temperatures and gray landscape.

    ____

11. ____ A. After three days of rain, the sun was bright in the blue sky.

    ____ B. After three days of rain, the sun was a welcome, returning friend.

    ____

12. ____ A. It was Liz's turn to wash the dishes, which were piled high in the sink.

    ____ B. It was Liz's turn to wash the dishes, which were a mountain in the sink.

    ____

Part B. Directions: On the back of this sheet, write three sentences of your own demonstrating examples of figurative language.

© 2002 by John Wiley & Sons, Inc.

Name ______________________________ Date ________________

3-14

Determining Which Reference Source to Use

Directions: Read each question and decide which reference source below will most likely provide the answer. Write the letter of the reference source on the blank before the question. Some questions may have more than one answer.

A. Dictionary	B. Thesaurus	C. Almanac
D. Atlas	E. Encyclopedia	

© 2002 by John Wiley & Sons, Inc.

1. _____ In what year did the island of Krakatoa experience a catastrophic volcanic eruption that destroyed much of the island?
2. _____ Where is the current island of Krakatoa located?
3. _____ What is the origin of the word “melancholy”?
4. _____ In which states are the Rocky Mountains located?
5. _____ What is a synonym for “spectacular”?
6. _____ What were Thomas Edison’s greatest inventions?
7. _____ What is the average annual precipitation of Miami, Florida?
8. _____ What is the latitude and longitude of Seattle, Washington?
9. _____ Which nation won the greatest number of gold medals in the 2000 Olympic Games?
10. _____ What is photosynthesis?
11. _____ What is the highest mountain in South America?
12. _____ What is the fastest land mammal?

Name ______________________________ Date ________________

3-15

This Isn't Goodbye

Part A. Directions: Read the story and place a check before the word or phrase that best completes each statement.

Raelyn Evans closed the book she had been trying to read and looked up at the round clock on the wall. It was 4:00, and she had been waiting here in the library for her best friend Keri Abernathy for the past hour. Through all the years since nursery school, the two of them had been inseparable. And that's what was wrong now.

During the past few weeks Keri had been spending most of her free time with Tess Willis. If there was an "in crowd" at Woodmont Junior High, it was Tess and her friends. They weren't bad kids, Raelyn had to admit, but they weren't Raelyn's kind, or, she thought, Keri's kind either. She wasn't sure of that anymore, though, and that was the reason she had asked Keri to meet her here after school.

Raelyn glanced up at the clock again. She doubted that Keri was coming, but just as she was about to leave, Keri hurried in.

"Hey," she said. "Sorry I'm late."

Raelyn looked toward the front door of the library and saw Tess and a few other girls waiting in the hall outside. "It's okay."

"So, what's going on?" asked Keri. "You sounded like you really wanted to talk about something."

"That's just it," said Raelyn. "We don't talk much anymore."

Keri remained silent for a moment, her eyes looking away from Raelyn. "You know how it is," she finally said.

Raelyn knew exactly. She wanted to blurt out that Tess Willis wasn't Keri's friend—that she, Raelyn, was—but she held the words back for deep inside she realized that they were unfair. Keri had every right to choose her friends and make her life as she wished.

But Raelyn couldn't let go that easily. "Are you busy Friday night?"

Keri nodded.

"What about Saturday?" Raelyn said. "I was thinking maybe we could—"

Keri stopped her with a slight frown. "That's bad, too. But maybe next week we can hang out." The words were flat, said without enthusiasm.

"Okay," said Raelyn. "That'll be great."

Keri looked at the hall where the other girls were still waiting. "I have to go."

Raelyn nodded. "Me too."

© 2002 by John Wiley & Sons, Inc.

Name ______________________________ Date ________________

3-15

This Isn't Goodbye *(continued)*

Keri started to leave, but then paused. "This isn't goodbye, or anything like that," she said. "You know that, right? I mean, we've been friends a long time."

Raelyn managed a small smile. "Of course it isn't goodbye," she said, knowing that it was.

"So, I'll be seeing you around," Keri said.

Raelyn nodded and watched her friend go.

1. Over the years Raelyn and Keri _____.

   _____ A. were acquaintances

   _____ B. knew each other since nursery school

   _____ C. seldom saw each other

   _____ D. were best friends

2. During the past few weeks, the relationship between Raelyn and Keri changed because _____.

   _____ A. they stopped liking each other

   _____ B. Keri became friends with Tess Willis

   _____ C. Keri decided that she did not like Raelyn

   _____ D. their schedules in school changed and they didn't see each other much

3. Raelyn felt _____ about the change in their relationship.

   _____ A. despondent

   _____ B. furious

   _____ C. puzzled

   _____ D. detached

© 2002 by John Wiley & Sons, Inc.

Name ______________________________ Date ________________

3-15

This Isn't Goodbye *(continued)*

4. The best word for describing how Keri likely felt about the meeting with Raelyn is _____.

   _____ A. pleased

   _____ B. angry

   _____ C. uncomfortable

   _____ D. disgusted

Part B. Directions: Answer these questions on the back of this sheet.

1. What does Raelyn mean when she describes Tess Willis and her friends as being the "in crowd" at Woodmont Junior High?
2. Why do you think Raelyn didn't tell Keri how much she missed their friendship? If you were Raelyn, what would you have done?
3. Do you think the girls will ever be "best" friends again? Explain.

© 2002 by John Wiley & Sons, Inc.

Name ________________________________ Date ________________

3-16

The Changing of the Earth

Part A. Directions: Read the essay and place a check before the phrase that best completes each statement.

Prior to the explosion of the human population, the Earth was a very different planet. Nature ruled and ecosystems the world over were in balance. With the increasing numbers of human beings, however, that changed.

We began to change the planet wherever we went. Animals were hunted for food and sport, forests were cut down to provide wood for building and land for farming, and minerals were taken from the land to manufacture countless products. Today, to maintain our standard of living, we consume the Earth's resources at a furious pace, in the process polluting our skies, fouling our water, and poisoning our soil.

While human advancement must go on, it should progress in a manner that takes into account the needs of the Earth, its resources, natural wonders, and life. Before embarking on a course of action that will affect the environment, we must ask ourselves what the consequences will be. Will we harm our Earth or ourselves? We need to explore how we can advance yet remain in harmony with our planet.

As we move into the 21st century, we must realize that we are a part of the Earth and that by changing it, we risk changing ourselves.

© 2002 by John Wiley & Sons, Inc.

1. The author describes the Earth prior to the human population explosion _____.

_____ A. as a nice place to live

_____ B. as a place that needed change

_____ C. as a place with few natural resources

_____ D. as a place where ecosystems were in balance

2. According to the author, after the human population increased, _____.

_____ A. people began to change the planet

_____ B. people began to live in many places

_____ C. human beings tried to live in harmony with nature

_____ D. there were not enough resources for people

Name ______________________________ Date ________________

3-16

The Changing of the Earth *(continued)*

Part B. Directions: Answer these questions.

1. Is the title, "The Changing of the Earth," appropriate for this essay? Explain. _____

____

____

____

____

2. Is the author opposed to human advancement? Explain. ________________

____

____

____

____

3. What might be a consequence if human beings continue to change the planet? _____

____

____

____

____

4. Do you agree with the author's ideas? Explain. ____________________

____

____

____

____

© 2002 by John Wiley & Sons, Inc.

Name ______________________________ Date ________________

3-17

Is Your Computer Protected Against Viruses?

Part A. Directions: Read the article and place a check before the phrase that best completes each statement.

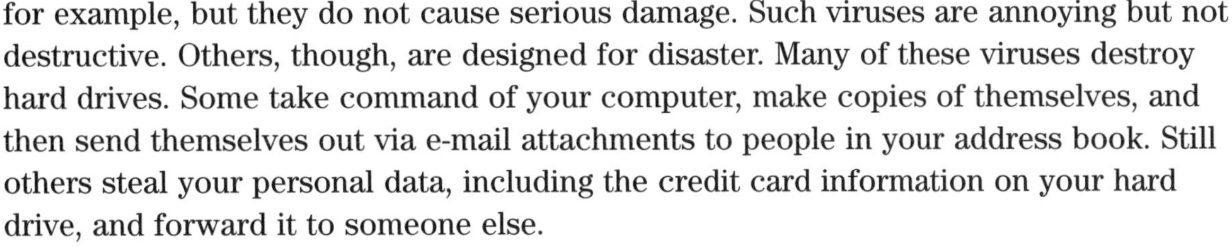

Everyone knows that a virus can cause a serious illness in a person, but not everyone knows that a computer virus can wreck a computer. Just like a biological virus can be bad for your health, a computer virus can be a calamity for your computer's software.

Computer viruses are commands that some individuals create for the purpose of disrupting your computer's operation. Some viruses are relatively benign; they may cause a silly message to appear on your screen, for example, but they do not cause serious damage. Such viruses are annoying but not destructive. Others, though, are designed for disaster. Many of these viruses destroy hard drives. Some take command of your computer, make copies of themselves, and then send themselves out via e-mail attachments to people in your address book. Still others steal your personal data, including the credit card information on your hard drive, and forward it to someone else.

The best way to prevent damage from a virus is to avoid the virus. Since that is becoming increasingly difficult, as thousands of viruses circulate in cyberspace, you need to exercise caution. Be wary when downloading files, especially free files from unfamiliar sources. Viruses can lurk in files. Be careful when opening e-mail attachments, which are a favorite hiding place for viruses. Many computer experts suggest immediately deleting any e-mail with an attachment you aren't expecting or one that comes from a stranger. Also be mindful that floppy disks can harbor viruses and that sharing disks can share viruses.

Aside from being cautious, you should invest in virus protection software. Several companies sell effective software at reasonable prices. The top companies provide protection updates through their websites. Once you obtain virus protection software, it is important to update the protection regularly because new viruses are constantly being created.

When you think of computer viruses, remember the old saying: "An ounce of prevention is worth a pound of cure."

© 2002 by John Wiley & Sons, Inc.

Name ________________________________ Date ________________

3-17

Is Your Computer Protected Against Viruses? *(continued)*

1. A computer virus _____.

   _____ A. may pass from the computer to the person operating the computer

   _____ B. may destroy a computer's hard drive

   _____ C. is a myth

   _____ D. is a mystery science has yet to solve

2. A computer can "catch" a virus through _____.

   _____ A. an e-mail attachment

   _____ B. an infected person

   _____ C. faulty wiring

   _____ D. a power surge

3. One of the best ways to prevent damage from a computer virus is to _____.

   _____ A. never use your computer

   _____ B. realize that a virus can destroy your computer's software

   _____ C. buy and use virus protection software

   _____ D. never share files with anyone, not even friends

© 2002 by John Wiley & Sons, Inc.

Part B. Directions: Answer these questions on the back of this sheet.

1. In the opening paragraph, what does the author compare a computer virus to? In your opinion, is this a good comparison? Why or why not?
2. The author concludes the article with this final advice: "An ounce of prevention is worth a pound of cure." How does this old saying apply to modern computers and computer viruses?

Name ______________________________ Date ________________

3-18

Strange Lights Over Sumner's Cove

Part A. Directions: Read the newspaper article and place a check before the phrase that best completes each statement.

March 3, 2002

Sumner's Cove — Strange lights appearing in the sky last night over Sumner's Cove resulted in numerous frantic calls to police by area residents. Although police were dispatched to several areas of alleged sightings, officers reported that they found nothing unusual.

When contacted late last night, Police Chief Ted Bower explained that a full investigation was already underway.

"Nearby airports were checked, but no flights in or out could have been responsible for the strange lights," the chief said. "Nothing unusual appeared on radar either."

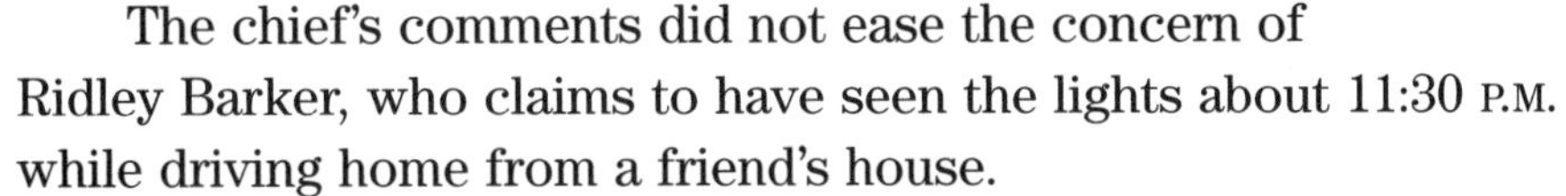

The chief's comments did not ease the concern of Ridley Barker, who claims to have seen the lights about 11:30 P.M. while driving home from a friend's house.

"There were about a dozen lights flashing on and off," he said. "They started in the northeast, then moved toward the northwest."

Maggie Simmons claims to have seen the lights when she arrived home from the supermarket. "It was about ten o'clock," she said. "I just got out of my car and I saw these lights overhead."

Other residents offered similar observations, even though they saw the lights at different times and from different parts of town.

"That's the most puzzling thing," said Chief Bower. "None of the sightings occurred at the same time or place. And all were before twelve o'clock."

The chief assures residents that the investigation will continue. He plans to stay outside tonight and hopes to see the lights for himself.

1. This article is about _____.

   _____ A. a prank in Sumner's Cove

   _____ B. people suffering hallucinations in Sumner's Cove

   _____ C. mysterious lights in the sky above Sumner's Cove

   _____ D. an alien invasion

© 2002 by John Wiley & Sons, Inc.

Name ________________________________ Date ________________

3-18

Strange Lights Over Sumner's Cove *(continued)*

2. The sightings occurred _____.

    _____ A. on March 2, 2002

    _____ B. on a Tuesday evening

    _____ C. on March 3, 2002

    _____ D. over a nearby airport

3. Ridley Barker witnessed the strange lights _____.

    _____ A. on his way home from work

    _____ B. on his way home from a friend's house

    _____ C. as he walked his dog

    _____ D. when he returned from shopping

4. According to Chief Bower, the most puzzling thing about the sightings is _____.

    _____ A. that police officers sent to investigate did not see anything

    _____ B. that only a few people witnessed the lights

    _____ C. that nearby airports could not have been responsible for the lights

    _____ D. that none of the sightings occurred at the same time or place, but all were before midnight

Part B. Directions: Answer this question on the back of this sheet.

The strange lights in the sky above Sumner's Cove were a mystery. What do you think might have caused the lights?

© 2002 by John Wiley & Sons, Inc.

Name ______________________________ Date ________________

3-19

Maggie Draper Walker

Part A. Directions: Read the biographical sketch and place a check before the phrase that best completes each statement.

Maggie Draper was born on July 15, 1867 in Richmond, Virginia. She was the daughter of a former slave.

Maggie graduated from the Armstrong Normal School in 1883 and went on to teach at the Lancaster School. She married Armstead Walker, Jr. in 1886.

After her marriage, Maggie worked for the Grand United Order of St. Luke, which was an African-American cooperative insurance society. Maggie showed exceptional business acumen and quickly worked her way up through the local offices. Maggie became executive secretary–treasurer in 1899 of the renamed Independent Order of St. Luke.

Maggie continued with her hard work. In 1903 she opened the St. Luke Penny Savings Bank, of which she was the president. Over the next several years, the bank grew under Maggie's guidance, eventually absorbing all of the other banks in Richmond owned by African Americans. The St. Luke Penny Savings Bank became the Consolidated Bank and Trust Company for which Maggie continued to serve as chairman of the board.

Maggie also was involved in Richmond's community life. She helped found the Richmond Council of Colored Women in 1912. Serving as its president, she helped raise money for the support of various educational and civic organizations.

Maggie Draper Walker was among the most successful African-American business women of her time.

© 2002 by John Wiley & Sons, Inc.

1. Maggie's first occupation was _____.

_____ A. being a teacher

_____ B. working in a bank

_____ C. working as an insurance agent

_____ D. working for the Grand United Order of St. Luke

Name ______________________________ Date ________________

3-19

Maggie Draper Walker *(continued)*

2. Under Maggie's guidance as its president, the St. Luke Penny Savings Bank _____.

   _____ A. became the best bank in Richmond

   _____ B. continued to grow and was renamed the Independent Order of St. Luke

   _____ C. eventually absorbed all of the other banks in Richmond that were owned by African Americans

   _____ D. proved that a company can sell insurance and also lend money successfully

3. The phrase "business acumen" means _____.

   _____ A. having good luck in business

   _____ B. growth in business

   _____ C. possessing mathematical and bookkeeping skill

   _____ D. having the ability to make wise business decisions

4. Maggie's interest in the Richmond community was shown by _____.

   _____ A. her willingness to lend people money

   _____ B. her help in founding the Richmond Council of Colored Women

   _____ C. her serving as president of the Consolidated Bank and Trust Company

   _____ D. her success as a business woman

Part B. Directions: Answer the following question on the back of this sheet.

Do you agree or disagree with the article's last statement? Explain.

© 2002 by John Wiley & Sons, Inc.

Name ______________________ Date ______________

3-20

Penguins: Birds of the Ice

Directions: Read the article and place a check before the word or phrase that best completes each statement.

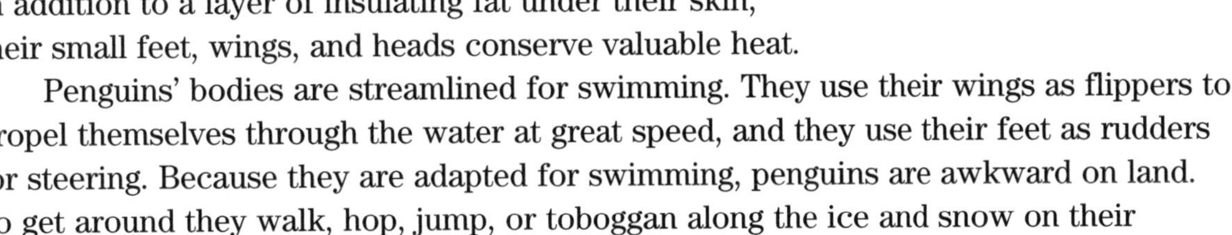

Penguins are aquatic, flightless birds most commonly found on Antarctica and the continent's nearby islands. Although their wings are small and are used as flippers, scientists believe that penguins have descended from flying birds.

Unlike most birds, penguins are specially adapted for the cold, harsh conditions of Antarctica. In addition to a layer of insulating fat under their skin, their small feet, wings, and heads conserve valuable heat.

Penguins' bodies are streamlined for swimming. They use their wings as flippers to propel themselves through the water at great speed, and they use their feet as rudders for steering. Because they are adapted for swimming, penguins are awkward on land. To get around they walk, hop, jump, or toboggan along the ice and snow on their stomachs, pushing themselves with their wings and feet.

Penguins are sociable birds and are usually found in flocks. On land, the birds congregate in colonies that may number hundreds of thousands.

© 2002 by John Wiley & Sons, Inc.

1. Penguins are best described as flightless, aquatic birds that are _____.

_____ A. solitary and distrustful of groups

_____ B. awkward swimmers

_____ C. adapted for the Antarctic environment

_____ D. happiest when they are tobogganing on their stomachs

2. The word "aquatic" means _____.

_____ A. having to do with cold

_____ B. agile

_____ C. having to do with water

_____ D. hardy

Name ______________________________ Date ________________

3-20

Penguins: Birds of the Ice *(continued)*

3. Penguins conserve heat _____.

   _____ A. by huddling together in big colonies to keep warm

   _____ B. by swimming toward the equator during the Antarctic winter

   _____ C. by building nests in the sun

   _____ D. through special adaptations such as an insulating layer of fat beneath their skin

4. One reason penguins are awkward on land is _____.

   _____ A. they prefer to swim

   _____ B. they have small feet

   _____ C. they like to hop and jump

   _____ D. they waddle when they walk

5. The primary habitat of most penguins is _____.

   _____ A. Antarctica and the region around it

   _____ B. the northern hemisphere

   _____ C. the Arctic

   _____ D. the islands of the southern hemisphere

© 2002 by John Wiley & Sons, Inc.

Name ______________________________ Date ________________

3-21

Thunder and Lightning

Part A. Directions: Read the Nigerian myth and place a check before the word or phrase that best completes each statement.

A long time ago, when the world was young, Thunder and Lightning lived among people. Thunder was a mother sheep and Lightning was her son, a ram.

The people of the village did not like Thunder and Lightning because whenever Lightning got angry, which was often, he would release sizzling bolts that would burn whatever they touched. Huts, corn bins, crops, and trees would be burned, and even those unlucky people who got in his way would be injured or killed. Whenever Lightning became enraged, his mother Thunder would yell at him, her deafening voice rumbling across the land and terrifying the people still more.

The people complained to the king about Thunder and Lightning, until the king finally ordered the two of them to move to the edge of the village. This was not far enough, however. Lightning still flew into rages and burned everything around him, and Thunder, his mother, shouted again and again for him to stop, her voice reverberating all around.

The king once again called Thunder and Lightning before him.

"I have given you a chance to live a better life," he said to them, "but you have not changed your ways."

The king then ordered them to move far away from the village and live in the forest.

Thunder and Lightning obeyed him, but Lightning was so furious that he set fire to the forest. As Thunder yelled at him to stop, the blaze raged out of control, destroying farms and homes.

At last, the king called his counselors together. They decided that there was only one thing to do. The king banished Thunder and Lightning to the sky, far from the Earth. Things proved to be a little better, but not much.

Lightning still becomes angry from time to time. Mostly his fire flashes across the sky, but sometimes it crackles down to the ground. After each flash, Thunder shouts in her loud voice, ordering her son to end his rage.

1. According to this myth, when Lightning lived among people and became angry, he would _____.

   _____ A. tell Thunder, his mother

   _____ B. burn whatever was near

   _____ C. streak across the sky

   _____ D. complain to the king

© 2002 by John Wiley & Sons, Inc.

Name ______________________________ Date ________________

3-21 Thunder and Lightning *(continued)*

2. After Lightning lost his temper, Thunder would _____.

   _____ A. hide in the clouds

   _____ B. warn the people to hide

   _____ C. seek shelter

   _____ D. yell loudly at him

3. The word "reverberating" means _____.

   _____ A. yelling

   _____ B. communicating

   _____ C. echoing

   _____ D. being able to hear

4. The people complained to the king about Lightning because _____.

   _____ A. Lightning was mischievous

   _____ B. Lightning was destructive

   _____ C. Lightning did no work around the village

   _____ D. Lightning did not listen to his mother

5. After the king sent Thunder and Lightning away from the village to live in the forest, Lightning _____.

   _____ A. was so angry that he set fire to the forest

   _____ B. took his mother to live in the sky

   _____ C. followed the king's order for many years

   _____ D. accidentally caused a fire in the forest

6. After meeting with his counselors, the king _____.

   _____ A. told Lightning that he must never start another fire

   _____ B. tried banishing Lightning to a cave where he could not cause any more damage

   _____ C. decided that there was no way to stop Lightning

   _____ D. banished Lightning and Thunder to the sky

Part B. Directions: Answer this question on the back of this sheet.

What do you think this Nigerian myth tried to explain?

© 2002 by John Wiley & Sons, Inc.

Name ______________________________ Date ______________

3-22

A Retelling of Pecos Bill and the Cyclone

Part A. Directions: Read the tall tale and place a check before the word or phrase that best completes each statement.

Ask any cowboy who the greatest cowboy of them all was and the answer will be Pecos Bill. Many stories are told about him, but one of the most famous is when Bill lassoed a cyclone.

The story started out in Texas, which was suffering through the worst drought anyone could remember. The rivers were dried up like deserts, and the parched grass was so hot under that blazing Texas sun that it just burned all by itself. Even the horses and cattle were drying up and blowing away in the dry wind.

Pecos Bill had to do something. First he lassoed water from the Rio Grande River, but there wasn't enough to wet all of Texas. Then he lassoed water from the Gulf of Mexico, but there still wasn't enough.

Just when it seemed that the whole state was about to dry up and shrivel away, Bill heard a roar of thunder beyond the mountains to the west. In the distance he saw a giant storm and twister. But it was going the wrong way!

Pecos Bill knew this was his chance. He lassoed that cyclone and pulled himself up on its back. Then he steered that twister over Texas, squeezing the rain out of it with his bare hands. Before he was done, Texas was flooded with fresh water. Just for fun, Bill then rode that twister through New Mexico, Arizona, and into California, dumping rain wherever he went. So much rain came down in one place that the land sank a few hundred feet under the weight of the water. Today we call that place Death Valley (and it hasn't gotten much rain since).

After he finally jumped off that twister, Pecos Bill looked back on the water-logged land and figured that it should be awhile before the next drought.

© 2002 by John Wiley & Sons, Inc.

1. This story of Pecos Bill starts in _____.

   _____ A. California

   _____ B. Arizona

   _____ C. New Mexico

   _____ D. Texas

Name ______________________________ Date ________________

3-22

A Retelling of Pecos Bill and the Cyclone *(continued)*

2. Pecos Bill is known as _____.

_____ A. an American superhero

_____ B. the greatest cowboy who ever lived

_____ C. a tornado chaser

_____ D. a Texas farmer worried about a drought

3. Pecos Bill first tried to bring water to Texas by _____.

_____ A. drawing water from the Gulf of Mexico

_____ B. steering rain clouds over Texas

_____ C. lassoing water from the Rio Grande River

_____ D. building irrigation canals

4. Pecos Bill finally ended the drought in Texas by _____.

_____ A. squeezing rain out of a tornado

_____ B. bringing rain from California

_____ C. stirring up rain clouds

_____ D. making it rain

© 2002 by John Wiley & Sons, Inc.

Part B. Directions: Answer these questions on the back of this sheet.

1. A characteristic of tall tales is great exaggeration. Give at least three examples of exaggeration in this tall tale.
2. In your opinion, why might people enjoy telling and retelling tall tales?

Name ______________________________ Date ________________

3-23

How to Bake Carrot Cake

Part A. Directions: Read the recipe and place a check before the phrase that best completes each statement.

> Many people like to bake, and many more like to eat what great bakers create. The following recipe is one of the best around for carrot cake. (**Note:** Do not attempt to bake or cook without the permission of your parent or guardian.)

© 2002 by John Wiley & Sons, Inc.

Ingredients for the cake:

- 4 eggs
- 2 cups all-purpose flour
- 2 tsp. cinnamon
- 2 tsp. baking soda
- 2 tsp. double-acting baking powder
- 2 cups shredded carrots
- 2 cups sugar
- 1 tsp. salt
- 1 cup cooking oil
- 1 cup chopped pecans

Ingredients for the icing:

- 8 oz. cream cheese (softened)
- 4 oz. butter (softened)
- 2 tsp. vanilla
- 1 box confectioners sugar

Preparation:

1. Preheat oven to 350°.
2. Sift together the all-purpose flour, cinnamon, baking soda, double-acting baking powder, and salt.
3. Mix sugar with oil.
4. Add sifted ingredients alternately with eggs to the sugar and oil.
5. Add shredded carrots and pecans.
6. Bake in a greased and floured tube pan for 1 hour.
7. Make the icing by mixing the butter and cream cheese. Then add the confectioners sugar and vanilla, and mix evenly.
8. After the cake has been removed from the pan and cooled, spread the icing on the cake.

Name ______________________________ Date ________________

3-23

How to Bake Carrot Cake *(continued)*

1. The first step to baking a carrot cake is to _____.

   _____ A. buy fresh carrots

   _____ B. obtain all of the ingredients

   _____ C. mix the ingredients

   _____ D. preheat the oven to 350°

2. In this recipe, "sift" means to _____.

   _____ A. apply various small particles by scattering (as if through a sieve)

   _____ B. organize materials into a cake mix before baking

   _____ C. decide which ingredients to use in the cake

   _____ D. separate, or break down, various particles

3. "Add sifted ingredients alternately with eggs" means to _____.

   _____ A. add all of the ingredients at once in a random manner and mix thoroughly

   _____ B. mix some of the sifted ingredients together, then add an egg and repeat the process until all of the materials are used

   _____ C. add all of the ingredients one at a time and then mix

   _____ D. add only the ingredients you prefer

Part B. Directions: Answer this question on the back of this sheet.

What might happen if the directions of the recipe are not followed closely?

© 2002 by John Wiley & Sons, Inc.

Name ______________________________ Date ________________

3-24

Songfest

Part A. Directions: Read the review and place a check before the word or phrase that best completes each statement.

Songfest, a tribute to the evolution of pop music from the 1960s to the present, opened last night at the Willow Brook Theater. With a cast of 75, a full orchestra, and the distinctive sounds of the top songs of the period, *Songfest* brought the packed house to its feet throughout the two-hour performance.

Although the cast is comprised mostly of unknowns with just a few of the performers having Broadway experience, it was hard to find anyone not satisfied with the show. Led by Tom Patterson and Marcy Howell, the cast sang songs from the top artists of the past 40 years with flair and excellence.

If there was a flaw in the overall top-notch performance, it was the pacing. In an effort to pack as much as he could into a two-hour show, Director Ronald McWilliams rushed performers from one act to another, resulting in a pace that at times became one of frenetic turmoil. At one point, two singers collided as one ran offstage and the other hurried on. Fortunately, the mini-collision did not disrupt the show, but the speed of the upcoming acts left little room for error and in some cases almost left the audience behind.

Minor mishaps aside, *Songfest* is a joy and a fine tribute to the past 40 years of pop music. The show may not quite be the best thing since Broadway, but it surely deserves four stars.

© 2002 by John Wiley & Sons, Inc.

1. *Songfest* is a show that pays tribute to pop music _____.

   _____ A. of the past few years

   _____ B. of the 1960s

   _____ C. since the 1960s

   _____ D. of Broadway

2. Most of the performers of *Songfest* _____.

   _____ A. have little experience

   _____ B. have performed on Broadway

   _____ C. are stars

   _____ D. come from local towns

Name ________________________________ Date __________________

3-24

Songfest *(continued)*

3. The phrase "frenetic turmoil" means _____.

_____ A. poor organization

_____ B. silly mistakes

_____ C. excited confusion

_____ D. not being prepared

4. The reviewer noted that the only weakness in the show was _____.

_____ A. the amateur singing

_____ B. the choice of songs

_____ C. the orchestra

_____ D. the pacing

5. According to the reviewer, the Willow Brook Theater was _____.

_____ A. a poor choice for the performance

_____ B. full

_____ C. too small for the crowd

_____ D. loud

© 2002 by John Wiley & Sons, Inc.

Part B. Directions: Answer these questions on the back of this sheet.

1. What do you think the reviewer's opinion of *Songfest* was? Use details from the review to support your answer.
2. Based on the review, if *Songfest* was to come to your town, would you be interested in attending a performance? Explain.

Name ______________________________ Date ________________

3-25

Charity Drive at Local Firehouse

Directions: Read the announcement of the charity drive and place a check before the phrase that best completes each statement.

Charity Drive

On March 10, North Jameston suffered the worst flooding of the Monassa River in 50 years. Over 30 homes and businesses were destroyed, with many others being severely damaged. Let's help our neighbors in their time of need.

- **Where:** North Jameston Firehouse
- **When:** Saturday, March 20 and Sunday, March 21, 9 A.M. to 3 P.M.
- **Items Needed:** Clothing, canned goods, children's toys, sheets, bedding, small household items. Cash donations gladly accepted.
- **Sponsored by:** North Jameston Council of Churches

All donations will go directly to the victims of the flood.

This is your chance to help!

© 2002 by John Wiley & Sons, Inc.

Name ______________________________ Date ________________

3-25

Charity Drive at Local Firehouse *(continued)*

1. The charity drive in North Jameston is being held in response to _____.

   _____ A. various natural disasters

   _____ B. a need of people to give to charity

   _____ C. a clothing drive

   _____ D. a severe flood

2. The charity drive is being held _____.

   _____ A. on a random Saturday and Sunday in March

   _____ B. on March 15

   _____ C. on Saturday and Sunday, March 20 and 21

   _____ D. on the upcoming weekend

3. If you intended to donate to the charity drive, you could not donate _____.

   _____ A. canned tomato soup

   _____ B. a child's toy

   _____ C. a sofa

   _____ D. a pillow

4. If you intended to donate to the charity drive, you would be able to donate between _____.

   _____ A. 8:30 A.M. and 9:00 A.M.

   _____ B. 1 P.M. and 1:30 P.M.

   _____ C. 3 P.M. to 5 P.M.

   _____ D. 10:00 P.M. to 11:30 P.M.

5. The charity drive is sponsored by _____.

   _____ A. the North Jameston Fire Department

   _____ B. the North Jameston Better Business Bureau

   _____ C. the North Jameston Council of Churches

   _____ D. a group of local citizens

© 2002 by John Wiley & Sons, Inc.

Name ______________________________ Date ________________

3-26

"Still Here" by Langston Hughes

Part A. Directions: Read the poem and place a check before the word that best completes each statement.

Still Here

I've been scarred and battered
My hopes the wind done scattered
Snow has friz me, sun has baked me
  Looks like between 'em
  They done tried to make me
Stop laughin', stop lovin', stop livin'—
  But I don't care!
  I'm still here! —LANGSTON HUGHES

From *The Collected Poems of Langston Hughes* by Langston Hughes, copyright 1994 by The Estate of Langston Hughes. Used by permission of Alfred A. Knopf, a division of Random House, Inc.

© 2002 by John Wiley & Sons, Inc.

1. The tone of the poem can best be described as _____.

_____ A. apologetic _____ C. defiant

_____ B. sorrowful _____ D. defeatist

2. The best word to describe the poet's experience in life is _____.

_____ A. jovial _____ C. easy

_____ B. difficult _____ D. successful

Part B. Directions: Answer these questions on the back of this sheet.

1. In describing his life, it is obvious that the poet has endured hardships. How do you know he has not given up?
2. It seems like the poet is speaking directly to the reader through the lines of his poetry. How does Langston Hughes achieve this effect?
3. Describe the person in this poem. What do you think he or she would be like?

Name ______________________________ Date ________________

3-27

Verse by Walt Whitman

Part A. Directions: Read the excerpt of Whitman's poem "Song of the Open Road" and place a check before the word or phrase that best completes each statement.

> Afoot and light-hearted, I take to the open road
> Healthy, free, the world before me,
> The long brown path before me, leading wherever I choose.
> Henceforth I ask not good-fortune, I myself am good-fortune,
> Henceforth I whimper no more, postpone no more, need nothing,
> Done with indoor complaints, libraries, querulous criticisms,
> Strong and content, I travel the open road. — WALT WHITMAN

1. The poem implies that the author is _____.

_____ A. looking for a new job

_____ B. returning home from work

_____ C. lost and trying to find his way

_____ D. setting out on his or her own

2. The best word to describe the poet's attitude is _____.

_____ A. uncertain

_____ B. confident

_____ C. arrogant

_____ D. frustrated

3. "Querulous criticisms" means _____.

_____ A. serious criticisms

_____ B. lies

_____ C. criticisms without much basis

_____ D. unfair accusations

Part B. Directions: Answer these questions on the back of this sheet.

1. Based on the poem, if the poet is faced with a problem, how do you think he will react? Explain your answer.
2. What do you think "open road" symbolizes? Explain.

© 2002 by John Wiley & Sons, Inc.

Name ______________________________ Date ________________

3-28

Following Directions

Part A. Directions: Read the "directions" below and place a check before the phrase that correctly completes each statement.

Carolyn's friend Gwen moved with her family to Hartsville last month. Recently Gwen sent these directions to Carolyn so that Carolyn and her mother could visit.

- Take Rt. 34 South to Tanner's Crossing and make a left at the first light. Stay in the right-hand lane and make the next right at the gas station. This is Carter Avenue.
- Continue on Carter Avenue for four blocks. Make a right at the stoplight. This is Hoover Drive.
- Make the first right onto Sydney Street. Follow Sydney to Route 78 North. Stay on 78 until Wallace Road. Take exit 45 onto Wallace Road and bear left. Go straight at the light onto New Haven Street.
- New Haven Street leads into Main Street, Hartsville. At the fifth light, turn left, then make an immediate right onto Hillcrest Road. Our house is number 12, the sixth house on the left.

© 2002 by John Wiley & Sons, Inc.

1. After Route 34 South, Carolyn and her mother must go to _____.

_____ A. Hoover Drive

_____ B. Carter Avenue

_____ C. Sydney Street

_____ D. Tanner's Crossing

2. To get onto Carter Avenue, they must _____.

_____ A. turn right at the stoplight

_____ B. turn left at New Haven Street

_____ C. take exit 45

_____ D. make a right at the gas station

Name ______________________________ Date ________________

3-28

Following Directions *(continued)*

3. Carolyn and her mother must follow Sydney Street to _____.

    _____ A. Wallace Road

    _____ B. Route 78 North

    _____ C. Main Street

    _____ D. Hoover Drive

4 To get to Hillcrest Road, they must _____.

    _____ A. turn left at the fifth light at Main Street, then make the immediate right

    _____ B. turn left at New Haven Street

    _____ C. turn right at Main Street, then look for the sixth house on the left

    _____ D. turn left at the fifth light at Main Street and continue on to the sixth house

5. Carolyn and her mother must get on Wallace Road from _____.

    _____ A. Main Street

    _____ B. Sydney Street

    _____ C. Route 78 North

    _____ D. Exit 45

Part B. Directions: Answer this question.

In your opinion, did Gwen give Carolyn clear directions? Explain. ______________

____

____

____

____

© 2002 by John Wiley & Sons, Inc.

Name ______________________________ Date ________________

3-29

Interpreting a Climograph

Part A. Directions: Study the climograph and place a check before the word or phrase that best completes each statement.

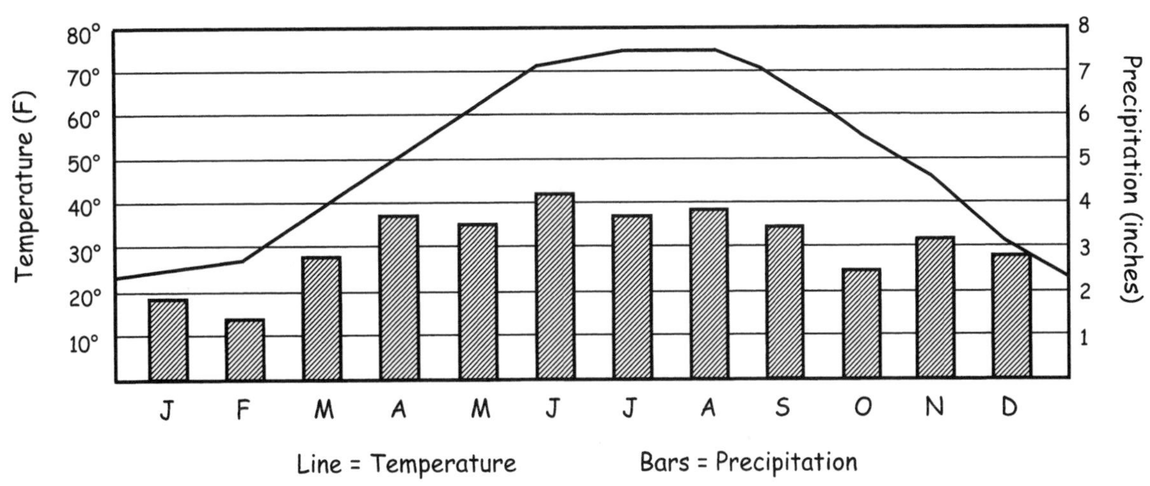

© 2002 by John Wiley & Sons, Inc.

1. This climograph shows the _____.

   _____ A. average annual temperature and rainfall of Chicago

   _____ B. average monthly precipitation and rainfall of Chicago

   _____ C. average monthly temperature and precipitation of Chicago

   _____ D. average monthly temperature and rainfall of Illinois

2. The average monthly temperature in Chicago for April is _____.

   _____ A. 3.5°

   _____ B. 38°

   _____ C. 52°

   _____ D. 50°

Name ______________________________ Date ________________

3-29

Interpreting a Climograph *(continued)*

3. The average monthly temperature for Chicago in October is _____.

_____ A. 50°

_____ B. 56°

_____ C. 60°

_____ D. 5.5°

4. The average monthly precipitation for Chicago in September is _____.

_____ A. 3.5 inches

_____ B. 3.9 inches

_____ C. 2.5 inches

_____ D. 4.0 inches

5. The month in which the average monthly precipitation is the lowest is _____.

_____ A. January

_____ B. February

_____ C. October

_____ D. December

Part B. Directions: Answer these questions on the back of this sheet.

1. How is this climograph useful?
2. Why must a person be careful when reading information on a climograph?

© 2002 by John Wiley & Sons, Inc.

Name ______________________________ Date ________________

3-30

Fast-Food Facts

Part A. Directions: Study the chart and place a check before the word or phrase that best completes each statement.

The Calories and Fat in Fast Food

Food	Total Fat (grams)	Calories
Regular hamburger	9.8	255
Quarter-pound hamburger	21.5	425
Double hamburger	32.0	560
Regular cheeseburger	14.3	310
Regular hot-dog	15.0	270
Large hot-dog	30.0	518
Fish sandwich	16.0	400
Fried chicken (drumstick)	8.0	136
Fried chicken (wing)	10.5	151
Fried chicken (thigh)	19.0	276
Medium French fries	10.0	214
Taco	8.0	185
Pizza	14.5	500

Note: The values of total fat and calories are derived from nutritional averages of the foods served at various fast-food chains.

© 2002 by John Wiley & Sons, Inc.

1. The food with the most calories and highest fat content is a _____.

    _____ A. cheeseburger

    _____ B. pizza

    _____ C. quarter-pound hamburger

    _____ D. double hamburger

Name ______________________ Date ______________

3-30

Fast-Food Facts *(continued)*

2. The fish sandwich contains more fat than the _____.

_____ A. chicken wing

_____ B. chicken thigh

_____ C. quarter-pound hamburger

_____ D. large hot-dog

3. The two foods that together would equal the lowest amount of calories and fat are the _____.

_____ A. taco and fried chicken drumstick

_____ B. regular hamburger and medium French fries

_____ C. fried chicken drumstick and medium French fries

_____ D. regular hamburger and friend chicken wing

© 2002 by John Wiley & Sons, Inc.

Part B. Directions: Answer the question.

Most people know that fast foods are high in calories and fat, yet millions of people eat at fast-food restaurants every year. Why are fast-food restaurants so popular? ______________________________

____

____

____

____

____

____

____

EIGHTH-GRADE LEVEL

Reading Comprehension

PRACTICE TESTS

© 2002 by John Wiley & Sons, Inc.

Reading Comprehension Practice Test I

Part 1. Directions: Read the story. Use the Answer Sheet to darken the letter of the answer that best completes each statement.

The Science Project

Damien, Jennifer, and Brady sat around the table in the library and stared at each other.

Finally, Jennifer shook her head.

"We can't just keep sitting here," she said, frustration thick in her voice.

"Why not?" said Brady.

His leering grin annoyed her, and she shot him an icy glare. "You may not worry about school, but some of us do," she said.

Brady rolled his eyes. "Relax. You worry too much."

"And you don't worry enough," she said. "Everybody knows you're flunking science."

"I'm not flunking," Brady said easily. "I'm close, but I'm still passing."

"And that's good enough?" said Jennifer.

"Yeah, it is," said Brady.

Jennifer could not believe the situation she was in. It was a nightmare. Their teacher had organized groups to work on science projects for the school's Science Fair, and Jennifer found herself working with Brady and Damien, two of the most unsuccessful students in the class. Brady hardly completed any work, and Damien, although he tried, was so disorganized that he seldom got anything done.

Damien, who had been silent since they met at the library, finally spoke. "The project is due in three days."

"That's right," said Jennifer, trying to keep sarcasm out of her voice. "Got any ideas?"

"No," said Damien.

She slumped back in her chair, as if the strength was draining out of her.

"I've suggested a half dozen topics, but you guys don't like any of them," Jennifer said.

"So?" said Brady.

"I've been trying to think of some," said Damien, "but . . . ." His voice trailed off.

"What are we going to do?" Jennifer demanded.

Brady smiled at her. "I guess it's up to you."

She turned to Damien for help, but he just shrugged.

"Okay," Jennifer said, realizing that if the project was to get done, she would have to take charge.

© 2002 by John Wiley & Sons, Inc.

1. The story suggests that _____.

   A. Brady is an outstanding athlete
   B. Brady and Damien are good friends
   C. Jennifer is a better student than either Brady or Damien
   D. the three kids will put their differences aside and work together to complete the science project

2. Jennifer thinks that being in a group with Brady and Damien is a nightmare. This means that _____.

   A. she is very unhappy having to work with them
   B. she feels that if the boys are willing to work together, their project can be successful
   C. she had an unpleasant dream about the science project last night
   D. she is disappointed she was not placed in a group with her best friends

3. The best words to describe Jennifer's feelings in this story are _____.

   A. displeased and forgiving
   B. frustrated and angry
   C. disappointed and pessimistic
   D. hopeless and bitter

4. The story suggests that Brady _____.

   A. is happy to be in a group with Jennifer and Damien
   B. does not enjoy science
   C. feels that Damien should have come to the meeting with an idea for a project
   D. is satisfied with poor grades, as long as he is passing

5. At the end of the story, Jennifer realizes that if the science project is to get done, she will have to take charge. This implies that _____.

   A. Jennifer will keep trying to convince the boys to help her
   B. Jennifer will rely on the boys to complete the project
   C. Jennifer will do what she must to complete the project, even if it means completing it herself
   D. Jennifer has decided to give up and no longer cares whether the project is completed

© 2002 by John Wiley & Sons, Inc.

Part 2. Directions: Read the myth. Use the Answer Sheet to darken the letter of the answer that best completes each statement.

Persephone

The ancient Greeks were a thoughtful and creative people who invented many myths to explain the mysteries of the world. One of these stories is of Persephone.

In the days when the gods ruled over people from Mt. Olympus, Persephone, the maiden of spring, was the daughter of Demeter, the goddess of the Earth.

One day, while Persephone was picking flowers, she noticed a flower of striking beauty. Unknown to Persephone, Hades, the god of the Underworld, had fallen in love with her and was watching her. When Persephone went to pick the flower, Hades, in his chariot drawn by powerful steeds, rose up and out of a chasm in the Earth. Seizing the girl, he carried her down into the Underworld to be his queen.

Persephone's cries echoed through the hills and across the seas, finally reaching her mother. Instantly, Demeter flew like a bird over land and sea, seeking her daughter, but she could not find her.

As Demeter continued wandering across the Earth in search of Persephone, her great anguish caused the world to grow desolate. Flowers and forests withered, crops died, and famine ravaged humanity.

Zeus, king of the gods, knew what had happened and worried that all of the Earth would perish. He sent various gods to Demeter in an attempt to ease her grief and anger.

But the goddess was adamant. "The Earth will not bear fruit again until I see my daughter," she told them.

At last Zeus realized that Hades must release Persephone or all life on the Earth would die. He ordered Hermes, the messenger of the gods, to travel down to the Underworld and bid Hades to release the girl.

Hades knew he must obey Zeus, but he loved Persephone. Before he let her go, he asked her to eat a pomegranate seed. Thinking that acceding to the god's wishes would hasten her release, Persephone ate the pomegranate seed, unaware that this was the food of the dead.

Not even Zeus's power could now keep the girl among the living, for once having tasted the food of the dead, Persephone belonged to Hades. Thus, the reunion between Demeter and her daughter was bittersweet for the girl could not remain with her mother.

In order to save the world from Demeter's grief, Zeus decreed a compromise, ruling that Persephone must return to Hades in the Underworld four months out of each year. During that time, when her daughter resides in the Underworld, Demeter's sorrow is such that plants die and the Earth becomes cold and gray. Only when Persephone reemerges in the spring and Demeter's grief is eased does life return to the land.

© 2002 by John Wiley & Sons, Inc.

1. According to this myth, Hades seized Persephone because _____.

   A. he wanted to exact a ransom for her

   B. he was angry at Zeus

   C. he had fallen in love with her

   D. she had picked his favorite flower

2. A "chasm" is _____.

   A. a big rock that marks a special location

   B. a gateway

   C. a valley

   D. a crack in the Earth's surface

3. An example of figurative language is _____.

   A. Hades, in his chariot drawn by powerful steeds, rose up and out of a chasm in the Earth

   B. Demeter flew like a bird over land and sea seeking her daughter

   C. Flowers and forests withered, crops died

   D. Zeus sent Hermes to the Underworld

4. Demeter's words "The Earth will not bear fruit again until I see my daughter" means _____.

   A. that apple trees would not bear apples until Persephone was freed

   B. that fruit trees all over the world would not have any fruit

   C. that plants would disappear forever from the Earth

   D. that plants would stop growing and die until Persephone was returned to her

5. Hades asked Persephone to eat the pomegranate seed because _____.

   A. he knew she would then have to return to him

   B. he knew that she was hungry

   C. pomegranates were his favorite food and he wanted to share some with her before she left

   D. he had nothing else to offer her as a parting gift

© 2002 by John Wiley & Sons, Inc.

6. The ancient Greeks likely created this story to _____.

   A. warn people to be careful when picking flowers

   B. explain the great love a mother has for her daughter

   C. explain why winter comes

   D. caution people not to eat pomegranates

Part 3. Directions: Read the selection. Use the Answer Sheet to darken the letter of the answer that best completes each statement.

The Earth today is undergoing a mass extinction. Just like 65 million years ago, when the dinosaurs disappeared, animals across the world are declining at an alarming rate. Unlike the dinosaurs, however, whose demise was brought about by a catastrophic meteor impact, the current extinctions are a result of human activity on our planet.

Animals in virtually every natural habitat are facing increasing pressure to survive. It has been estimated that over 60% of the world's bird population is declining, with close to 5% of the world's species of birds endangered. This means that they are likely to become extinct soon unless their decline is stopped. Close to 25% of the Earth's species of mammals are declining rapidly, with 10% on the endangered list. The numbers are no less grave for reptiles, amphibians, and fish. Frog populations are decreasing worldwide, and vast schools of fish, which once numbered in the millions, have disappeared from many of the world's seas.

Why is this happening? The reasons are complex, but the major factor is human activity. Habitat destruction, overhunting, and pollution are the primary culprits. Each of these factors is a byproduct of the growing human population and the development of natural resources necessary for human progress.

What can be done? Most important, people need to be educated so that they understand the complex interaction of life on Earth. This understanding can then be transformed into positive actions. Efforts need to be made to reduce habitat destruction, limit hunting and fishing of species whose numbers are in decline, and curtail pollution that affects life on the Earth.

With proper initiatives, the mass extinction currently in progress can be at least slowed, perhaps stopped, and hopefully reversed. Everyone must be willing to do his or her part to save life on the Earth.

© 2002 by John Wiley & Sons, Inc.

1. This selection is an example of _____.

   A. science fiction

   B. a persuasive essay

   C. a science article

   D. an informational article

Reading Comprehension Practice Test I *(continued)*

2. In the article the phrase "endangered species" refers to _____.

   A. a kind of animal that is in danger of becoming extinct soon

   B. a species that is overhunted

   C. a species whose only living members are found in zoos and special wildlife refuges

   D. a kind of animal that biologists are unable to find in the wild, but believe still exist

3. According to the author, one of the direct causes of mass extinction is _____.

   A. endangered species

   B. industry

   C. habitat loss

   D. the changing Earth

4. The statement that best summarizes this article is _____.

   A. animals are dying all over the world and something must be done to stop this

   B. pollution is a major cause of animal extinctions

   C. animal extinctions are occurring worldwide, but nothing can be done

   D. the Earth is in the midst of a mass extinction, which people must try to stop

5. The author's purpose in writing this article is to _____.

   A. provide information about endangered animals

   B. show how the mass extinctions going on today are similar to the extinction of the dinosaurs

   C. inform people of the mass extinctions and offer suggestions on how to prevent the decline of animals

   D. encourage people to accept a simple life that will ease the pressure on the habitats of animals

© 2002 by John Wiley & Sons, Inc.

Reading Comprehension Practice Test II

Part 1. Directions: Read the article. Use the Answer Sheet to darken the letter of the answer that best completes each statement.

How to Solve Problems

Everybody has problems. Most of the time our problems are small, but sometimes they can be complicated and distressing. Whatever kind of problem you may have, you need to solve it as soon as possible. If left unsolved, even little problems can grow into big problems that can be a challenge to overcome.

The first step to solving any problem is to *define the problem.* This is essential. It is unlikely that you will be able to solve a problem unless you know exactly what you are trying to solve. Try to state the problem in a single sentence. If you can't state it in a single sentence, you may be trying to solve the wrong problem, or maybe the problem confronting you is actually several problems.

The next step is to *understand the problem.* To do this, you must gather information. Find out what is causing the problem. This may require speaking to other people or conducting research, but it is vital to learn as much as you can about the problem and its causes.

Once you understand the problem, you must *develop a plan for its solution.* Look at the problem from different angles and try to come up with different ways to solve it. You may realize that you need more information, which will require you to gather more facts.

After you have developed plans to solve your problem, you must consider each one carefully and *choose the best plan.* Since some plans will be better than others, try to anticipate the possible implications of each. After careful evaluation, pick the plan that is most likely to solve the problem efficiently.

As you use your plan to solve the problem, *monitor your progress.* You may find that your plan is not achieving the results you thought it would. In this case, you may have to switch to another plan.

Remember, most problems we face are solvable. Using the steps detailed above will improve your chances of successfully solving the problems you encounter.

1. According to the article, it is important to solve little problems because _____.

   A. no problem should go unsolved

   B. little problems can grow into big problems

   C. it is the right thing to do

   D. sometimes little problems are actually big problems in disguise

© 2002 by John Wiley & Sons, Inc.

2. The first step in solving any problem is _____.

   A. finding a solution

   B. asking others for help

   C. waiting patiently for the problem to go away

   D. defining the problem

3. Gathering information is necessary _____.

   A. to understand a problem

   B. to discuss a problem

   C. only for finding the solution to big problems

   D. because everybody has problems

© 2002 by John Wiley & Sons, Inc.

4. According to the article, most problems _____.

   A. are big

   B. are connected to other problems

   C. can be solved

   D. may require several solutions

5. As you are attempting to solve a problem, you should monitor your progress because _____.

   A. you may find that your plan is not working and you will need to switch to another

   B. if you don't monitor your progress, you may solve the problem and not realize it

   C. you will learn more about the problem

   D. you will be in better control of the problem

6. This selection is an example of _____.

   A. an editorial

   B. an essay

   C. an informational article

   D. a narrative

Part 2. Directions: Read the information below. Use the Answer Sheet to darken the letter of the answer that best completes each statement.

Assume that a new game you purchased for your computer has the following system requirements:

- Windows® 95 or higher
- Pentium® processor 133 or higher
- at least 32MB RAM
- 2MB video card with 16-bit color
- direct X version 5.2 sound card or higher
- at least 40MB free disk space
- at least 8X CD-ROM drive
- 640 × 480 with 256 colors screen

1. The "system requirements" for this game refers to _____.

   A. your skill to play the game
   B. the age of your computer
   C. the capability of your computer system
   D. your computer's connection to the Internet

2. Of the following capabilities of a computer, which is likely to cause a problem in the operation of this game?

   A. Windows® 98
   B. 16MB RAM
   C. 240MB free disk space
   D. 16X CD-ROM drive

3. Which of the following is not a requirement to play this game?

   A. a printer
   B. a sound card
   C. a screen
   D. a CD-ROM drive

© 2002 by John Wiley & Sons, Inc.

4. Understanding the capabilities of a computer system and the system requirements of computer games _____.

   A. allows you to purchase any game you wish

   B. helps you to avoid making mistakes while playing the game

   C. enables you to buy games that will operate on your computer

   D. enables you to fix the game when something goes wrong

Part 3. Directions: Read the poem. Use the Answer Sheet to darken the letter of the answer that best completes each statement.

Untitled

When I was young
every day was as a beginning
of some new thing.
And every evening ended
with the glow of the next day's dawn.

—An Arctic Eskimo Poem

© 2002 by John Wiley & Sons, Inc.

1. The first line of the poem implies that the author is _____.

   A. a child

   B. an old man who is recalling the past

   C. thinking about tomorrow

   D. old enough to think about a time when he or she was young

2. The last two lines of the poem suggest that the author _____.

   A. looked forward to each day

   B. worried about the next day

   C. expected the next day to be sunny

   D. doesn't like the night

3. Of the following, the best title for this poem is _____.

   A. An Eskimo Child's Thoughts

   B. Reflecting on Yesterday

   C. Morning Follows Day

   D. Thinking about Sunrise

4. The phrase "glow of the next day's dawn" most likely refers to _____.

   A. a bright sunny day

   B. a warm day for the Arctic

   C. the next day

   D. sunrise

5. The mood created by the author of this poem is best described as _____.

   A. sorrowful

   B. gloomy

   C. wistful

   D. disappointed

© 2002 by John Wiley & Sons, Inc.

Reading Comprehension Practice Test III

Part 1. Directions: Read the article. Use the Answer Sheet to darken the letter of the answer that best completes each statement.

The Thomas Watson Exhibit opened yesterday at the Stonehill Museum on Main Street in Stonehill. Mr. Watson is the descendant of Walter Watson, the founder in 1744 of the quarry that bore his name. The town of Stonehill eventually was built around the quarry.

Although the original quarry was torn down and replaced by private homes in the 1850s, much of the Watson family remained in town until well into the 20th century. Today, however, Thomas Watson and his wife, Emily, are the only Watsons still residing in Stonehill. Because of the family's long residence in the town, the Watsons possess one of the most extensive collections of Colonial furniture, household items, and art in the state. It is this collection that is on display at the museum, now through May 5.

Over 300 pieces of furniture, cooking pots, quilts, farm tools, and paintings, all in excellent condition, are displayed on the museum's second floor. The exhibit creates a mood in which visitors are transported to an earlier time in our nation's history. Guides are available to explain the various items, and a slide show offering a brief history of Stonehill is presented at the top of every hour in the East Room.

While the exhibit is a must for history buffs, even those with just a casual interest in the past will find the period pieces fascinating. A visit to the exhibit will be time well spent.

© 2002 by John Wiley & Sons, Inc.

1. According to the article, _____.

   A. Thomas Watson built a quarry in 1744

   B. the town of Stonehill was built before the quarry

   C. Thomas Watson is a descendent of Walter Watson

   D. Thomas Watson owns the Stonehill Museum

2. The Thomas Watson Exhibit contains _____.

   A. photos of the original quarry

   B. Colonial furniture

   C. numerous photographs and memoirs of the family of Thomas Watson

   D. a guided tour of the quarry

3. The words "The exhibit creates a mood in which visitors are transported to an earlier time in our nation's history" mean _____.

   A. the display is so authentic that visitors feel like they are in the past

   B. visitors are unsettled by the realism of the exhibit

   C. visitors like learning about the past

   D. visitors are mysteriously sent back in time to the mid 1700s

4. The author's purpose for writing this article is to _____.

   A. convince people to visit the Thomas Watson Exhibit

   B. inform readers about the life of Thomas Watson

   C. inform readers about the Thomas Watson Exhibit

   D. provide a complete history of Stonehill

5. Based on the article, the reader can conclude that the Thomas Watson Exhibit is _____.

   A. one of the finest exhibits in the country

   B. only for Stonehill residents

   C. designed for people highly interested in world history

   D. a comprehensive collection of Colonial items

© 2002 by John Wiley & Sons, Inc.

Part 2. Directions: Read the selection. Use the Answer Sheet to darken the letter of the answer that best completes each statement.

William Sidney Mount (1807–1868) was one of the first American painters to reject European styles of art and instead use his talent to celebrate the developing United States. In the early 19th century, most American painters followed the lead of European painters whose work focused on scenes from literature, history, and religion.

Unlike other American artists of his time, Mount chose to paint scenes of America. Although he was widely respected for his portraits, one of which was Daniel Webster, Mount is best remembered as the inventor of American genre painting for his work that showed American life in realistic settings. Mount's paintings helped to show what America was like, and gave Americans throughout the country an opportunity to see the vastness of the nation.

1. In the early 19th century, most American painters painted scenes based on _____.

   A. natural settings

   B. American life

   C. history, literature, and religion

   D. portraits of famous Americans

2. The phrase “genre painting” means _____.

   A. the painting of portraits

   B. paintings that concentrate on religion

   C. a style of painting in which the painter mixes various different scenes together to create something entirely new

   D. a style of painting that shows scenes and subjects of ordinary life

3. William Sydney Mount is considered to be _____.

   A. the first American painter to paint a portrait

   B. the inventor of American genre painting

   C. an outspoken critic of European art

   D. a painter who preferred to paint historical scenes

4. William Sydney Mount can best be described as _____.

   A. the first true American painter

   B. an American painter who enjoyed experimenting with various art forms

   C. an American painter whose paintings of everyday life helped to show what America was like

   D. an American painter whose style was closely based on the style of leading European painters

© 2002 by John Wiley & Sons, Inc.

Part 3. Directions: Study the climograph. Use your Answer Sheet to darken the letter of the answer to each question.

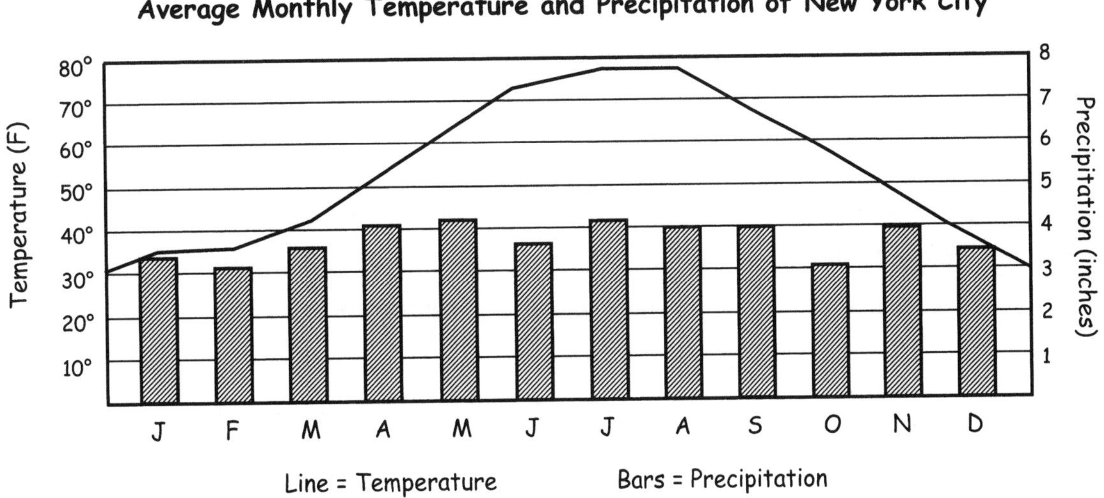

Reading Comprehension Practice Test III *(continued)*

1. What is the average temperature of New York City in March?

   A. 48°
   B. 42°
   C. 40°
   D. 38°

2. What is the average temperature of New York City in July?

   A. 80°
   B. 73°
   C. 68°
   D. 77°

3. What is the average precipitation for New York City in May?

   A. 4.6 inches
   B. 5 inches
   C. 4.2 inches
   D. 3.9 inches

4. Of the following, which month is the wettest in New York City?

   A. March
   B. May
   C. August
   D. September

5. Which of the following months averages the least amount of precipitation?

   A. March
   B. April
   C. October
   D. December

6. Based on the information of the graph, the best description of New York City's climate is _____.

   A. hot summers, warm winters, little precipitation
   B. warm summers, cold winters, moderate precipitation throughout the year
   C. cool summers, cold winters, heaviest precipitation in summer
   D. hot summers, cold winters, heaviest precipitation in winter

© 2002 by John Wiley & Sons, Inc.

Name ________________________________ Date ________________

Reading Comprehension

PRACTICE TEST I: ANSWER SHEET

Directions: Darken the circle above the letter of the correct answer.

Part 1

1. ○ A ○ B ○ C ○ D
2. ○ A ○ B ○ C ○ D
3. ○ A ○ B ○ C ○ D
4. ○ A ○ B ○ C ○ D
5. ○ A ○ B ○ C ○ D

Part 2

1. ○ A ○ B ○ C ○ D
2. ○ A ○ B ○ C ○ D
3. ○ A ○ B ○ C ○ D
4. ○ A ○ B ○ C ○ D
5. ○ A ○ B ○ C ○ D
6. ○ A ○ B ○ C ○ D

Part 3

1. ○ A ○ B ○ C ○ D
2. ○ A ○ B ○ C ○ D
3. ○ A ○ B ○ C ○ D
4. ○ A ○ B ○ C ○ D
5. ○ A ○ B ○ C ○ D

© 2002 by John Wiley & Sons, Inc.

Name ______________________________ Date ________________

Reading Comprehension

PRACTICE TEST II: ANSWER SHEET

Directions: Darken the circle above the letter of the correct answer.

Part 1

1. ○ A ○ B ○ C ○ D
2. ○ A ○ B ○ C ○ D
3. ○ A ○ B ○ C ○ D
4. ○ A ○ B ○ C ○ D
5. ○ A ○ B ○ C ○ D
6. ○ A ○ B ○ C ○ D

Part 2

1. ○ A ○ B ○ C ○ D
2. ○ A ○ B ○ C ○ D
3. ○ A ○ B ○ C ○ D
4. ○ A ○ B ○ C ○ D

Part 3

1. ○ A ○ B ○ C ○ D
2. ○ A ○ B ○ C ○ D
3. ○ A ○ B ○ C ○ D
4. ○ A ○ B ○ C ○ D
5. ○ A ○ B ○ C ○ D

© 2002 by John Wiley & Sons, Inc.

Name ____________________ Date ____________

Reading Comprehension

PRACTICE TEST III: ANSWER SHEET

Directions: Darken the circle above the letter of the correct answer.

Part 1

1. ○ A ○ B ○ C ○ D
2. ○ A ○ B ○ C ○ D
3. ○ A ○ B ○ C ○ D
4. ○ A ○ B ○ C ○ D
5. ○ A ○ B ○ C ○ D

Part 2

1. ○ A ○ B ○ C ○ D
2. ○ A ○ B ○ C ○ D
3. ○ A ○ B ○ C ○ D
4. ○ A ○ B ○ C ○ D

Part 3

1. ○ A ○ B ○ C ○ D
2. ○ A ○ B ○ C ○ D
3. ○ A ○ B ○ C ○ D
4. ○ A ○ B ○ C ○ D
5. ○ A ○ B ○ C ○ D
6. ○ A ○ B ○ C ○ D

© 2002 by John Wiley & Sons, Inc.

Reading Comprehension

KEY TO PRACTICE TEST I

Part 1

	A	B	C	D
1.	○	○	●	○
2.	●	○	○	○
3.	○	●	○	○
4.	○	○	○	●
5.	○	○	●	○

Part 2

	A	B	C	D
1.	○	○	●	○
2.	○	○	○	●
3.	○	●	○	○
4.	○	○	○	●
5.	●	○	○	○
6.	○	○	●	○

Part 3

	A	B	C	D
1.	○	●	○	○
2.	●	○	○	○
3.	○	○	●	○
4.	○	○	○	●
5.	○	○	●	○

© 2002 by John Wiley & Sons, Inc.

Reading Comprehension

KEY TO PRACTICE TEST II

Part 1

	A	B	C	D
1.	○	●	○	○
2.	○	○	○	●
3.	●	○	○	○
4.	○	○	●	○
5.	●	○	○	○
6.	○	○	●	○

Part 2

	A	B	C	D
1.	○	○	●	○
2.	○	●	○	○
3.	●	○	○	○
4.	○	○	●	○

Part 3

	A	B	C	D
1.	○	○	○	●
2.	●	○	○	○
3.	○	●	○	○
4.	○	○	○	●
5.	○	○	●	○

© 2002 by John Wiley & Sons, Inc.

Reading Comprehension

KEY TO PRACTICE TEST III

Part 1

1. ○ A ○ B ● C ○ D
2. ○ A ● B ○ C ○ D
3. ● A ○ B ○ C ○ D
4. ○ A ○ B ● C ○ D
5. ○ A ○ B ○ C ● D

Part 2

1. ○ A ○ B ● C ○ D
2. ○ A ○ B ○ C ● D
3. ○ A ● B ○ C ○ D
4. ○ A ○ B ● C ○ D

Part 3

1. ○ A ● B ○ C ○ D
2. ○ A ○ B ○ C ● D
3. ○ A ○ B ● C ○ D
4. ○ A ● B ○ C ○ D
5. ○ A ○ B ● C ○ D
6. ○ A ● B ○ C ○ D

© 2002 by John Wiley & Sons, Inc.

Section 4

Spelling

The ability to spell is a basic skill, closely linked to reading and writing. Good spellers are usually better readers and writers than those students who have weak spelling skills. Because of its importance, spelling is a prominent component of standardized tests.

While every student may not be able to attain perfect scores in spelling, most students can become proficient spellers. You can support the efforts of your students by distributing the following study sheets:

- Study Sheet 4-A, "Study Strategies for Spelling"
- Study Sheet 4-B, "Steps to Improve Your Spelling"
- Study Sheet 4-C, "Basic Spelling Rules"
- Study Sheet 4-D, "Spelling Word List"

The best time to distribute Study Sheets 4-A, 4-B, and 4-C is within the first few weeks of the school year. Handing them out on different days enables students to concentrate on the sheets one at a time. Discuss the information on the sheets with your students and encourage them to utilize the suggestions that are provided. Emphasize that people are not born with good spelling "genes"; people become competent spellers through study, reading, awareness of words, and the use of specific spelling strategies. Utilizing these study sheets will help your students improve their spelling.

While most students will find each of the study sheets helpful, Study Sheet 4-D, "Spelling Word List," is particularly beneficial because it contains words that are frequently found on eighth-grade standardized tests. All students, even your top spellers, should be familiar with these words before the test date.

A practical way to familiarize your students with these words is to divide the list into groups of 15–20 words and provide them to your students in regular intervals. A weekly or biweekly schedule should be practical for most people. To ensure that your students are exposed to all of the words on the list, you will probably need to start distributing groups of words several weeks prior to the test. Encourage your students to learn the spelling of these words by administering periodic quizzes.

Since it is likely that many of these words will appear in the material you teach, you may incorporate the words with your students' language, literature, or other spelling activities. Whichever way you decide to present the words of the list, avoid handing them out all at once. This will be overwhelming for your students and will likely result in few benefits and plenty of frustration.

This section also contains 12 spelling worksheets and two practice tests. The words contained on the worksheets are common in eighth-grade curriculums and are candidates for appearing on standardized tests. Sprinkled throughout the worksheets and tests are words from Study Sheet 4-D.

You should utilize the worksheets in a manner that best suits the needs of your students. You may assign all of the worksheets, or you may pick those you feel will be of most benefit. For the best results, distribute the worksheets periodically in advance of the test. In addition, suggest that your students write any words they have trouble spelling in a notebook for future reference. Not only will this help them to remember the words, it will also enable them to easily review words that they find difficult to spell.

Effective preparation for any test is critical for boosting achievement. Students who study words likely to appear on standardized spelling tests almost always improve their scores.

Teaching Suggestions for the Worksheets

4-1: Finding Misspelled Words I

Begin this exercise by explaining the importance of being able to spell. Quite simply, the companies and institutions of business, industry, and public service expect people to be able to spell words correctly. Note that through study and use of dictionaries most people can become competent spellers.

For this worksheet, your students are given sets of four words, of which one of the words is misspelled. They are to circle the misspelled word. Caution your students to consider each word carefully, because while some mistakes are glaring, others are subtle. Such words are commonly misspelled and at first glance may appear to be correct.

When your students have completed the worksheet, go over their answers. Point out the words that caused the most confusion and suggest that your students write these words in a notebook to which they may refer later.

4-2: Finding Misspelled Words II

This worksheet is similar to Worksheet 4-1 and provides your students with more practice in identifying misspelled words. Begin the exercise by explaining that the worksheet presents sets of four words, of which one word is misspelled. Students are to circle the misspelled word in each set.

When your students have finished the activity, correct the worksheets. Encourage your students to record and practice any words they did not identify correctly.

4-3: Finding Misspelled Words III

This activity provides additional practice in finding misspelled words and is similar to the previous worksheets of this section. Your students will be given sets of four words, of which one word is misspelled. They are to circle this word on the worksheet. Once your students have completed the worksheet, correct their work and encourage them to record and practice any misspelled words they did not identify.

4-4: Finding Misspelled Words IV

This exercise is like the previous three worksheets. The worksheet presents students with sets of four words, one of which is misspelled. Your students are to find the misspelled word and circle it on the worksheet. Upon completion of the worksheet, correct the answers and encourage your students to record and practice the words they did not identify as being misspelled.

4-5: Finding Misspelled Words in Phrases I

Introduce this activity by explaining that this worksheet presents sets of four phrases, each of which has an underlined word. In one of the phrases, the underlined word is spelled incorrectly. Instruct your students to read each phrase carefully. They are to place a check in the space before the phrase that contains the misspelled word.

Upon completion of the activity, correct the worksheets. Encourage your students to record and learn any words that they did not identify correctly.

4-6: Finding Misspelled Words in Phrases II

This worksheet is similar to Worksheet 4-5. Introduce the activity by explaining that the worksheet contains sets of four phrases, each of which contains an underlined word. Your students are to decide which phrase contains an underlined word that is misspelled and place a check in the space before that phrase. Upon completion of the worksheet, go over the phrases so that your students realize their mistakes. Encourage them to record and study the words they did not recognize as being misspelled.

4-7: Finding Misspelled Words in Phrases III

This exercise is modeled after Worksheets 4-5 and 4-6. Your students are given four sets of phrases, each of which contains an underlined word. One of the underlined words is misspelled. Your students are to find this word and place a check in the space before the phrase. When your students are done with the activity, correct the worksheet and encourage them to record and study any words they got wrong.

4-8: Finding the Correct Word I

Begin this activity by explaining that this worksheet presents sentences that are to be completed. Your students are given four words with which to complete each sentence, but only one of the choices is spelled correctly. They are to circle the correct word. Remind your students to carefully consider each possibility before making their selection. It is easy to make careless mistakes in spelling.

When your students have completed the worksheet, correct their answers so that they can see their mistakes. Encourage them to record and study any words they got wrong.

4-9: Finding the Correct Word II

This exercise is similar to Worksheet 4-8. Your students must complete sentences. They will be given four words as possible answers, and they are to circle the word that is spelled correctly. Caution your students to consider each potential answer to avoid making careless mistakes.

Upon completion of the worksheet, correct the answers and review any words that your students found difficult. Suggest that they record and practice the words they did not identify correctly.

4-10: Finding the Correct Word III

This exercise is similar to Worksheets 4-8 and 4-9. Start the activity by explaining that the worksheets contain sentences that must be completed by choosing a correctly spelled word. Your students should circle their answers. When your students are done, go over their work and encourage them to record and study any words they did not identify correctly.

4-11: Proofreading for Misspelled Words I

Begin this exercise by explaining that we may make mistakes in spelling when we write. This is often a result of mixing up a letter or two or through just plain carelessness. The best way to overcome errors in spelling in our writing is to carefully proofread our material.

For this worksheet, your students are to proofread a selection and identify 10 misspelled words. They are to first circle each misspelled word in the selection, then write each word correctly on the lines that follow. After your students complete the activity, correct their work and review any words they had trouble spelling. Encourage them to record and study these words.

4-12: Proofreading for Misspelled Words II

Start this activity by explaining that it is similar to Worksheet 4-11. Your students are to read a selection and circle any misspelled words they find. They should find 10. Next they are to write the words correctly on the lines after the selection.

Upon completion of the worksheet, go over the selection and review any words your students found troublesome. Encourage your students to record and study these words.

Spelling Practice Tests I and II

This section contains two practice tests. You may assign either or both. The tests follow the formats of the worksheets—finding misspelled words in sets of four words, finding misspelled words in phrases, and finding the correctly spelled word to complete sentences. The first test draws words mostly from Worksheets 4-1 through 4-6, while the second test is comprised of words taken from Worksheets 4-7 through 4-12.

Your students should use the Answer Sheets with these tests. Using the answer sheets will give them practice marking answers on the answer sheets that accompany standardized tests.

Answer Key for Section 4

4-1. **1.** inflexible **2.** retrieve **3.** preliminary **4.** meager **5.** balance **6.** punctually **7.** changeable **8.** forfeit **9.** persist **10.** celebrity **11.** sacrifice **12.** boredom **13.** informant **14.** memoir **15.** loathe

4-2. **1.** politician **2.** investigate **3.** saturate **4.** extraordinary **5.** wondrous **6.** surplus **7.** scandalous **8.** optimistic **9.** momentous **10.** harass **11.** encouraged **12.** gruesome **13.** descendant **14.** incredible **15.** crescent

4-3. **1.** icicle **2.** frugal **3.** symbolic **4.** torturous **5.** favorable **6.** vaccination **7.** curiosity **8.** erroneous **9.** development **10.** subscription **11.** cemetery **12.** distress **13.** criticize **14.** bacteria **15.** placid

4-4. **1.** inheritance **2.** knowledge **3.** fascinate **4.** scenic **5.** juvenile **6.** gaseous **7.** career **8.** murmur **9.** capillary **10.** deficiency **11.** identical **12.** boundary **13.** disbelief **14.** preference **15.** tributary

4-5. **1.** B **2.** A **3.** C **4.** D **5.** C **6.** D **7.** C **8.** A **9.** B **10.** D **11.** C **12.** B

4-6. **1.** B **2.** D **3.** C **4.** B **5.** A **6.** D **7.** C **8.** B **9.** A **10.** B **11.** D **12.** C

4-7. **1.** A **2.** D **3.** C **4.** C **5.** B **6.** D **7.** A **8.** C **9.** B **10.** A **11.** D **12.** C

4-8. **1.** exasperates **2.** invited **3.** thermometer **4.** invasion **5.** abstract **6.** detective **7.** edible **8.** interfered **9.** bewildering **10.** violent **11.** knowledge **12.** compromise

4-9. **1.** descended **2.** inhabitant **3.** enormous **4.** reliability **5.** ignored **6.** gauge **7.** esteem **8.** retrieving **9.** preparation **10.** receipt **11.** monopoly **12.** vigorous

4-10. **1.** attendance **2.** detergent **3.** sufficient **4.** precious **5.** certified **6.** bilingual **7.** immediately **8.** nominated **9.** microbes **10.** irresistible **11.** versatile **12.** questionnaire

4-11. **1.** difficulty **2.** individuals **3.** selecting **4.** interests **5.** humorous **6.** particular **7.** magazines **8.** browsing **9.** hesitate **10.** fascinating

4-12. **1.** occurred **2.** subsided **3.** estimated **4.** propelled **5.** debris **6.** navigate **7.** literally **8.** coastal **9.** original **10.** catastrophe

Study Sheet 4-A

Study Strategies for Spelling

Use the following steps to study spelling.

1. Find a quiet place to study. Avoid watching TV, listening to music, and having other distractions while you are studying.
2. Look at the word and concentrate.
3. Say the word. Be sure you are pronouncing it correctly.
4. Say the letters of the word.
5. Note syllables and special letter combinations, for example, double vowels or consonants.
6. Close your eyes and see the word in your mind.
7. Focus your mind on the letters of the word.
8. Spell the word.
9. Write the word.
10. Check that you have spelled the word correctly.
11. If you have spelled it correctly, spell the word again to yourself, focusing on each letter. This will help you to remember it.
12. If you have misspelled the word, repeat Steps 2–10.

Here's an additional tip: Take notice of words in your reading, in advertisements, and on signs. Pay attention to how words are spelled. This will help you recall how to spell words.

© 2002 by John Wiley & Sons, Inc.

Study Sheet 4-B

Steps to Improve Your Spelling

The following can help you improve your spelling.

1. Always try to spell words correctly.
2. Use a dictionary if you are not sure of a word's spelling.
3. Learn to spell long words by syllables.
4. Learn basic spelling rules.
5. Learn the meanings of homophones. Knowing the meanings of homophones will help you to use and spell them correctly.
6. Learn the meanings of easily confused words, such as "desert," a dry wasteland, and "dessert," a tasty food served at the end of a meal. This will help you to spell such words correctly.
7. Pay special attention to "tricky" words that are often misspelled.
8. Keep a notebook of words you have trouble spelling.
9. Always proofread your writing carefully for spelling mistakes.
10. If you are using a computer for writing, be sure to use *spell check* to verify your spelling.
11. Always study for spelling tests.
12. When you find that you have spelled a word incorrectly, study the correct spelling and try to memorize it.

© 2002 by John Wiley & Sons, Inc.

Study Sheet 4-C

Basic Spelling Rules

Knowing the following rules can help you spell words correctly.

1. For words with **ie** and **ei**:

   - When the sound of a word is **e**, spell the word with **ie**, except after **c**.

     Examples of the **e** sound: brief, piece, relieve

     Examples "except after **c**": perceive, ceiling

   - When the sound of a word is not **e**, spell the word **ei.** This is especially true if the sound is **a**.

     Examples: weight, freight, sleigh

   - There are exceptions to the rules above: either, friend, weird.

2. For adding **s** and **es**:

   - An **s** can be added to many words without a spelling change.

     Examples: car—cars, walk—walks, beaver—beavers

   - For words that end in **ch, s, sh, x,** or **z,** add **es**.

     Examples: church—churches, genius—geniuses, bush—bushes, box—boxes

3. For most words ending in **f** or **fe**:

   - When adding **s** or **es,** change the **f** to **v**, then add **s** or **es**.

     Examples: wife—wives, knife—knives, loaf—loaves

   - There are exceptions to the rule above: roof—roofs, chief—chiefs

4. For most words ending in **o**:

   - If the **o** follows a vowel, add **s** to form the plural.

     Examples: radio—radios, rodeo—rodeos

   - If the **o** follows a consonant, add **es** to form the plural.

     Examples: hero—heroes, potato—potatoes

© 2002 by John Wiley & Sons, Inc.

Study Sheet 4-C

Basic Spelling Rules *(continued)*

5. For most words ending in a consonant and **y**:

   - Change the **y** to **i** before an ending that does not begin with **i**.

     Examples: lady—ladies, try—tried

6. For most words ending in a vowel and **y**:

   - Keep the **y** when adding an ending.

     Examples: stay—stayed, employ—employing

7. For most one-syllable words that end in one vowel and one consonant:

   - Double the consonant when adding an ending that starts with a vowel.

     Examples: thin—thinner, glad—gladder, run—running

8. For most two-syllable words that end in one vowel and one consonant:

   - Double the consonant only if the accent is on the second syllable.

     Examples: begin—beginning, refer—referred

9. Irregular nouns defy spelling rules when changing from singular to plural forms:

   - Some irregular nouns change their form.

     Examples: mouse—mice, goose—geese, ox—oxen, child—children, man—men, woman—women

   - Some irregular nouns have the same form when they are singular or plural.

     Examples: deer—deer, sheep—sheep, moose—moose

   - *Note:* The best strategy for spelling the plurals of irregular nouns is to learn the plural forms, and consult a dictionary if you are unsure.

© 2002 by John Wiley & Sons, Inc.

Study Sheet 4-D

Spelling Word List

Practice spelling the following words

abbreviation
abrupt
absurd
academy
accommodate
accumulate
acquaintance
acquire
acquittal
adapt
adequate
adjustment
aerial
aisle
allegiance
ambiguous
anonymous
anxiety
appearance
appendix
approximate
architect
ardently
arrival
atrocious
beautician
believable
beneficial
bewildering
bigoted
bilingual
boredom
boundary
brevity
brilliant
brochure
buoyant
bureau
business
campaign
capillary
captivating
career
catastrophe
caution
cavity
celebrity
changeable
chapter
chronicle
collapse
colossal
commerce
competitive
conspicuous
contemplate
contempt
continuous
controversy
crescent
curiosity
decimal
deficiency
deliberation
dependent
detergent
devastating
disastrous
disguise
disregard
distress
disturbance
dynamic
eccentric
edible
eligible
embellish
encourage
endeavor
erroneous
escapade
esteem
estuary
exaggerate
excessive
excitable
exorbitant
expansion
experience
extensive
extraordinary
faculty
fallacy
fascinate
feasible
ferocity
fictitious
fiery
foreign
forfeit
furious
gadget
generous
genius
government
grandeur
grateful
grievance
gruesome
guarantee
harassment
healthy
hesitate
hindrance
humanity
humidity
humorous
hysterical
ignore
illiterate

© 2002 by John Wiley & Sons, Inc.

Study Sheet 4-D

Spelling Word List *(continued)*

imagery
immaculate
impeccable
implication
impudent
incessant
inconspicuous
incredulous
indecision
indelible
independent
indestructible
inflexible
inquisitive
interfere
invasion
investigate
involve
isle
isolation
jealousy
jewelry
judicial
junction
knowledge
laudable
legislate
leisure
liable
limitation
literacy

loathe
loneliness
magazine
maximum
meager
melancholy
melodious
memorable
menace
miniature
minimum
miraculous
mischievous
misplaced
momentum
monopoly
morale
murmur
mysterious
napkin
nausea
necessary
negligence
negotiate
nervous
noticeable
nourishment
nuisance
obedience
obligation
obscure

obstacle
occasional
occurrence
official
ominous
opportunity
original
outrageous
override
pageantry
parallel
particular
perceive
permissible
perseverance
persist
perspiration
persuade
phenomenon
philosophy
physical
placate
placid
plausible
precious
predictable
preference
prejudice
premature
prevalent
privilege

propaganda
proprietor
punctually
quadrant
quantity
questionnaire
quorum
quotation
radiation
realize
rebellion
receipt
receive
recipient
recommend
recycle
redemption
reflection
reimburse
reiterate
reliability
reluctant
rendezvous
repetition
replenish
represent
reticent
retrieve
reverse
rhythm
sabotage

© 2002 by John Wiley & Sons, Inc.

Study Sheet 4-D

Spelling Word List *(continued)*

sacrifice
salvage
sarcastic
satire
saturate
savanna
scandalous
scenic
scholar
scrutiny
seize
sensible
separation
sequence
several
siege
sierra
sieve
significance
similarity
slogan
society
solemn

solitary
stationary
strenuous
surplus
suspicious
symbolic
symmetric
tangible
tariff
tedious
temperament
temperature
temporary
tenacious
tenant
tendency
terrestrial
territorial
theory
thistle
tolerant
tomorrow
torrid

torturous
tranquil
treasurer
tremendous
trilogy
turbulence
twelfth
tyranny
ultimately
unanimous
unconscious
underground
unexpected
unilateral
unique
unity
universal
usage
vaccination
vacuum
variety
vengeance
verify

versatile
vertical
vicious
vigilance
vigorous
village
violent
visible
volcanoes
volunteer
waive
waltz
wary
weather
weird
wharf
wondrous
wreckage
yacht
zeros
zoology

© 2002 by John Wiley & Sons, Inc.

Name ______________________________ Date ________________

4-1

Finding Misspelled Words I

Directions: Circle the misspelled word in each group of words.

1.	dandelion	processor	inflexable	generous
2.	quotation	retreive	various	intellect
3.	cycle	attraction	library	preliminery
4.	meeger	bazaar	redeem	prudent
5.	athlete	balence	yacht	saxophone
6.	intercede	chimney	punctualy	environment
7.	ingenious	guarantee	curtail	changable
8.	forfit	criteria	influential	prosecution
9.	pursist	receive	irrelevant	delivery
10.	atrocious	chapter	celebritty	insult
11.	prominent	sacrefice	organization	irresponsible
12.	curriculum	interruption	multiple	bordom
13.	stanza	triumphant	customer	informent
14.	extinguish	inheritance	memoire	feasible
15.	lothe	matrix	fiery	pageantry

© 2002 by John Wiley & Sons, Inc.

Name ______________________________ Date ________________

4-2

Finding Misspelled Words II

Directions: Circle the misspelled word in each group of words.

1.	facade	extensive	recognize	politisian
2.	investagate	grievous	hearty	legislative
3.	waltz	saterate	roommate	sequence
4.	superstition	adequate	exterordinary	biography
5.	fictitious	disobey	wonderous	cruelty
6.	difference	serplus	ingredient	satellite
7.	verified	invited	pamphlet	scandilous
8.	optomistic	junction	omission	intrigue
9.	invincible	humanity	momentus	obscure
10.	essence	deliberation	gadget	harrass
11.	encuraged	dictionary	illustration	furniture
12.	prescribe	grusome	genuine	suppress
13.	capitalism	strenuous	chocolate	desendant
14.	incredable	cinema	parallel	analysis
15.	brevity	cresent	impartial	plateau

© 2002 by John Wiley & Sons, Inc.

Name ________________________________ Date ____________________

4-3

Finding Misspelled Words III

Directions: Circle the misspelled word in each group of words.

1.	abstract	isicle	grandeur	furniture
2.	frugle	exaggerate	raisins	juggle
3.	prosperity	invoke	translation	cymbolic
4.	liable	torterous	redemption	proportion
5.	collectible	bisect	faverable	cyclical
6.	vacinnation	similarity	quotation	cherish
7.	architect	memorable	dynasty	curiousity
8.	intentional	eroneous	devastating	protein
9.	inflation	embargo	developement	survivor
10.	radiation	correspondent	ascent	subscribtion
11.	alleviate	cemetary	bilingual	dazzling
12.	distres	ignition	discussion	porpoise
13.	melodious	movable	criticise	depression
14.	exclude	cowardice	government	backteria
15.	industrious	plasid	licorice	opera

© 2002 by John Wiley & Sons, Inc.

Name ______________________________ Date ________________

4-4

Finding Misspelled Words IV

Directions: Circle the misspelled word in each group of words.

1.	courtesy	inheritence	alliance	inquisitive
2.	pyramid	humorous	knowlege	plausible
3.	efficient	facinate	necessary	mythology
4.	seenic	prophecy	obedient	legitimate
5.	disrupt	calculator	information	juvenle
6.	columnist	identify	gasous	foreign
7.	dwindle	carreer	illusion	excitable
8.	masterpiece	custodian	murmer	professor
9.	capilary	realize	persuasion	jealousy
10.	oppress	deficency	implication	pastime
11.	identicle	official	mutation	capsule
12.	miserable	embassy	ecosystem	boundery
13.	banquet	disbeleif	energetic	automotive
14.	quantity	territory	preferance	velocity
15.	procession	slender	nucleus	tributory

© 2002 by John Wiley & Sons, Inc.

Name ______________________________ Date ________________

4-5

Finding Misspelled Words in Phrases I

Directions: Place a check before each phrase with a misspelled word.

1. ___ A. frozen with indecision
   ___ B. dropped her napken
   ___ C. gourmet foods
   ___ D. intermediate grades

2. ___ A. ineligable for the position
   ___ B. possessing exceptional eyesight
   ___ C. an interesting theory
   ___ D. the high plateau

3. ___ A. the obstacle course
   ___ B. an unconstitutional law
   ___ C. a tranqul day
   ___ D. the province of Quebec

4. ___ A. lost luggage
   ___ B. a complex system of irrigation
   ___ C. an irrelevant discussion
   ___ D. an enjoyable musicle

5. ___ A. the burglar's accomplice
   ___ B. the incessant noise of the jackhammer
   ___ C. an uncomfortable, torid day
   ___ D. punishment to fit the crime

6. ___ A. a strange phenomenon
   ___ B. salvage the sunken ship
   ___ C. recycle the newspaper
   ___ D. the Italian resteraunt

7. ___ A. poison ivy
   ___ B. a lively debate
   ___ C. extensiv storm damage
   ___ D. the volcanic eruption

8. ___ A. an embarassing situation
   ___ B. a dynamic personality
   ___ C. a terrible disease
   ___ D. a detailed questionnaire

9. ___ A. a prudent decision
   ___ B. the widespread rebelion
   ___ C. the mountainous landscape
   ___ D. ride in a limousine

10. ___ A. a confusing assignment
    ___ B. a severe infection
    ___ C. lack of adequate information
    ___ D. a colassal statue

11. ___ A. an impatient child
    ___ B. a hardy individual
    ___ C. a large envelop
    ___ D. the grouchiest man in town

12. ___ A. the new millennium
    ___ B. modernise the computer system
    ___ C. maximum effort
    ___ D. a minor traffic violation

© 2002 by John Wiley & Sons, Inc.

Library Resource Center
Renton Technical College
3000 N.E. 4th St.
Renton, WA 98056

Name ____________________ Date ____________

4-6

Finding Misspelled Words in Phrases II

Directions: Place a check before each phrase with a misspelled word.

1. ___ A. an adjacent room
   ___ B. an incredable sight of a UFO
   ___ C. a swarm of mosquitoes
   ___ D. a tall cypress tree

2. ___ A. the plume of smoke
   ___ B. the unabridged version
   ___ C. a temporary delay in their flight's takeoff
   ___ D. the sophmore class

3. ___ A. the treasurer of the 8th-grade class
   ___ B. the group's interaction
   ___ C. a solenm occasion
   ___ D. the student government

4. ___ A. the country's expanding economy
   ___ B. a strange disappearence
   ___ C. hydroelectric power
   ___ D. dissatisfied with the test results

5. ___ A. a fundamentle law
   ___ B. took the car for inspection
   ___ C. the study of philosophy
   ___ D. a ridiculous story

6. ___ A. a contestant on the game show
   ___ B. the math assignment on polygons
   ___ C. an employee at the diner
   ___ D. her weekly allowence

7. ___ A. the thermostat set to 68°
   ___ B. receive a letter
   ___ C. choclate candy
   ___ D. a computer programmer

8. ___ A. an informative lecture
   ___ B. cloudy day with intermittant drizzle
   ___ C. suffering with allergies
   ___ D. the school district

9. ___ A. never disregaurd the rules
   ___ B. generous charitable contribution
   ___ C. the shrubbery around the house
   ___ D. a hearty appetite

10. ___ A. a severe cold
    ___ B. greatful for the gift
    ___ C. illegible handwriting
    ___ D. a heated discussion

11. ___ A. excellent achievement
    ___ B. lunch in the cafeteria
    ___ C. an impulsive decision
    ___ D. a disasterous storm

12. ___ A. a preliminary conclusion
    ___ B. a biographical sketch
    ___ C. the candidate's acceptence speech
    ___ D. the car's ignition system

© 2002 by John Wiley & Sons, Inc.

Name ______________________________ Date ________________

4-7

Finding Misspelled Words in Phrases III

Directions: Place a check before each phrase with a misspelled word.

1. ___ A. superior accomodations
   ___ B. a police informant
   ___ C. the glistening snow
   ___ D. the state's acting governor

2. ___ A. a pleasant temperament
   ___ B. a valuable lesson
   ___ C. an involuntary reaction
   ___ D. an exagerated story

3. ___ A. the "now" generation
   ___ B. the faculty of the school
   ___ C. studying fractions and decimels
   ___ D. a delicate flower

4. ___ A. stinging criticism
   ___ B. crisp morning air
   ___ C. an inflamable material
   ___ D. a customer service representative

5. ___ A. natural immunity to some diseases
   ___ B. a reluctent witness
   ___ C. the prosecution in the case
   ___ D. an inconvenient schedule

6. ___ A. numerous craters on the moon
   ___ B. an overseas correspondent
   ___ C. cleaning with ammonia
   ___ D. a far-reaching consperacy

7. ___ A. antiqe furniture
   ___ B. carnivorous animals
   ___ C. transmit a radio message
   ___ D. an impatient individual

8. ___ A. a dance troupe
   ___ B. possessing a suspicious nature
   ___ C. start her own busness
   ___ D. the subconscious mind

9. ___ A. believes in superstition
   ___ B. sign the patition
   ___ C. remnants of an ancient village
   ___ D. reflection of the sun on the pond

10. ___ A. a great oppertunity
    ___ B. a perennial flower
    ___ C. the original story
    ___ D. nucleus of an atom

11. ___ A. lifeguard at the pool
    ___ B. subscribe to a periodical
    ___ C. a primitive society
    ___ D. a sensable decision

12. ___ A. a gradual improvement in the weather
    ___ B. the evacuation before the storm
    ___ C. miniture scale model of the town
    ___ D. look through the binoculars

© 2002 by John Wiley & Sons, Inc.

Name ______________________ Date ______________

4-8

Finding the Correct Word I

Directions: Complete each sentence by circling the word that is spelled correctly.

1. Greg's mischievous nature _____ his teachers.

   ecasperates   exasperates   exaspirates   exasparates

2. Rochelle _____ over 50 friends to her pool party.

   envited   invitid   unvited   invited

3. According to the _____, the temperature was –3° this morning.

   thermometer   thermoneter   thermomiter   termometer

4. After watching the movie about an alien _____ of Earth, Teri suffered nightmares for a week.

   invashun   invasion   envasion   innvasion

5. Tom always found math to be _____ and difficult.

   abstrack   abstrak   abstract   abstractk

6. Carissa's ambition is to be a police _____ someday.

   detektive   detective   ditective   detectiv

7. Only certain kinds of wild mushrooms are _____.

   edable   edibel   eddible   edible

© 2002 by John Wiley & Sons, Inc.

Name ______________________________ Date ______________

4-8

Finding the Correct Word I *(continued)*

8. After working just two weeks, Brad realized his job _____ with his school work.

   interfered interferred intafered interfared

9. Because of the confusing directions, Shawna found the requirements for the science project to be _____.

   beweldering biwildering bewildering bewilderring

10. The thunderstorm, with its brilliant lightning, powerful winds, and deafening thunder, was one of the most _____ in memory.

    vilent violent violunt vilant

11. The guest speaker's _____ about mountain climbing came from his personal experiences.

    knowlege knoledge knowlidge knowledge

12. The members of the committee for preserving open space in the town reached a _____ over the sale of the forest land.

    compromise comprimise compromize compremise

© 2002 by John Wiley & Sons, Inc.

Name ______________________________ Date ________________

4-9

Finding the Correct Word II

Directions: Complete each sentence by circling the word that is spelled correctly.

1. The plane _____ through the clouds on its landing approach.

   desended decended descended discended

2. The strange little man claimed to be an _____ of Mars.

   inhabitent inhabitant inhabatant inhabiten

3. Evacuating the island's residents before the storm on such short notice was an _____ problem.

   enormous enormus enormas inormous

4. Because of its reputation for _____, Jason was surprised when his new car would not start.

   reliabilty realibity relyability reliability

5. The firefighters _____ the danger and rushed inside the building to search for people who may have been trapped.

   ignord egnored ignored iggnored

6. Even though Tony had just filled the car's tank with gas, the fuel _____ indicated that the tank was almost empty.

   gage gague gaige gauge

7. All of the students felt Mrs. Santiago was an excellent teacher, and they held her in high _____.

   esteem esteam esteme estheem

© 2002 by John Wiley & Sons, Inc.

Name ______________________________ Date ________________

4-9

Finding the Correct Word II *(continued)*

8. The puppy enjoyed _____ the ball.

   retreving retreeving retreveing retrieving

9. In _____ for the dance competition, Ali practiced three hours each day.

   prepairation preperation preparation prepiration

10. Because she had misplaced the sales _____, Charlene was unable to return the sweater for a cash refund.

    receipt receit receept reseipt

© 2002 by John Wiley & Sons, Inc.

11. Until the opening of the new mall, the local shops had enjoyed a _____ in the valley.

    monopoli monopoly munopoly monapoly

12. Trying to get ready for the season opener, the coach put the team through several _____ practice sessions.

    vigerous vigarous vigorous vigorus

Name ______________________________ Date ________________

4-10

Finding the Correct Word III

Directions: Complete each sentence by circling the word that is spelled correctly.

1. Jennifer was the only student in her homeroom to have perfect _____ last year.

   attendence atendance attendance attendanz

2. Conor was proud of himself for doing his own laundry, until he realized he had forgotten to add _____.

   detergent ditergent detergant datergant

3. The leaders of the colony believed they had _____ resources to last through the winter.

   sufficent sufficient suficient sufficeint

4. Gold is considered to be a _____ metal.

   presous preshus pracious precious

5. Before Tamara can begin her job as a lifeguard at the community pool, she needs to be _____.

   certafied certified sertified certifide

6. Because they are able to speak both English and French, many Canadians are _____.

   bylingual bilinguel bilingual bilingal

© 2002 by John Wiley & Sons, Inc.

Name ______________________________ Date ____________________

4-10

Finding the Correct Word III *(continued)*

7. The reception was to _____ follow the wedding service.

   immediately immediatley imediately immedetialy

8. Melanie felt honored that her classmates _____ her to represent them in the Student Council.

   nomanated nomimated nominated nomonated

9. Only a small percentage of _____ causes disease in humans.

   microboes mycrobes microwbes microbes

10. Taylor found chocolate ice cream _____.

    irasistible irresistible irresistable iresistible

11. Nikki is a _____ athlete; she excels at several sports.

    versatile versitile versitle versotile

12. The Better Lunch Committee designed a _____ to find out what kinds of lunches students preferred.

    questionaire questonnaire questionnaire questoneer

© 2002 by John Wiley & Sons, Inc.

Name ______________________________ Date ________________

4-11

Proofreading for Misspelled Words I

Directions: Read the article and circle the 10 misspelled words. Then write the words correctly on the lines after the article.

Some people who enjoy reading have dificulty finding books they like. If you are one of these indeviduals, the following information may be helpful.

Before silecting any book to read, think about your intrests. What do you like to do? What hobbies do you have? How do you like spending your time? What kinds of TV shows and movies do you watch? For example, if you are a person who likes action, you should consider adventure stories. If you like comedies, you might like humerous books. Or, if you like love stories, picking a romance is probably a good choice.

Once you find a book you like, you should consider similar books. If you come to enjoy the writing of a particuler author, try other books he or she has written. You will probably enjoy these books, too.

You can also find great books by reading book reviews in newspapers and magazeens. Many Sunday editions of newspapers have entire sections devoted to reviews.

Browzing in the library or bookstore is yet another way to find books to read. Don't hesatate to ask your librarian if he or she knows of any facinating titles.

It may take a little time to obtain books that you will come to love. But be assured that they are available, just waiting for you to find them.

© 2002 by John Wiley & Sons, Inc.

1. ____________________ 6. ____________________

2. ____________________ 7. ____________________

3. ____________________ 8. ____________________

4. ____________________ 9. ____________________

5. ____________________ 10. ____________________

Name ______________________________ Date ____________________

4-12

Proofreading for Misspelled Words II

Directions: Read the article and circle the 10 misspelled words. Then write the words correctly on the lines after the article.

On the morning of May 20, 1883, Krakatoa was a seemingly peaceful volcanic island in the Pacific Ocean, located between Java and Sumatra. The only known eruption, which had been a moderate one, had occured in 1680. On May 20, however, one of the island's volcanic cones became active. The activity subsidid by the end of the month, only to begin again on June 19 and continue on and off through much of the summer. This activity gave no hint as to what was to come.

At about 10 A.M. on August 27, the island blew up. The explosions, heard over 2,000 miles away in Australia, are thought to be the loudest noise ever heard. It is estamated that the force of the explosion was 100 megatons, about five times more powerful than the first atomic bombs. The dust, smoke, and ash that were propeled into the sky blocked the sun and blanketed the region in darkness for two days. Huge masses of floating pumice and debre were so thick that ships could not navegate through the nearby waters.

While a great amount of the island was literaly "blown to bits," much of the remaining land sank below the ocean, triggering a tsunami (tidal wave) that reached 120 feet in height. The wave crashed into nearby islands, washing away coastle towns and villages and killing 36,000 people.

The originel Krakatoa had an area of about 18 square miles. After the catastrophy, the island was reduced to about six square miles.

© 2002 by John Wiley & Sons, Inc.

1. ______________________
2. ______________________
3. ______________________
4. ______________________
5. ______________________
6. ______________________
7. ______________________
8. ______________________
9. ______________________
10. ______________________

EIGHTH-GRADE LEVEL

Spelling

PRACTICE TESTS

© 2002 by John Wiley & Sons, Inc.

Spelling Practice Test I

Part 1. Directions: Find the misspelled word in each set. Use the Answer Sheet to darken the letter of your answer.

	A.	B.	C.	D.
1.	A. loathe	B. prominant	C. disinfect	D. punctually
2.	A. essential	B. function	C. extensive	D. gruesom
3.	A. cemetery	B. chapter	C. critacize	D. adjourn
4.	A. courtessy	B. dominoes	C. capillary	D. fascinate
5.	A. accuse	B. torturous	C. urgent	D. limosine

Part 2. Directions: Find the misspelled word in each set of phrases. Use the Answer Sheet to darken the letter of your answer.

1. A. writing her memoirs
   B. an incredible concert
   C. the cresent moon in the sky
   D. a new housing development

2. A. vacinnation for measles
   B. magazine subscription
   C. identical twins
   D. a Chinese restaurant

3. A. a career in government
   B. a hopeful prophecy for world peace
   C. shopping for new furniture
   D. a plausable theory

4. A. a forest ecosystem
   B. a newspaper columist
   C. the space capsule
   D. the legitimate heir to the throne

© 2002 by John Wiley & Sons, Inc.

Spelling Practice Test I *(continued)*

5. A. an <u>invincible</u> castle

   B. <u>parallel</u> lines

   C. a <u>memorible</u> vacation

   D. a communications <u>satellite</u>

Part 3. Directions: Find the word that is spelled correctly and completes the sentence. Use the Answer Sheet to darken the letter of your answer.

1. Coach Harper always _____ his players to do their best on the field and in life.

   A. encurages B. encourages C. incourages D. incuriges

2. Meg knew she would have to _____ time with her friends if she was to play field hockey.

   A. sacrefice B. sacrofice C. sacrifice D. sakrifice

3. After working out on his own for several weeks, Brendon was _____ about his chances of making the track team.

   A. optimistic B. optomistic C. opimistic D. optmistic

4. Because of successful fundraising events, the eighth-grade class's Activity Fund contained a _____.

   A. surples B. serplus C. seerplus D. surplus

5. Tia is _____ of her class.

   A. treasurer B. tresurer C. trashurer D. treaserer

© 2002 by John Wiley & Sons, Inc.

Spelling Practice Test II

Part 1. Directions: Find the misspelled word in each set. Use the Answer Sheet to darken the letter of your answer.

	A.	B.	C.	D.
1.	A. molecule	B. aerial	C. depression	D. chronikle
2.	A. decimal	B. inflexible	C. solitery	D. tedious
3.	A. exagerate	B. faculty	C. immaculate	D. specific
4.	A. bigoted	B. subordinate	C. adapt	D. reluctent
5.	A. dynamic	B. reliabilty	C. wary	D. auxiliary

Part 2. Directions: Find the misspelled word in each set of phrases. Use the Answer Sheet to darken the letter of your answer.

1. A. an interesting magazine
   B. the original copy
   C. the mimimum amount to open a checking account
   D. a sales receipt

2. A. a bitter controversy
   B. excessive worry
   C. an example of abstrac art
   D. a violent storm

3. A. the antique shop
   B. use an abbreveation
   C. a primitive society
   D. reach a compromise

4. A. prosperity because of a strong economy
   B. an obligation to join the committee
   C. the majority of the students
   D. make an ajustment

© 2002 by John Wiley & Sons, Inc.

Spelling Practice Test II *(continued)*

5. A. an apreciation of music

   B. a dependable person

   C. a certified accountant

   D. a partition between the rooms

Part 3. Directions: Find the word that is spelled correctly and completes the sentence. Use the Answer Sheet to darken the letter of your answer.

1. Tom's grandfather had an exciting _____ as a diplomat.

   A. carrer B. carear C. career D. carreer

2. The students circulated a _____ in support of school-sponsored dances.

   A. petition B. patition C. petishun D. potition

3. The thief tried to remain _____ as he checked the layout of the bank.

   A. inconspicous B. inconspicuous C. inconspicus D. inconspicious

4. The little girl loved the _____ dollhouse her grandfather had made for her.

   A. miniture B. miniachure C. minature D. miniature

5. Being able to work at the animal hospital was a great _____ for Melissa, who wanted to be a veterinarian someday.

   A. opportunity B. opportoonity C. opertunity D. opportunitty

© 2002 by John Wiley & Sons, Inc.

Name ______________________________ Date ________________

Spelling

PRACTICE TEST I: ANSWER SHEET

Directions: Darken the letter above the circle that best answers the question.

Part 1

1. ○ A ○ B ○ C ○ D
2. ○ A ○ B ○ C ○ D
3. ○ A ○ B ○ C ○ D
4. ○ A ○ B ○ C ○ D
5. ○ A ○ B ○ C ○ D

Part 2

1. ○ A ○ B ○ C ○ D
2. ○ A ○ B ○ C ○ D
3. ○ A ○ B ○ C ○ D
4. ○ A ○ B ○ C ○ D
5. ○ A ○ B ○ C ○ D

Part 3

1. ○ A ○ B ○ C ○ D
2. ○ A ○ B ○ C ○ D
3. ○ A ○ B ○ C ○ D
4. ○ A ○ B ○ C ○ D
5. ○ A ○ B ○ C ○ D

© 2002 by John Wiley & Sons, Inc.

Name ______________________________ Date ________________

Spelling

PRACTICE TEST II: ANSWER SHEET

Directions: Darken the letter above the circle that best answers the question.

Part 1

1. ○ A ○ B ○ C ○ D
2. ○ A ○ B ○ C ○ D
3. ○ A ○ B ○ C ○ D
4. ○ A ○ B ○ C ○ D
5. ○ A ○ B ○ C ○ D

Part 2

1. ○ A ○ B ○ C ○ D
2. ○ A ○ B ○ C ○ D
3. ○ A ○ B ○ C ○ D
4. ○ A ○ B ○ C ○ D
5. ○ A ○ B ○ C ○ D

Part 3

1. ○ A ○ B ○ C ○ D
2. ○ A ○ B ○ C ○ D
3. ○ A ○ B ○ C ○ D
4. ○ A ○ B ○ C ○ D
5. ○ A ○ B ○ C ○ D

© 2002 by John Wiley & Sons, Inc.

Spelling

KEY TO PRACTICE TEST I

Part 1

	A	B	C	D
1.	○	●	○	○
2.	○	○	○	●
3.	○	○	●	○
4.	●	○	○	○
5.	○	○	○	●

Part 2

	A	B	C	D
1.	○	○	●	○
2.	●	○	○	○
3.	○	○	○	●
4.	○	●	○	○
5.	○	○	●	○

Part 3

	A	B	C	D
1.	○	●	○	○
2.	○	○	●	○
3.	●	○	○	○
4.	○	○	○	●
5.	●	○	○	○

© 2002 by John Wiley & Sons, Inc.

Spelling

KEY TO PRACTICE TEST II

Part 1

	A	B	C	D
1.	○	○	○	●
2.	○	○	●	○
3.	●	○	○	○
4.	○	○	○	●
5.	○	●	○	○

Part 2

	A	B	C	D
1.	○	○	●	○
2.	○	○	●	○
3.	○	●	○	○
4.	○	○	○	●
5.	●	○	○	○

Part 3

	A	B	C	D
1.	○	○	●	○
2.	●	○	○	○
3.	○	●	○	○
4.	○	○	○	●
5.	●	○	○	○

© 2002 by John Wiley & Sons, Inc.

Section 5

Language Mechanics and Word Usage

Because of their significance to written and spoken communication, language mechanics and word usage are major topics in every eighth-grade language arts curriculum. They also account for a significant portion of standardized tests.

One of the most practical ways to teach language mechanics and word usage is through the daily writing and speaking of your students. Consistent emphasis on the correct use of English raises the level of the importance of these topics in your classes.

All written work, for example, from formal writing assignments to short answers on homework questions, should demonstrate correct mechanics and usage. Complete sentences, along with the use of capital letters, punctuation, and effective word choice should be required. You should also confer with your students often about their writing and show them how to improve their use of English. Organizing a system of peer editors in which students proofread, comment on, and offer suggestions about a partner's writing is yet another way to foster the learning of mechanics and usage, as well as improve the overall quality of writing in your classes. If your students are not experienced with peer editing, you should model how they can read a friend's work and offer constructive comments. It is through the practical experience of their written work that most students learn the fundamentals of mechanics and usage.

Just as you encourage your students to write correctly, you should encourage them to speak correctly. Politely correct them when they make mistakes with constructions such as faulty agreement ("Britney and Naomi is in the same dance class"), incorrect use of pronouns ("Joe and me went to the basketball game yesterday"), and double negatives ("We don't have no homework tonight"). If you advocate correct usage consistently, your students will gain a better understanding of English. Many will carry over this understanding into testing.

To supplement your instruction of language mechanics and word usage, the following study sheets are provided:

- Study Sheet 5-A, "Rules for Using End Marks"
- Study Sheet 5-B, "Rules for Using Commas"

- Study Sheet 5-C, "Rules for Using Colons and Semicolons"
- Study Sheet 5-D, "Rules for Using Apostrophes"
- Study Sheet 5-E, "Rules for Using Quotation Marks and Underlining (Italics)"
- Study Sheet 5-F, "Rules for Using Parentheses, Dashes, and Hyphens"
- Study Sheet 5-G, "A Proofreader's Checklist"
- Study Sheet 5-H, "Rules for Capitalization"
- Study Sheet 5-I, "Sentences, Fragments, and Run-ons"
- Study Sheet 5-J, "Common and Proper Nouns"
- Study Sheet 5-K, "Singular and Plural Nouns"
- Study Sheet 5-L, "Possessive Nouns"
- Study Sheet 5-M, "Regular and Irregular Verbs"
- Study Sheet 5-N, "Helping Verbs and Verb Phrases"
- Study Sheet 5-O, "Verb Tenses"
- Study Sheet 5-P, "Subjective Case and Objective Case Pronouns"
- Study Sheet 5-Q, "Possessive Pronouns"
- Study Sheet 5-R, "Indefinite Pronouns"
- Study Sheet 5-S, "Who, Whom, Whose, and Who's"
- Study Sheet 5-T, "Negative Words and Double Negatives"
- Study Sheet 5-U, "Friendly Letter Model"
- Study Sheet 5-V, "Business Letter Model"

Probably the best time to distribute copies of Study Sheet 5-A, "Rules for Using End Marks," Study Sheet 5-B, "Rules for Using Commas," Study Sheet 5-C, "Rules for Using Colons and Semicolons," Study Sheet 5-D, "Rules for Using Apostrophes," Study Sheet 5-E, "Rules for Using Quotation Marks and Underlining (Italics)," and Study Sheet 5-F, "Rules for Using Parentheses, Dashes, and Hyphens," is at the beginning of the year. These study sheets cover the basics of punctuation. To avoid overloading your students, hand out each study sheet on a different day over a period of a week or two. Review the rules and examples on the sheets and answer any questions your students may have. For most of your students, the information on these sheets will probably be a review. Nonetheless, suggest that your students keep the study sheets in a folder or binder for future reference.

You might also prefer to hand out copies of Study Sheet 5-G, "A Proofreader's Checklist," at the beginning of the year. Explain that proofreading can be a difficult task, and that this sheet is a guide that can help people look for mistakes and oversights in their writing. Go over the information on the sheet with your students and answer any questions they may have. You may wish to devote some class time for students to use this study sheet as they proofread some of their writing. As they work, circulate around the class, offering guidance in the proofreading process and emphasizing the importance of reading carefully to find oversights and errors in written work. Suggest that your students keep the copy of the study sheet in a folder or binder to which they may refer as necessary throughout the year.

The remaining study sheets of this section can be used to introduce topics, supplement lessons, or reinforce material that has already been taught. You might, for example, hand out Study Sheet 5-H, "Rules for Capitalization," when you are explaining or reviewing which types of words must be capitalized. Study Sheet 5-L, "Possessive Nouns," can be used to summarize the rules for showing the possessive case, while Study Sheet 5-P, "Subjective Case and Objective Case Pronouns," can be used to introduce or review pronouns. Each study sheet stands alone and can be used in a manner that best suits the needs of your students.

This section also contains 26 worksheets and three practice tests. The worksheets and practice tests concentrate on language mechanics and word usage skills found in the typical eighth-grade curriculum with particular emphasis given to those skills that regularly appear on standardized tests. Like the study sheets, each worksheet and practice test stands alone, and you may assign all of them or only those that you feel will be of most benefit to your students.

Teaching Suggestions for the Worksheets

5-1: Using Capitalization and Punctuation Correctly I

Start this activity by emphasizing to your students that capital letters and punctuation are essential to written English. Without mastery of these important topics, a person will be unable to write the simplest paragraph correctly.

Depending upon the abilities of your students, you might find it helpful to review the basics of capitalization and punctuation through the following study sheets:

- 5-A, "Rules for Using End Marks"
- 5-B, "Rules for Using Commas"
- 5-C, "Rules for Using Colons and Semicolons"
- 5-D, "Rules for Using Apostrophes"
- 5-E, "Rules for Using Quotation Marks and Underlining (Italics)"
- 5-F, "Rules for Using Parentheses, Dashes, and Hyphens"
- 5-H, "Rules for Capitalization"

Go over the instructions of the worksheet and remind your students to correct all mistakes as they rewrite the sentences. Note that most sentences contain more than one error. Once your students have finished the worksheet, correct the sentences and discuss the sentences that your students had difficulty rewriting correctly.

5-2: Using Capitalization and Punctuation Correctly II

Begin this activity by explaining that understanding capitalization and punctuation is necessary if a person is to demonstrate mastery of written English. If you have previously assigned Worksheet 5-1, note that this worksheet is similar and provides additional practice for the topics. If necessary, review the basics of punctuation and capitalization on Study Sheets 5-A, 5-B, 5-C, 5-D, 5-E, 5-F, and 5-H.

Go over the instructions of the worksheet and note that your students are to rewrite the sentences, correcting errors in capitalization and punctuation. Remind them that some sentences have several mistakes. When your students have finished the worksheet, correct the sentences and answer any questions they may have.

5-3: Singular and Plural Nouns

Introduce this activity by discussing the definition of a noun, which is a word that names a person, place, thing, or idea. Note that singular nouns refer to one, and that plural nouns refer to more than one. Depending upon the abilities of your students, you may wish to distribute and review Study Sheet 5-K, "Singular and Plural Nouns." (If your students need help in recognizing nouns, hand out copies of Study Sheet 5-J, "Common and Proper Nouns.")

Go over the directions on the worksheet with your students. Note that they are to read the paragraph, and circle all singular nouns and underline all plural nouns. You may wish to mention that there are 12 singular and 11 plural nouns in the paragraph. (You may also wish to mention that although Babbage and Byron created detailed plans for their machines, the state of technology at the time prevented them from building any of them. In the early 1990s, however, British scientists built a working model of a machine called Difference Engine No. 2, based on the inventors' original plans.) Once your students have completed the worksheet, go over their work and make sure they are able to identify all of the nouns.

5-4: Finding Verbs and Verb Phrases

Introduce this exercise by explaining that verbs and verb phrases make up predicates in sentences. Predicates may be a single verb, or a verb phrase containing a main verb and one or more helping verbs.

You may find it helpful to hand out copies of Study Sheet 5-N, "Helping Verbs and Verb Phrases." Review the examples on the study sheet with your students.

For the worksheet, make sure your students understand that they are to underline the verb or verb phrase in each sentence and circle the main verb in each phrase. Mention that not all sentences contain verb phrases. Upon completion of the worksheet, correct the sentences and discuss any that proved to be difficult for your students.

5-5: Understanding Irregular Verbs I

Begin this activity by explaining that most verbs in English form their past tense by simply adding *d* or *ed*. These verbs are called *regular* verbs. Verbs that do not form their past tense in this manner are known as *irregular* verbs. Because they do not follow the standard pattern of conjugation, the various forms of irregular verbs can be confusing.

To help your students improve their understanding of irregular verbs, hand out copies of Study Sheet 5-M, "Regular and Irregular Verbs." Discuss the information on the sheet, focusing special attention on the past and past participle forms of the irregular verbs. Point out the varying forms and mention to your students that when they are doubtful of a particular form, they should consult a dictionary or an author's style book. Most English textbooks also contain lists of irregular verbs.

Go over the instructions on the worksheet and note that students are to use the correct form of the verb in parentheses to complete the sentences. Upon completion of the worksheet, correct the sentences and note any verbs that caused particular trouble. Suggest to your students that they try to memorize the forms of the verbs they had gotten wrong.

5-6: Understanding Irregular Verbs II

This worksheet is similar to Worksheet 5-5 and provides students with additional practice with the forms of irregular verbs. Begin the exercise by asking for a volunteer to explain the difference between regular and irregular verbs. Regular verbs form their past tense by adding *d* or *ed*; irregular verbs do not. The past tense and past participle forms of irregular verbs vary, resulting, unfortunately, in much confusion.

You may find it helpful to review Study Sheet 5-M, "Regular and Irregular Verbs," with your students. Since there are no rules that address the conjugation of irregular verbs, suggest that they try to learn the forms of as many of the irregular verbs as they can. Note that every time they use the forms correctly, they will be reinforcing the correct forms in their minds.

For this worksheet, your students are to fill in the blank with the correct form of the verbs in parentheses to complete each sentence. When your students are done with the worksheet, correct the sentences and discuss the verbs that were troublesome.

5-7: Understanding Verb Tenses

Start this exercise by explaining that the tense of a verb indicates whether the action of a sentence took place in the past, is happening now in the present, or will (or might) happen in the future. Maintaining consistency of tenses is necessary for clear expression.

To help your students with their understanding of tenses, hand out copies of Study Sheet 5-O, "Verb Tenses." Note that along with simple past, present, and future, there are perfect past, perfect present, and perfect future tenses. Such an assortment of tenses enables speakers and writers to be very specific about action that has, is, or will take place. Review the various tenses with your students and discuss the examples on the study sheet.

Note that the worksheet has two parts. For Part A, your students are to write the tense of the verb or verb phrase on the line after the sentence. For Part B, they are to write sentences of their own, demonstrating each tense. Upon completion of the worksheet, go over both parts. For Part B, ask volunteers to read their sentences to the class. Discuss any of the tenses that gave your students trouble.

5-8: Understanding Contractions

Begin this activity by explaining that a contraction is a word composed of two words from which one or more letters have been dropped. Ask volunteers to name some examples of contractions, which you may write on the board or an overhead projector. Explain that an apostrophe is used to indicate missing letters.

This worksheet consists of two parts. For Part A, your students are to write the contraction of the underlined words on the line after the sentence. For Part B, they are to write the words that make up the contraction on the line after the sentence. Upon completion of the worksheet, go over the contractions.

5-9: Finding the Subjects of Sentences

Introduce this activity by explaining that the subject of a sentence is the *doer* of the action. Note that every sentence has a subject.

Write this example on the board or an overhead projector: *Sharon finished her homework.* The doer of the action (which is finishing homework) is Sharon.

While the subject is fairly obvious in most sentences, the subject may not appear in imperative or exclamatory sentences, but rather is understood.

Offer your students this example: *Don't fall!* The subject here is understood to be "you," which is to whom the sentence refers.

Caution your students not to be tricked by thinking a noun in an opening phrase or clause is the subject of a sentence. Suggest that they look for the action of the sentence and identify who or what performs the action.

Offer this example: *Late last night Billy found his brother sleepwalking.* "Night" is the first noun, but "Billy" found his brother sleepwalking. Billy, therefore, is the subject.

Upon completion of the worksheet, correct the sentences and discuss any subjects that your students had trouble identifying.

5-10: Finding Simple Predicates

Introduce this exercise by explaining that just as every sentence must have a subject, it must also have a predicate. Simple predicates are made up of verbs, words that express action or indicate that something exists.

Write this example on the board or an overhead projector: *The car skidded on the wet road.* The action, obviously, is "skidded." Suggest that an effective way to identify action verbs is to try to visualize what is happening in a sentence.

Now offer your students this example: *She is here.* The verb "is" indicates a state of existence. You might remind students that "is" is a form of the verb *to be,* along with *am, are, was, were, be,* and *being.* All verb phrases ending in *be* or *been* are also forms of the verb *to be.*

For this worksheet, your students are to underline the simple predicates of each sentence. Point out that some predicates may contain verb phrases. Once your students have finished the worksheet, correct the sentences and discuss any that your students found confusing.

5-11: Finding Compound Subjects and Compound Predicates

Start this activity by reviewing simple subjects and predicates. The subject of a sentence is the doer of the action, and the predicate is the action or a state of being. Explain that compound subjects are two or more subjects that have the same predicate. Likewise, compound predicates are two or more verbs that have the same subject. A sentence may have both a compound subject and a compound predicate.

Write the following examples on the board or an overhead projector, noting the compound subjects and compound predicates:

- *Sara and Michelle play instruments in the school band.* (Sara and Michelle are the compound subject.)
- *Mr. Harris designs and builds wooden furniture.* (Designs and builds are the compound predicate.)
- *Peter and his brother swim and fish in the lake.* (Peter and his brother are the compound subject; swim and fish are the compound predicate.)

The worksheet has two parts. For Part A, note that students are to underline each compound subject and circle each compound predicate. Caution them that not all sentences will have both a compound subject and compound predicate. For Part B, your students are to write sentences of their own, demonstrating compound subjects and compound predicates. Upon completion, correct the sentences for Part A and discuss any sentences that your students found confusing. Ask volunteers to share their sentences for Part B and have other students identify the compound subjects and predicates.

5-12: Subject and Predicate Agreement I

Begin this exercise by explaining the importance of agreement between subjects and predicates. If the subject of a sentence is singular, the verb must be in its singular form. If the subject of a sentence is plural, its verb must be plural. While most students will have little trouble with agreement when the predicate directly follows the subject, intervening words can cause confusion.

Write this example on the board or an overhead projector: *The cookies in the box are on the table.* At first glance, it might seem that "box" is the subject of the sentence and therefore would require "is" for its predicate. However, "in the box" is an intervening phrase, and the subject is "cookies" which agrees with "are."

Caution your students to read the sentences of the worksheet carefully to choose the form of the verb that agrees with the subject. Upon completion of the worksheet, correct the sentences and answer any questions your students might have.

5-13: Subject and Predicate Agreement II

This worksheet is similar to Worksheet 5-12 and provides students with more practice with agreement. Begin the activity by discussing the importance of agreement between subjects and predicates. A singular subject requires the singular form of a verb, while a plural subject requires a plural form.

For this worksheet, your students are to select the correct word from the parentheses and complete each sentence. Remind them to pay close attention to phrases that are positioned between subjects and predicates, because the nouns in such phrases can often be mistaken for subjects. Once your students have finished the worksheet, correct the sentences and discuss any sentences that caused confusion.

5-14: Understanding Subject and Object Pronouns

Begin this activity by explaining that a pronoun is a word that takes the place of a noun. There are different types of pronouns, of which personal pronouns are among the most common. Personal pronouns may be used as subjects or objects in sentences. Subjective case pronouns may only be used as subjects of sentences or as predicate pronouns following a linking verb. Objective case pronouns may only be used as direct or indirect objects, or as the object of a preposition in a prepositional phrase. Adding to the confusion is the fact that everyday, informal speech doesn't always take into account the strict rules of grammar.

To help your students better understand pronouns, distribute copies of Study Sheet 5-P, "Subjective Case and Objective Case Pronouns." Review the pronouns and the examples.

Explain that for this worksheet your students must select the correct pronoun to complete each sentence. Encourage them to read each sentence carefully and determine whether the missing pronoun is used in the subjective or objective case. This will determine what answer they will choose. Upon completion of the worksheet, correct the sentences and answer any questions your students may have.

5-15: Understanding Pronouns and Antecedents

Begin this activity by explaining that the antecedent of a pronoun is the word to which the pronoun refers. Pronouns must always agree in number and gender with their antecedents. Explain that while this may seem obvious, ensuring the agreement of pronouns and their antecedents can become tricky, especially in long sentences or in the case of indefinite pronouns.

Note that this worksheet contains two parts. For Part A, your students must complete the sentences by writing the correct pronoun. For Part B, they are to rewrite the sentences, correcting instances where pronouns and antecedents do not agree. Once your students have finished, correct their work and discuss pronouns and antecedents that proved to be confusing.

5-16: Understanding Indefinite Pronouns and Agreement with Verbs

Start this activity by explaining that indefinite pronouns are pronouns that refer to nouns in general. Some are singular, some are plural, and some may be singular or plural, depending upon their use in a sentence. When used as a subject, an indefinite pronoun must agree with its verb.

To help your students better understand indefinite pronouns, hand out copies of Study Sheet 5-R, "Indefinite Pronouns." Review the information on the sheet with your students.

For this worksheet, students are to complete sentences by writing the form of a verb that agrees with the indefinite pronoun. Warn your students to pay close attention to intervening words and phrases that can lead to mistakes. After your students have finished the worksheet, correct the sentences and discuss any that your students found difficult.

5-17: Using Who, Whom, Whose, and Who's Correctly

Introduce this activity by explaining that many people find the pronouns *who, whom, whose,* and *who's* confusing. Learning a few rules is the key to using them correctly.

Explain that *who* and *whom* are used as interrogative pronouns, which ask a question, or as relative pronouns, which introduce a subordinate clause. *Who* is the nominative form and *whom* is the objective form.

To help your students with their understanding of these pronouns, hand out copies of Study Sheet 5-S, "Who, Whom, Whose, and Who's." Review the information and discuss the examples, emphasizing how students can determine which pronoun to use. (You may wish to note that for simplicity, the suggestions on the study sheet say to substitute *he* and *him* for *who* and *whom,* but that any similar case pronoun will do. Instead of *he,* one might substitute *she, they,* or *we.* Instead of *him,* one might substitute *her, them,* or *us.*)

Instruct your students to read the sentences on the worksheet carefully, for it is easy to make mistakes with these pronouns. Upon completion of the worksheet, correct the sentences and discuss those that your students found confusing.

5-18: Using Comparisons of Modifiers Correctly

Start this exercise by explaining that adjectives and adverbs are modifiers, or words that describe other words. Adjectives modify nouns or pronouns; adverbs modify verbs, adjectives, or other adverbs.

All modifiers have three forms: positive, comparative, and superlative. Offer your students this example: *long* (positive), *longer* (comparative), and *longest* (superlative). The comparative form of an adjective or adverb is used to compare two items, and the superlative form is used to compare three or more.

Note that modifiers with three or more syllables generally use the words *more* and *most* (or *less* and *least*) for the comparative and superlative forms. Offer the example of *colorful, more* (or *less*) *colorful,* and *most* (or *least*) *colorful.*

For this worksheet, students are to choose the correct form of the modifier to complete each sentence. When they are done with the worksheet, correct their sentences and answer any questions they may have.

5-19: Correcting Fragments and Run-ons

Begin this activity by explaining that a sentence expresses a complete thought. It must have a subject and predicate. A fragment is a phrase or group of words that lacks a subject or predicate, or both. A run-on is a sentence in which two or more complete sentences are strung together without connecting words or the correct punctuation.

To help your students understand fragments and run-ons, distribute copies of Study Sheet 5-I, "Sentences, Fragments, and Run-ons," and review the information and examples. Explain that fragments can be corrected by completing the sentence, while run-ons can be corrected by separating the sentences with a period or a comma and a conjunction such as *and, but, or, for,* or *nor.*

Note that the worksheet has two parts. For Part A, students are to correct the fragments, and for Part B they are to correct run-ons. When they are done, go over their work and answer any questions they may have.

5-20: Correcting Double Negatives

Start this exercise by explaining that a double negative is a construction in which two negative words are used. Double negatives are glaring examples of incorrect usage, because the two negative words cancel each other out, resulting in the opposite of what the speaker or writer wants to say.

Distributing copies of Study Sheet 5-T, "Negative Words and Double Negatives," will help your students to recognize double negatives. Review the examples and emphasize that double negatives can be easily corrected by eliminating one of the negative words. Upon completion of the worksheet, correct the sentences and discuss any that might have caused your students trouble.

5-21: Using Quotation Marks and Underlining (Italics) Correctly

Introduce this activity by explaining that quotation marks and underlining (italics) are forms of punctuation that indicate dialogue, titles, and emphasis. You may find it helpful for your students to review copies of Study Sheet 5-E, "Rules for Using Quotation Marks and Underlining (Italics)." Discuss the information and examples on the study sheet. Mention that underlining indicates italics and is most often used when printing or writing in script.

For the worksheet, students are to rewrite sentences, correcting quotation marks and underlining or italics that are misused. Note that some sentences may have more than one mistake. Once your students are done, correct the worksheets and discuss any sentences that caused difficulty.

5-22: Understanding Friendly Letters

Begin this exercise by explaining that a friendly letter is a letter a person sends to a friend, relative, or close acquaintance. Friendly letters have a standard form.

To help your students understand the format of friendly letters, distribute copies of Study Sheet 5-U, "Friendly Letter Model." Review the example of the friendly letter with your students, pointing out the return address with commas between city and state and day and year, the greeting (which is followed by a comma), and the closing (in which only the first word is capitalized and which is followed by a comma).

Your students are to rewrite and correct the letter on a separate sheet of paper. You might wish to mention that the letter contains 10 mistakes. Upon completion, correct the rewritten letters and answer any questions your students have.

5-23: Understanding Business Letters

Begin this activity by explaining that a business letter is a letter that an individual writes to a company or organization. It is more formal than a friendly letter and has a slightly different format.

Hand out copies of Study Sheet 5-V, "Business Letter Model," to show your students an example of a semi-block form business letter. Note that business letters may also be written in block form, in which all lines start at the left margin, including the heading and closing. Emphasize that the beginnings of paragraphs are not indented in block form.

As you review the model, note the correct form for the heading, business address, greeting (which is followed by a colon), and the closing (the first word of which is capitalized and which is followed by a comma). Also point out that a business letter requires a signature and a printed name.

For this worksheet, your students are to rewrite and correct the business letter. You might mention that the letter contains 10 mistakes. Upon completion, correct the letters and answer any questions your students may have.

5-24: Proofreading I

Start this activity by explaining that your students are to proofread the paragraph and identify the mistakes in punctuation and capitalization. You may wish to distribute copies of Study Sheet 5-G, "A Proofreader's Checklist," to help them with their efforts. You might mention that the paragraph contains 10 mistakes. After your students have completed rewriting the paragraph, correct their work and point out the mistakes and how they should have been revised.

5-25: Proofreading II

This worksheet is similar to Worksheet 5-24, except that along with mistakes in punctuation and capitalization, mistakes are also made in usage. Instruct your students to read the paragraph and identify all the mistakes. Your students may find it helpful to refer to Study Sheet 5-G, "A Proofreader's Checklist," as they work. You may mention that the paragraph contains 10 mistakes. When your students have finished rewriting the paragraph, correct their work and point out the mistakes that they should have found.

5-26: Proofreading III

This worksheet is similar to Worksheets 5-24 and 5-25. Instruct your students to read the paragraph and identify mistakes in punctuation, capitalization, and usage. They may find it helpful to refer to Study Sheet 5-G, "A Proofreader's Checklist." You might mention that the paragraph contains 10 mistakes. Your students are to rewrite the paragraph, correcting the mistakes. When they are done, correct the paragraphs and note the mistakes that they should have corrected.

Language Mechanics & Usage Practice Tests

You may assign any or all of the three practice tests. Test I focuses on punctuation and capitalization. Test II centers around the identification of subjects and predicates, and the correct use of pronouns. Test III concentrates on agreement, usage, and the correct form and punctuation of a business letter. Your students should use the Answer Sheets with these tests, which will give them practice in using standardized answer sheets.

Answer Key for Section 5

5-1. **1.** Sara's family goes out for Chinese food every Friday night. **2.** Centerville's Historical Society meets every Tuesday evening in the library at 7:30. **3.** Although she loved her little brother, Maria found his high energy level to be exasperating. **4.** Last summer our family visited Yellowstone National Park during our vacation. **5.** Exam week tired everyone out, especially Callie. **6.** One of my favorite books is *The Sword in the Stone* by T. H. White. **7.** Tina, Valerie's cousin, lives in Scranton, Pennsylvania. **8.** "Let's plan on going to a movie on Saturday," said Brian. **9.** Sheila thought about all she had to do on Saturday: go to soccer practice, go shopping with her mom, watch her younger sister, do homework, and go to Erin's party. **10.** "What is the weather report for tomorrow?" asked Randy. **11.** Of course, Jess never saw a puppy she didn't love. **12.** "Watch out!" Cheryl cried, and she pulled Beth out of the way of the speeding car.

5-2. **1.** Lisa is a gifted athlete and excels at field hockey and softball. **2.** Jan asked, "What's for dinner tonight?" **3.** "If we want to see the start of the game," Jerry said, "we'd better leave now." **4.** Tom's grandfather served under General Patton during World War II. **5.** According to a popular theory, a giant asteroid impact caused the extinction of the dinosaurs. **6.** Manuel accepted the compromise; Conor would not. **7.** My father reads *The Wall Street Journal* every morning. **8.** Amy's favorite poem is "Mushrooms" by Sylvia Plath. **9.** Indira plans to try out for her school's field hockey team. **10.** "If we start now," said Angela, "we should be finished with the project by six." **11.** "What time does the concert start?" asked Wil. **12.** The coach told the team that they should play hard, try their best, and remember that the game isn't over until the final whistle.

5-3. *Singular Nouns:* invention, century, computer, Charles Babbage, Augusta Ada Byron, number, engine, store, information, mill, printer, record *Plural Nouns:* people, computers, historians, roots, years, mathematicians, machines, problems, conceptions, operations, results

5-4. **1.** sponsored **2.** slipped **3.** had been raining (raining is main verb) **4.** had studied (studied) **5.** had been fascinated (fascinated) **6.** scolded **7.** soared **8.** was scheduled (scheduled) **9.** caused **10.** is **11.** was tired (tired) **12.** will be sailing (sailing)

5-5. **1.** broken **2.** fell **3.** crept **4.** known **5.** born **6.** fled **7.** flown **8.** eaten **9.** set **10.** stung **11.** written **12.** shrunk

5-6. **1.** slew **2.** swum **3.** taught **4.** shone (or shined) **5.** threw **6.** blew **7.** flung **8.** came **9.** caught **10.** seen **11.** sung **12.** sprang

5-7. **Part A.** **1.** past **2.** present **3.** present perfect **4.** future **5.** past perfect **6.** past **7.** future perfect **8.** present **9.** present perfect **10.** future perfect **Part B.** Accept reasonable sentences.

5-8. **Part A.** **1.** He's **2.** couldn't **3.** it'll **4.** What's **5.** They'd **6.** mustn't **Part B.** **1.** team is **2.** would have **3.** should not **4.** did not **5.** They have **6.** will not

5-9. **1.** Martin **2.** shower **3.** moon **4.** dog **5.** Sara **6.** weather **7.** you (understood) **8.** author **9.** clouds **10.** game **11.** one **12.** rocket

5-10. **1.** howled **2.** towered **3.** extended **4.** will be going **5.** spends **6.** is **7.** were supposed **8.** had enjoyed **9.** felt **10.** blared **11.** cascaded **12.** was rescheduled

5-11. **Part A.** **1.** *predicates:* hurried, started **2.** *subjects:* Lauren, Danny; *predicates:* set, prepared **3.** *subjects:* Jill, Mavis **4.** *predicates:* issued, cautioned **5.** *subjects:* Jennifer, Lara; *predicates:* danced, sang **6.** *predicates:* stung, caused **7.** *subjects:* fog, drizzle; *predicates:* obscured, made **8.** *subjects:* Billy, Teri, Carla **9.** *predicates:* sprained, twisted **10.** *subjects:* Patricia, Jeanette **Part B.** Accept reasonable sentences.

5-12. **1.** erodes **2.** interact **3.** play **4.** encourages **5.** leads **6.** suppresses **7.** creak **8.** quote **9.** prescribe **10.** returns **11.** enjoy **12.** wants

5-13. **1.** beckons **2.** invites **3.** publish **4.** revises **5.** consider **6.** believes **7.** prefer **8.** provokes **9.** participate **10.** organizes **11.** prevents **12.** impresses

5-14. **1.** her **2.** he **3.** They **4.** us **5.** them **6.** me **7.** him **8.** I **9.** he **10.** she **11.** we **12.** He

5-15. **Part A.** **1.** her **2.** their **3.** his or her **4.** she **5.** he, her **6.** their, they, their **Part B.** **1.** When Darlene left for college, her younger brother got her room. **2.** Scott did the best he could on the test. **3.** The members of the dance team did their best at the dance contest. **4.** Gwen's sister Karen is taller than she. **5.** The student who lost his (or her) keys should report to the office. **6.** Phil and Zak think their science project is the most original in class.

5-16. **1.** is **2.** has **3.** are **4.** fails **5.** tells **6.** was **7.** has **8.** know **9.** believe **10.** leaves **11.** is **12.** raise

5-17. **1.** Whom **2.** Who **3.** Who's **4.** Whose **5.** Who **6.** Whose **7.** Whom **8.** who **9.** whom **10.** who **11.** whose **12.** Who's

5-18. **1.** harshest **2.** good **3.** earlier **4.** greatest **5.** most spectacular **6.** more entertaining **7.** well **8.** more strenuous **9.** worst **10.** more sensible **11.** healthier **12.** friendliest

5-19. **Part A.** Accept reasonable sentences. **Part B.** Answers may vary; following are some possible answers. **1.** Blue whales are the largest animals on Earth. They can grow to be over 100 feet long and weigh up to 150 tons. **2.** Jennifer had never seen such a big mall, and she decided she could spend days shopping there. **3.** Rick's favorite sport is baseball, but his father's favorite sport is football. **4.** Dan has never flown before, and he looked forward to takeoff. **5.** Maria enjoys ice-skating, but she doesn't like roller-skating. **6.** Kara could watch a movie, or she could listen to music.

5-20. Answers may vary; following are some possible answers. **1.** Because of the snowstorm, there wasn't any school today. **2.** None of the kids had any ideas for which music to play at the party. **3.** They did not have enough snow to build a snowman. **4.** There will be no homework over the long weekend. **5.** With the computers down, no one in the school could send e-mail. **6.** Suresh couldn't find his keys anywhere. **7.** Despite having searched all day, the investigators hadn't found any clues. **8.** None of the sources they checked provided information. **9.** In some areas of the river, fish can't live because of the pollution. **10.** Progress wasn't made until the group decided on an interesting topic. **11.** After practicing her gymnastics routine for three hours, Liz couldn't practice anymore. **12.** Tom believes there's no career more important than being a doctor.

5-21. **1.** "I received five phone calls from her today," said Jimmy. **2.** His favorite book is <u>Something Wicked This Way Comes</u> by Ray Bradbury. **3.** "We got lost," said Monica, "and by the time we finally found her house, the party was half over." **4.** "Did you get caught in the storm?" asked Mr. Taylor. **5.** Kate loved the poem "The Road Not Taken" by Robert Frost. **6.** Meg's father reads the <u>New York Times</u> every morning at breakfast. **7.** Pat titled her article "How to Take Care of Your Puppy." **8.** "What do you want to do Friday night?" Tyler asked. **9.** Many readers find <u>The Diary of Anne Frank</u> to be one of the most memorable books they have ever read. **10.** The coach said, "Do your best." **11.** "It's already dinner time," said Tania into the phone to her friend, "and I still haven't started my homework." **12.** One of my mother's favorite magazines is <u>Good Housekeeping.</u>

5-22.

203 Sunset St.
Riverville, PA 12435
January 15, 2003

Dear Mark,

How are you doing? Everything is great here. I'm looking forward to your visit next month over the winter break.

My dad has offered to take us to Philadelphia to a basketball game. I can't wait.

Write back soon.

Your friend,
Billy

5-23.

654 Main St.
Center City, FL 98762
Nov. 15, 2003

Bright Color Art, Inc.
139 Coast Blvd.
Ocean Town, GA 89763

Dear Sir:

I would like to order your Pro Oil Paint Set, catalog number 86029. The cost of the set is $39.95, which includes shipping and handling. I have enclosed payment.

Thank you.

Sincerely,
Janet Williams
Janet Williams

5-24.

The cause of the extinction of the dinosaurs some 65 million years ago has been debated for decades. Although the disappearance of the dinosaurs is often thought of as having occurred in a great, momentary catastrophe, in fact, many of the dinosaur families became extinct one by one over the course of many years. Various theories have been offered to explain the extinction, including major climate change, the explosion of a nearby star that bathed the Earth in excessive lethal radiation, or a giant asteroid impact, which would have resulted in mass destruction, dark clouds blocking the sun's light and heat, and a worldwide collapse of the food chain. Whatever caused the disappearance of the dinosaurs also made it possible for mammals to become Earth's dominant species.

5-25.

The blue whale is the largest animal that has ever lived. An adult blue whale may attain a length of 100 feet and weigh 150 tons (300,000 pounds). Despite its size, the blue whale isn't an active predator that seeks and attacks prey. Instead of teeth, blue whales have baleen plates connected to their upper jaws. The plates have bristles on their inner edges, which are used to capture plankton, the main diet of the whales. When feeding, the blue whale swims with its mouth open, gulping seawater and plankton. Then the whale shuts its mouth and forces the water out through the bristles, trapping the plankton. Found in all oceans, blue whales were once hunted extensively. Now they are an endangered species, protected by law.

5-26.

The Internet is more than just a medium for e-mail, shopping, and electronic entertainment. It contains information on virtually every topic. A search for a common topic such as Abraham Lincoln may come up with over 250,000 hits, or websites with information about Lincoln. A search for a less familiar topic, for example, the Komodo dragon, a lizard that lives on some small Indonesian islands in the Pacific Ocean, can yield over 100,000 hits. While this great abundance of material proves to be helpful to millions of people every day, it can also be a source of confusion. Depending on the sponsors of the website, this information may or may not be reliable. It is necessary for the researcher to make sure that the information is accurate. This can be done by visiting websites sponsored by respected individuals and organizations and by checking information against other sources. The value of the Internet far outweighs any potential problems it might cause.

Study Sheet 5-A

Rules for Using End Marks

Periods, question marks, and exclamation points are called end marks because they come at the end of sentences.

Periods

1. Use a period to end a statement (declarative sentence). *Example:*

   It is cold outside.

2. Use a period after a command (imperative sentence). *Example:*

   Close the door.

3. Use a period at the end of an abbreviation. *Examples:*

   Dr. Mrs. Sun. Jan.

4. Use a period with initials. *Examples:*

   Ursula K. Le Guin S. E. Hinton O. Henry

Question Marks

Use a question mark after a question (interrogative sentence). *Example:*

What time is it?

Exclamation Points

Use an exclamation point after a sentence with strong emotion (exclamatory sentence). *Example:*

Look out!

© 2002 by John Wiley & Sons, Inc.

Study Sheet 5-B

Rules for Using Commas

Commas have many uses in sentences, addresses, letters, and numbers.

1. Use a comma between the words, phrases, and clauses in a series. *Examples:*

   apples, peaches, and pears

   Mandy came home from school, did her homework, and called Kim.

2. Use a comma between the names of cities and states. *Examples:*

   Philadelphia, Pennsylvania Houston, Texas

3. Use a comma between the day and year in dates. *Example:*

   January 1, 2003

4. Use a comma to set off nouns in direct address. *Example:*

   Ramiro, it is time for lunch.

5. Use a comma to set off direct quotations in a sentence. *Example:*

   "We have math homework tonight," Alyssa said.

6. Use a comma in front of *and, but, or,* or *nor* in a compound sentence. *Examples:*

   - They hiked to the top of the hill, *and* they made camp near the oak tree.
   - Sonia loves pretzels, *but* Billy likes potato chips.
   - Patrick will do a report on pollution, *or* he will do one on weather.
   - Trish did not understand the assignment, *nor* did the other students in her group.

© 2002 by John Wiley & Sons, Inc.

Study Sheet 5-B

Rules for Using Commas *(continued)*

7. Use a comma to set off an appositive. *Example:*

   Justin, a computer whiz, enjoys creating new computer games.

8. Use a comma to separate adjectives of equal importance. *Example:*

   The tall, distinguished man was a stranger in town.

9. Use a comma after an introductory word, phrase, or clause in a sentence. *Examples:*

   - Yes, it is raining outside.
   - Terrified by the thunder and lightning, the puppy crawled under the couch.
   - If the snowstorm begins during the night, school will probably be canceled.

10. Use commas to set off parenthetical and nonessential expressions. *Example:*

    Of course, we'll be glad to help with the charity drive.

11. Use a comma after the greeting of a friendly letter and after the closing of all letters. *Examples:*

    Dear Aunt Janet,   Yours truly,

12. Use commas in numbers of more than three digits. *Examples:*

    1,436   23,985   108,735   7,309,576

© 2002 by John Wiley & Sons, Inc.

Study Sheet 5-C

Rules for Using Colons and Semicolons

Colons and semicolons have a variety of uses in written material.

Colons

1. Use a colon to set off words in a list following an independent clause. *Example:*

   Natalie packed the following for the picnic: a salad, sandwiches, cake, and a jug filled with iced tea.

2. Use a colon between hours and minutes. *Examples:*

   10:15 A.M. 2:45 P.M.

3. Use a colon after the greeting of a business letter. *Examples:*

   Dear Mr. Smith: Dear Miss Jones:

4. Use a colon to set off an important idea. *Example:*

   Directions: Read the story and answer the questions.

© 2002 by John Wiley & Sons, Inc.

Semicolons

1. Use a semicolon between independent clauses not joined by *and, but, or,* or *nor. Example:*

   Tom was in agreement; Brad was not.

2. Use a semicolon between main clauses if there are commas in one or both of the clauses. *Example:*

   Knowledge of computers, more so now in the 21st century than ever before, is necessary for a successful career; and fortunately many American students use computers every day in school and at home.

Study Sheet 5-D

Rules for Using Apostrophes

Apostrophes are used with contractions and to show possessive nouns.

1. Use an apostrophe in contractions to show what letters are missing. *Examples:*

   can not—can't will not—won't would not—wouldn't

2. Use an apostrophe to show possessive nouns.

   Examples for singular nouns:

   Sara's kitten the puppy's toy James's book

   Examples for plural nouns:

   the puppies' toys

   the men's shoe department

   the twin sisters' room

   the mice's nest

© 2002 by John Wiley & Sons, Inc.

Study Sheet 5-E

Rules for Using Quotation Marks and Underlining (Italics)

Quotation marks and underlining (italics) serve many purposes in written language.

Quotation Marks

1. Use quotation marks to set off the direct words of a speaker. *Examples:*

   "It is a great day," he said.

   "If it rains," said Ali, "the game will be postponed."

   Dara asked, "What is the math homework for tonight?"

2. Use quotation marks around the titles of short stories, articles, songs, poems, or the titles of chapters in books. *Examples:*

   "The Open Window" (story)

   "The Star-Spangled Banner" (song)

   "How to Train a Puppy" (article)

   "The Road Not Taken" (poem)

© 2002 by John Wiley & Sons, Inc.

Underlining (Italics)

1. Underline (or italicize) the titles of books, movies, and works of art. *Examples:*

   Night (book)

   Star Wars: Episode I—The Phantom Menace (movie)

   The Mona Lisa (painting)

2. Underline (or italicize) the names of newspapers, magazines, ships, trains, planes, and spacecraft. *Examples:*

   The New York Times (newspaper)

   Atlantic Monthly (magazine)

   U.S.S. Enterprise (ship)

3. Underline (or italicize) words for special emphasis. *Example:*

   There is a difference between advice and advise.

Note: Underlining is used mostly for handwriting and typed material. Most word processors provide the use of italics.

Study Sheet 5-F

Rules for Using Parentheses, Dashes, and Hyphens

The following have special uses in written material.

Parentheses

Use parentheses to enclose information that is added to a sentence, but which is not of critical importance. *Example:*

During exams (now through next Tuesday) Sari will concentrate on studying.

Note: In some cases, commas or dashes can be used in place of parentheses.

Hyphens

1. Use a hyphen to connect two or more words to form compound words. *Examples:*

   up-to-date   double-header   merry-go-round

2. Use a hyphen to break words into syllables. *Examples:*

   fol-low   base-ball   let-ter

3. Use a hyphen when writing certain numbers. *Examples:*

   twenty-three   eighty-nine   one hundred forty-five

Dashes

Use a dash to signal a break in thought. *Example:*

If I do well on the test tomorrow—and I'm sure I will because I studied more than half the night—I'll get an "A" in history this quarter.

© 2002 by John Wiley & Sons, Inc.

Study Sheet 5-G

A Proofreader's Checklist

Check the following when you proofread your written work.

- ☐ Sentences begin with capital letters and end with the correct end mark.
- ☐ Sentences are complete thoughts. Fragments and run-ons have been revised.
- ☐ The beginning of each paragraph is indented.
- ☐ Commas are used in compound sentences; between the words of a list; after introductory words, phrases, and clauses; and with appositives.
- ☐ Apostrophes are used correctly for contractions and possessive nouns.
- ☐ Verb tenses are correct.
- ☐ Subjects and predicates agree.
- ☐ Pronouns are used correctly.
- ☐ Quotation marks are used for dialogue, and for the titles of short stories, poems, and songs.
- ☐ Underlining (italics) is used for the titles of books, movies, and works of art, and also for the names of newspapers, magazines, ships, trains, and planes.
- ☐ Any parentheses, dashes, and hyphens are used correctly.
- ☐ Spelling is correct.

© 2002 by John Wiley & Sons, Inc.

Study Sheet 5-H

Rules for Capitalization

Use the following rules to capitalize correctly.

1. Capitalize proper nouns and proper adjectives. *Examples:*

   George Washington   the Lincoln Tunnel   Chinese food

2. Capitalize initials. *Examples:*

   John F. Kennedy   H. H. Munroe   J. K. Rowling

3. Capitalize titles when they are attached to a name. *Examples:*

   Doctor Brown   General Adams   Captain Sanchez
   Uncle Bob   Aunt Joan   Pastor Hardy

4. Capitalize the pronoun "I."

5. Capitalize the days of the week. *Examples:*

   Sunday   Tuesday   Thursday   Saturday

6. Capitalize the months of the year. *Examples:*

   January   March   July   October   December

7. Capitalize the names of public and religious holidays. *Examples:*

   Fourth of July   Easter   Yom Kippur   Ramadan

8. Capitalize the names of cities, states, countries, and continents. *Examples:*

   Chicago   California   United States of America   Asia

9. Capitalize the names of rivers, oceans, mountains, and other geographical sites. *Examples:*

   Mississippi River   Atlantic Ocean   Rocky Mountains

© 2002 by John Wiley & Sons, Inc.

Study Sheet 5-H

Rules for Capitalization *(continued)*

10. Capitalize the names of streets and avenues. *Examples:*

    Thomas Street   Sunset Avenue   Deer Run Road

11. Capitalize the names of companies, organizations, and clubs. *Examples:*

    The Hillside Hikers Club

    General Motors

    The Federal Bureau of Investigation (FBI)

12. Capitalize the first word in a sentence. *Example:*

    School is canceled today because of the snowstorm.

13. Capitalize the first word in a quotation. *Example:*

    Tommy said, "Let's go to the movies Friday night."

14. Capitalize all of the words of the greeting of a letter. Only capitalize the first word of a closing of a letter. *Examples:*

    Dear Miss Williams,   Yours truly,

15. Capitalize the first word and all important words in the titles of books, poems, songs, movies, plays, and works of art. *Examples:*

    The Outsiders (book)

    "The Raven" (poem)

    "America the Beautiful" (song)

    "Lift Every Voice and Sing" (work of art)

© 2002 by John Wiley & Sons, Inc.

Study Sheet 5-I

Sentences, Fragments, and Run-ons

Complete sentences are the foundation of written English.

1. A sentence must have a subject and predicate. It begins with a capital letter and ends with a period, a question mark, or an exclamation point. *Examples:*

   It rained all night. *(declarative sentence)*

   Please close the door. *(imperative sentence)*

   Where did I leave my keys? *(interrogative sentence)*

   Watch out! *(exclamatory sentence)*

2. A compound sentence contains two sentences joined by a comma and the words *and, but, or,* or *nor. Example:*

   Cody likes to watch TV, but Jimmy likes to listen to music.

3 A complex sentence contains a main clause and one or more subordinate clauses. *Example:*

   Because the snowstorm closed New York's airports,
   Brad was unable to fly home until the weekend.

4. A sentence fragment is an incomplete thought. Fragments should always be corrected. *Examples:*

   A letter to Uncle Bob. *(fragment)*

   I sent a letter to Uncle Bob. *(correct)*

   Went hiking. *(fragment)*

   We went hiking in the park. *(correct)*

5. A run-on sentence connects two or more sentences without the proper punctuation. The sentences should either be written separately, or should be joined by a comma and a word such as *and, but, or,* or *nor.* Run-ons should always be corrected. *Example:*

   Tanya did her homework, she went shopping with her mother. *(run-on)*

   Tanya did her homework, and she went shopping with her mother. *(correct)*

© 2002 by John Wiley & Sons, Inc.

Study Sheet 5-J

Common and Proper Nouns

A noun is a word that names a person, place, thing, or idea. Nouns may be common or proper.

A common noun names any person, place, thing, or idea. A proper noun names a specific person, place, thing, or idea. Proper nouns are always capitalized.

Examples of Common Nouns

- *Persons:* student child man doctor
- *Places:* town valley country shopping mall
- *Things:* book table house tree kitten
- *Ideas:* happiness sadness courage truth

© 2002 by John Wiley & Sons, Inc.

Examples of Proper Nouns

- *Persons:* Jennifer Doctor Smith Mrs. Morales
- *Places:* Boston Texas Walt Disney World
- *Things:* the George Washington Bridge the Lincoln Memorial the Declaration of Independence
- *Ideas:* Equal Rights

Note:

- A proper adjective is an adjective formed from a proper noun. Proper adjectives always begin with capital letters. *Examples:*

  English German Spanish Chinese Japanese

Study Sheet 5-K

Singular and Plural Nouns

Nouns may be singular and name one person, place, thing, or idea. Nouns may be plural and name more than one person, place, thing, or idea.

- *Examples of singular nouns:* dog tree lunch puppy child woman ox goose
- *Examples of plural nouns:* dogs trees lunches puppies children women oxen geese

How to Form Plural Nouns

- For most nouns, add **s**. *Examples:* kid—kids chair—chairs book—books
- For nouns that end in **s**, **x**, **ch**, **sh**, or **zz**, add **es**. *Examples:* guess—guesses fox—foxes church—churches bush—bushes buzz—buzzes
- For nouns that end with a vowel and **y**, add **s**. *Examples:* day—days monkey—monkeys
- For nouns that end with a consonant and **y**, change the **y** to **i** and add **es**. *Examples:* county—counties berry—berries
- For some nouns that end in **f** or **fe**, change the **f** to **v** and add **es**. Add **s** to other nouns that end in **f**. *Examples:* wife—wives calf—calves cliff—cliffs
- For nouns that end with a vowel and **o**, add **s**. *Examples:* video—videos radio—radios
- For nouns that end with a consonant and **o**, add **s** or **es**. *Examples:* halo—halos hero—heroes
- Some nouns have special plural forms. *Examples:* goose—geese mouse—mice tooth—teeth foot—feet man—men woman—women child—children
- Some nouns have the same forms in singular and plural. *Examples:* sheep—sheep deer—deer moose—moose

© 2002 by John Wiley & Sons, Inc.

Study Sheet 5-L

Possessive Nouns

<u>Possessive nouns</u> show ownership. An apostrophe (') is used to show the possessive case. *Example:*

Jennifer's bicycle was in the garage. *(The apostrophe and* **s** *tell the reader that the bicycle belongs to Jennifer.)*

How to Form Possessive Nouns

- For singular nouns, add an apostrophe and an **s**. *Examples:*

  the cat's toy　　Charles's pen　　Aunt Ella's house

  Note: When a singular noun ends with two or more successive "s" or "z" sounds, an apostrophe may be used without addition of another **s**. *Example:*

  Moses'

© 2002 by John Wiley & Sons, Inc.

- For plural nouns ending with **s**, add an apostrophe. *Examples:*

  the girls' soccer team　　the wolves' territory

  the boys' clubhouse　　the puppies' box

- For plural nouns not ending with **s**, add an apostrophe and an **s**. *Examples:*

  children's books　　mice's nest　　women's gloves

Study Sheet 5-M

Regular and Irregular Verbs

A verb is a word that shows action, a condition, or that a thing exists.

Most verbs are regular verbs, which form their past tense by adding **d** or **ed**. *Examples:*

walk—walked	start—started
watch—watched	miss—missed
enjoy—enjoyed	finish—finished

When helping verbs like *has, have*, or *had* are used with a verb, they form a verb phrase called the past participle. *Example:*

He had finished earlier than anyone else.

Irregular verbs do not form their past tense by adding **ed**. These verbs have different forms. Following are common irregular verbs.

Present Tense	Past Tense	Past Participle
bear	bore	has, have, had borne
beat	beat	has, have, had beaten
become	became	has, have, had become
begin	began	has, have, had begun
bite	bit	has, have, had bitten
blow	blew	has, have, had blown
break	broke	has, have, had broken
bring	brought	has, have, had brought
burst	burst	has, have, had burst
catch	caught	has, have, had caught
choose	chose	has, have, had chosen
come	came	has, have, had come
creep	crept	has, have, had crept
do	did	has, have, had done
draw	drew	has, have, had drawn
drink	drank	has, have, had drunk

© 2002 by John Wiley & Sons, Inc.

Study Sheet 5-M

Regular and Irregular Verbs *(continued)*

Present Tense	Past Tense	Past Participle
drive	drove	has, have, had driven
eat	ate	has, have, had eaten
fall	fell	has, have, had fallen
fight	fought	has, have, had fought
flee	fled	has, have, had fled
fling	flung	has, have, had flung
fly	flew	has, have, had flown
freeze	froze	has, have, had frozen
give	gave	has, have, had given
go	went	has, have, had gone
grow	grew	has, have, had grown
know	knew	has, have, had known
lay	laid	has, have, had laid
lie	lay	has, have, had lain
lose	lost	has, have, had lost
make	made	has, have, had made
ride	rode	has, have, had ridden
ring	rang	has, have, had rung
rise	rose	has, have, had risen
run	ran	has, have, had run
say	said	has, have, had said
see	saw	has, have, had seen
seek	sought	has, have, had sought
set	set	has, have, had set
shake	shook	has, have, had shaken
shine	shone	has, have, had shone
shrink	shrank	has, have, had shrunk

© 2002 by John Wiley & Sons, Inc.

Study Sheet 5-M

Regular and Irregular Verbs *(continued)*

Present Tense	Past Tense	Past Participle
sing	sang	has, have, had sung
sink	sank	has, have, had sunk
sit	sat	has, have, had sat
slay	slew	has, have, had slain
speak	spoke	has, have, had spoken
spin	spun	has, have, had spun
spring	sprang	has, have, had sprung
steal	stole	has, have, had stolen
stick	stuck	has, have, had stuck
sting	stung	has, have, had stung
strive	strove	has, have, had striven
swear	swore	has, have, had sworn
swim	swam	has, have, had swum
swing	swung	has, have, had swung
take	took	has, have, had taken
teach	taught	has, have, had taught
tear	tore	has, have, had torn
throw	threw	has, have, had thrown
wear	wore	has, have, had worn
write	wrote	has, have, had written

© 2002 by John Wiley & Sons, Inc.

Study Sheet 5-N

Helping Verbs and Verb Phrases

A verb phrase is a group of words consisting of a main verb and one or more helping verbs. *Example:*

We are going to the movies tonight.

"Are going" is the verb phrase. "Going" is the main verb and "are" is the helping verb.

The following are common helping verbs.

be	been	am	are	is	was	were
do	does	did	have	has	had	can
could	will	would	may	might	shall	should

© 2002 by John Wiley & Sons, Inc.

Study Sheet 5-O

Verb Tenses

Verb tense helps to show when something happened in a sentence. The three main tenses are simple present, simple past, and simple future.

- **Present tense verbs** show action that is happening now. *Example:*

  Joanie walks home with Rachel after school.

- **Past tense verbs** show action that has already happened. *Example:*

  Joanie walked home with Rachel yesterday.

- **Future tense verbs** show action that has not yet happened. *Example:*

  Joanie will walk home with Rachel tomorrow.

Along with the simple present, past, and future tenses, verbs may have perfect tenses. These tenses use *has*, *have*, or *had* with the past participle.

- **Present perfect tense** shows an action that started in the past and continues in the present. It requires *has* or *have* with the past participle. *Example:*

  Joanie has walked home with Rachel after school.

- **Past perfect tense** shows a past action that ended before another past action started. It requires *had* with the past participle. *Example:*

  Joanie had walked home with Rachel after school.

- **Future perfect tense** shows a future action that will have ended before another action starts. It requires *shall have* or *will have* with the past participle. *Example:*

  Joanie will have walked home with Rachel after school.

© 2002 by John Wiley & Sons, Inc.

Study Sheet 5-P

Subjective Case and Objective Case Pronouns

A pronoun is a word that takes the place of a noun. Two important types of pronouns are subjective case pronouns and objective case pronouns. Each type of pronoun must be used correctly.

Subjective Case Pronouns

	Singular	Plural
First Person:	I	we
Second Person:	you	you
Third Person:	he, she, it	they

Subjective case pronouns take the place of nouns that are subjects of a sentence. They also take the place of nouns that follow a linking verb, in which case they are known as predicate pronouns.

© 2002 by John Wiley & Sons, Inc.

Objective Case Pronouns

	Singular	Plural
First Person:	me	us
Second Person:	you	you
Third Person:	him, her, it	them

Objective case pronouns take the place of nouns that are direct or indirect objects of a sentence. They may also take the place of nouns that are the object of prepositions, which are words such as *for, at, to, between, with, in,* or *toward.*

Examples of incorrect and correct usage:

Incorrect: Tom and me studied for the test together.
Correct: Tom and I studied for the test together.

Incorrect: Her and Sara went to the movies.
Correct: She and Sara went to the movies.

Incorrect: The package came for Danny and I.
Correct: The package came for Danny and me.

Example of a predicate pronoun:

Incorrect: It was me who found the wallet.
Correct: It was I who found the wallet.

Study Sheet 5-Q

Possessive Pronouns

Possessive pronouns show ownership. Some are used before nouns. Some are used alone.

Possessive Pronouns Used before Nouns

	Singular	Plural
First Person:	my	our
Second Person:	your	your
Third Person:	his, her, its	their

Possessive Pronouns Used Alone

	Singular	Plural
First Person:	mine	ours
Second Person:	yours	yours
Third Person:	his, her, its	theirs

Be careful not to confuse possessive pronouns with contractions.

Possessive Pronoun	Contraction
your	you're (you are)
its	it's (it is)
their	they're (they are)

© 2002 by John Wiley & Sons, Inc.

Study Sheet 5-R

Indefinite Pronouns

An indefinite pronoun refers to a person, place, or thing without specifying which particular one. Some indefinite pronouns are singular, some are plural, and some can be either singular or plural.

Singular	Plural	Singular or Plural
another	both	all
anybody	few	any
each	many	more
either	others	most
everyone	several	none
everything		some
much		
neither		
no one		
nothing		
one		
other		
somebody		
someone		
something		

© 2002 by John Wiley & Sons, Inc.

Study Sheet 5-S

Who, Whom, Whose, and Who's

Who and whom are used as interrogative pronouns, which ask a question, or as relative pronouns, which introduce a subordinate clause.

Who is a nominative case pronoun. Use *who* whenever the pronoun *he* can be substituted for it. *Examples:*

Who ate the last of the pie?
He ate the last of the pie.

Jason Randall, who is in eighth grade, is the winner of the essay contest.
. . . who is in eighth grade . . .
. . . he is in eighth grade . . .

Whom is an objective case pronoun. Use *whom* whenever you can turn the question into a statement and substitute the pronoun *him* for *whom*. *Examples:*

Whom have you called today?
You have called him today.

With whom are you online?
You are online with him.

Whose is a possessive pronoun showing ownership. Who's is a contraction for *who is*. To check if you are using *who's* and *whose* correctly, break the contraction apart and see if the sentence makes sense. *Examples:*

Incorrect: Who's coat is that? (*Who is* coat is that?)
Correct: Whose coat is that?

Incorrect: Whose there?
Correct: Who's there? (*Who is* there?)

© 2002 by John Wiley & Sons, Inc.

Study Sheet 5-T

Negative Words and Double Negatives

A negative word is a word that means "no" or "not." Contractions that are formed with "not" are negative words.

Common Negative Words						
no	not	none	nobody	nothing	no one	never
isn't	aren't	won't	can't	couldn't	mustn't	shouldn't
doesn't	didn't	don't	haven't	hasn't	hadn't	wouldn't

© 2002 by John Wiley & Sons, Inc.

Using more than one negative in a sentence is incorrect. This is called a double negative. Double negatives can easily be corrected by changing one negative word to a positive word.

Incorrect: We don't have no gym today.

Correct: We don't have gym today.

Correct: We have no gym today.

Incorrect: We never see no deer during our hikes.

Correct: We never see any deer during our hikes.

Correct: We see no deer during our hikes.

Incorrect: Josh doesn't have no brothers.

Correct: Josh doesn't have any brothers.

Correct: Josh has no brothers.

Study Sheet 5-U

Friendly Letter Model

A friendly letter is a letter sent to a friend or relative. Its purpose is to tell the reader about something. Here is a sample.

123 Fairfield Street
West Valley, NJ 00112 **(Heading)**
March 15, 2002

Dear Uncle George, **(Greeting)**

Thank you very much for the fishing pole you sent for my birthday. With trout season opening next week, I'm sure I'll be able to put it to good use. Mom says that you'll be visiting in a few weeks. We'll have to go fishing. I found a great spot behind Wilson's Bridge. Thanks again. **(Body)**

Sincerely, **(Closing)**

Carl **(Signature)**

© 2002 by John Wiley & Sons, Inc.

Study Sheet 5-V

Business Letter Model

A business letter is a letter sent to a company or organization. It has a slightly different form than a friendly letter. This letter uses a semi-block format.

342 Hilltop Street
Albertville, NY 90872 **(Heading)**
April 8, 2002

L. J. Print Company
578 River Road **(Inside Address)**
Summer's Port, DE 77653

Dear Sir or Madam: **(Greeting)**

I would like to order your Mountain Mist poster, catalog number MM-8943123. I have enclosed $9.95 for the cost of the poster and for shipping. **(Body)**

Thank you.

Yours truly, **(Closing)**

Tara Jones **(Signature)**

Tara Jones **(Name)**

Note: Another format for a business letter is the *block form* in which there are no indentations. The heading, inside address, greeting, closing, signature, and name all start at the left margin. There are no indentations for paragraphs.

© 2002 by John Wiley & Sons, Inc.

Name ______________________ Date ______________

5-1

Using Capitalization and Punctuation Correctly I

Directions: Rewrite each sentence, correcting mistakes in capitalization and punctuation. (There may be more than one error in each sentence.)

1. Saras family goes out for chinese food every friday night.

____

____

2. Centerville's Historical society meets every Tuesday Evening in the library at 7,30.

____

____

3. Although she loved her little brother Maria found his high energy level to be exasperating?

____

____

4. Last Summer our family, visited Yellowstone National park during our vacation.

____

____

5. Exam week tired everyone out; especially Callie

____

____

6. One of my favorite books is "The Sword in The Stone" by T. h. White.

____

____

© 2002 by John Wiley & Sons, Inc.

Name ______________________________ Date ________________

5-1

Using Capitalization and Punctuation Correctly I *(continued)*

7. Tina, Valeries Cousin lives in Scranton Pennsylvania.

____

____

8. "Let's plan on going to a movie on Saturday." Said Brian.

____

____

9. Sheila thought about all she had to do on Saturday go to soccer practice go shopping with her mom watch her younger sister do homework, and go to Erin's party.

____

____

10. What is the weather report for tomorrow," asked Randy.

____

____

11. Of course, Jess never saw, a puppy, she didn't love.

____

____

12. "Watch out," Cheryl cried and she pulled Beth out of the way of the speeding car!

____

____

© 2002 by John Wiley & Sons, Inc.

Name ______________________________ Date ________________

5-2

Using Capitalization and Punctuation Correctly II

Directions: Rewrite each sentence, correcting mistakes in capitalization and punctuation. (There may be more than one error in each sentence.)

1. Lisa is a gifted Athlete and excels at field hockey, and softball.

____

____

2. Jan asked, whats for dinner tonight?

____

____

3. “If we want to see the start of the game”, Jerry said, “We’d better leave now.”

____

____

4. Tom’s grandfather served under general Patton during world War II.

____

____

5. According to a popular Theory a giant asteroid impact caused, the extinction of the dinosaurs

____

____

6. manuel accepted the compromise Conor would not.

____

____

© 2002 by John Wiley & Sons, Inc.

Name ______________________ Date ______________

5-2

Using Capitalization and Punctuation Correctly II *(continued)*

7. My father, reads "The Wall Street Journal" every morning.

____

____

8. Amys favorite poem is, "Mushrooms" by Sylvia Plath.

____

____

9. Indira plans to try out for her schools field hockey team

____

____

10. If we start now, said Angela, "we should be finished with the project by six."

____

____

11. "What time does the concert start," asked Wil?

____

____

12. The coach told the team that they should play hard try their best and remember that, the game isn't over until the final whistle.

____

____

© 2002 by John Wiley & Sons, Inc.

Name ______________________________ Date ________________

5-3

Singular and Plural Nouns

Directions: Read the selection. Underline all singular nouns and circle all plural nouns.

Although most people think of computers as being an invention of the 20th century, historians trace the roots of the modern computer back about 170 years. That was when two British mathematicians, Charles Babbage and Augusta Ada Byron, conceived a number of machines designed to handle complex mathematical problems. One of their conceptions, called an analytical engine, had a store for saving information, a mill for mathematical operations, and a primitive printer that produced a record of results.

© 2002 by John Wiley & Sons, Inc.

Name ________________________________ Date ____________________

5-4

Finding Verbs and Verb Phrases

Directions: Read each sentence. Underline the verb or verb phrase and circle the main verb in each verb phrase. (Not all sentences contain verb phrases.)

1. The student council sponsored a spring dance at the end of March.
2. Marla slipped into her seat moments before the late bell.
3. It had been raining all day.
4. Over the past three days Vinnie had studied several hours for his history exam.
5. Tiago always had been fascinated with how mechanical devices operated.
6. Sandy gently scolded her puppy for ruining her slipper.
7. The eagle soared majestically across the sky.
8. The math test was scheduled for Tuesday.
9. The storm caused power outages across the county.
10. The continent of Antarctica is one of the most inhospitable places on Earth.
11. After watching the movie until 2 A.M. last night, Sean was tired in the morning.
12. For our family's vacation this year, we will be sailing to the Bahamas.

© 2002 by John Wiley & Sons, Inc.

Name ________________________________ Date ________________

5-5

Understanding Irregular Verbs I

Directions: Complete each sentence by writing the correct form of the verb in parentheses in the blank.

1. The weight of the ice from the freezing rain had ______________ several branches on the tree. **(break)**
2. The temperature ______________ into the twenties last night. **(fall)**
3. The kitten ______________ stealthily up to the toy mouse. **(creep)**
4. Marissa and Kelly have ______________ each other just about all their lives. **(know)**
5. The puppies were ______________ in the spring. **(bear)**
6. The refugees ______________ the war-torn country. **(flee)**
7. Becky was nervous as the plane taxied down the runway because she had never ______________ before. **(fly)**
8. Having not ______________ since breakfast, Tom was famished by dinner time. **(eat)**
9. Melissa had ______________ the table for dinner before any of her guests arrived. **(set)**
10. The hornet ______________ Sam on his arm. **(sting)**
11. Mia was certain she had ______________ her best paper of the entire year. **(write)**
12. After doing his own wash, Jay realized all of his jeans had ______________. **(shrink)**

© 2002 by John Wiley & Sons, Inc.

Name ______________________________ Date ______________

5-6

Understanding Irregular Verbs II

Directions: Complete each sentence by writing the correct form of the verb in parentheses in the blank.

1. The brave prince ______________ the horrifying dragon. **(slay)**
2. While on vacation, they had ______________ every day in the hotel's pool. **(swim)**
3. Mrs. Adams ______________ eighth grade for 30 years. **(teach)**
4. The early sun's rays first ______________ on the mountains, then warmed the valley. **(shine)**
5. While playing catch, the boy accidentally ______________ the ball through the neighbor's window. **(throw)**
6. The winter wind ______________ icily across the field. **(blow)**
7. Chad ______________ the stone, skipping it over the pond. **(fling)**
8. Antonio's grandparents ______________ from Florida to visit for the holidays. **(come)**
9. On their last fishing trip, Lisa and her father ______________ several bass. **(catch)**
10. Vanessa had ______________ the movie three times, but she always enjoyed it. **(see)**
11. The chorus has ______________ at every school concert this year. **(sing)**
12. The grasshopper ______________ out of reach of the curious puppy. **(spring)**

© 2002 by John Wiley & Sons, Inc.

Name ______________________________ Date ________________

5-7

Understanding Verb Tenses

Part A. Directions: Write whether the tense is simple present, past, or future, or present perfect, past perfect, or future perfect on the line after each sentence.

1. Tom rehearsed his speech until it was perfect. ________________
2. Tiffany receives dozens of e-mail messages from her friends each day. ________________
3. The class has visited the Museum of Natural History earlier in the year. ________________
4. Mr. Hastings will be flying to Italy for a business conference. ________________
5. We had finished the project a week before the due date. ________________
6. Last week's ski trip was canceled because of the unusually mild weather. ________________
7. The research group will have completed their experiments by the end of next year. ________________
8. Liz jogs three miles before school each morning. ________________
9. Carlos has worked every Saturday in his father's store since the beginning of school this year. ________________
10. In four more years the class will have finished high school. ________________

Part B. Directions: On the back of this sheet, write sentences that show each of the following tenses:

- simple present
- simple past
- simple future
- present perfect
- past perfect
- future perfect

© 2002 by John Wiley & Sons, Inc.

Name ______________________________ Date ________________

5-8

Understanding Contractions

Part A. Directions: Write the contractions for the underlined words on the line after each sentence.

1. He is planning to attend medical school next year. __________
2. Jenna could not recall Trish's e-mail address. __________
3. According to the weather forecast, it will probably rain tomorrow. __________
4. "What is for lunch?" Melissa asked. __________
5. They had expected to arrive by six in the evening. __________
6. She must not forget to hand the paper in by Friday. __________

© 2002 by John Wiley & Sons, Inc.

Part B. Directions: Write the words that make up each contraction on the line after each sentence.

1. The soccer team's going to the state championship. ______________
2. They would've preferred to go to the concert instead of visiting their relatives.

   ____
3. Since he left earlier than usual, James shouldn't be late for class.

   ____
4. Ashlee left her science book in school and didn't finish her homework.

   ____
5. They've gone to California to visit their aunt. ______________
6. The boys won't go camping if the forecast calls for rain. ______________

Name ______________________________ Date ________________

5-9

Finding the Subjects of Sentences

Directions: Underline the simple subject in each sentence.

1. Martin searched everywhere for his house keys.

2. The meteor shower created a fantastic show in the night sky.

3. The moon, a bright glowing ball, rose slowly above the distant hills.

4. Upon recognizing his owner, the old dog wagged his tail affectionately.

5. In the middle of the night, Sara heard strange sounds outside.

6. The weather was unusually mild for the beginning of winter.

7. Please close the door.

8. Lori's favorite author is Judy Blume.

9. The clouds, dark and grim, foretold of a coming storm.

10. Tied at the end of the fourth period, the basketball game went into overtime.

11. Only one of the applicants for the job had the right qualifications.

12. The rocket, a testimony to technology, lifted off from its launch pad.

© 2002 by John Wiley & Sons, Inc.

Name ______________________________ Date ________________

5-10

Finding Simple Predicates

Directions: Underline the simple predicate in each sentence. (Some predicates may be verb phrases.)

1. Like a wolf, the wind howled through the night.

2. The white-capped mountains towered over the surrounding plains.

3. The vast desert extended for miles in all directions.

4. Sandy and Evie will be going shopping later today.

5. Alan spends hours on the Internet.

6. Alaska is the largest state in the country.

7. Students were supposed to vote in the school elections yesterday.

8. Rhonda had enjoyed her visit to the Space Museum.

9. Gliding down the hill on his snowboard, Kyle felt as free as the wind.

10. At 3:30 A.M., the alarm blared.

11. The river, swollen with water from melting snow, cascaded down the mountain and into the valley.

12. The rained-out softball game was rescheduled for Saturday afternoon.

© 2002 by John Wiley & Sons, Inc.

Name ______________________________ Date ________________

5-11

Finding Compound Subjects and Compound Predicates

Part A. Directions: Underline each compound subject and circle each compound predicate. (Some sentences may not have a compound subject. Some may not have a compound predicate. Some may have both.)

1. After school Adrienne hurried home and started her math project.
2. Last night Lauren and Danny set the table and prepared dinner for their parents.
3. Jill and Mavis are co-captains of the girls' field hockey team.
4. The weather bureau issued a severe storm warning and cautioned people to remain indoors.
5. Jennifer and Lara danced and sang in the Eighth-Grade Talent Show.
6. The cold rain stung Mari's face and caused her to shiver.
7. The fog and drizzle obscured the road and made driving difficult.
8. Billy, Teri, and Carla checked several sources for information for their report on Shakespeare.
9. Dave sprained his ankle and twisted his knee on the same play.
10. Patricia and Jeanette are cousins and best friends.

© 2002 by John Wiley & Sons, Inc.

Part B. Directions: On the back of this sheet, write one sentence of your own with a compound subject, another sentence with a compound predicate, and a third sentence with a compound subject and compound predicate.

Name ______________________________ Date ______________

5-12

Subject and Predicate Agreement I

Directions: Complete the sentences by writing the correct predicate from the pairs of verbs in parentheses.

1. Every rainstorm ______________ the hill further. **(erode, erodes)**
2. The groups ______________ as they try to find a solution to the problem. **(interact, interacts)**
3. Rebecca and her sister ______________ soccer, but they are on different teams. **(play, plays)**
4. Mr. Samuels ______________ his students to always do their best. **(encourage, encourages)**
5. That flight of stairs ______________ up to the balcony. **(lead, leads)**
6. In some countries, the government ______________ information it does not want its citizens to know. **(suppress, suppresses)**
7. The hinges on the old door ______________ when the door opens. **(creak, creaks)**
8. Reporters often ______________ eyewitnesses in their stories. **(quote, quotes)**
9. Most doctors ______________ antibiotics when they suspect infections caused by bacteria. **(prescribe, prescribes)**
10. Halley's Comet ______________ at intervals that average about 76 years. **(return, returns)**
11. Tom and Jason ______________ playing video games in their spare time. **(enjoy, enjoys)**
12. Neither Kim nor Amy ______________ to give the first speech. **(want, wants)**

© 2002 by John Wiley & Sons, Inc.

Name ______________________________ Date ________________

5-13

Subject and Predicate Agreement II

Directions: Complete the sentences by writing the correct predicate from the pairs of verbs in parentheses.

1. The first snowfall ____________ Casey to the ski slopes. **(beckon, beckons)**
2. Every year at the end of school, Alyssa ____________ all of her friends to a pool party at her house. **(invite, invites)**
3. Greg and Jim ____________ a magazine for teens on the Internet. **(publish, publishes)**
4. Natalie always ____________ her writing assignments thoroughly before handing them in. **(revise, revises)**
5. The people of Carterville ____________ Mayor Harper to be a capable public servant. **(consider, considers)**
6. Neither her friends nor Shannon ____________ in ghosts. **(believe, believes)**
7. Stacy and Cara, of all the kids in their homeroom, ____________ vanilla ice cream. **(prefer, prefers)**
8. Violence almost always ____________ more violence. **(provoke, provokes)**
9. Sue, Tom, and Peter ____________ in a work–study program. **(participate, participates)**
10. Either Jill or Gordon ____________ the charity drive each spring. **(organize, organizes)**
11. Common sense ____________ many accidents. **(prevent, prevents)**
12. Mr. Dotson, who has visited many of the world's great cities, ____________ people with his experiences. **(impress, impresses)**

© 2002 by John Wiley & Sons, Inc.

Name ______________________________ Date ________________

5-14

Understanding Subject and Object Pronouns

Directions: Complete each sentence by writing the correct pronoun from the pair of pronouns in the parentheses.

1. Mary Ellen's uncle Bob sent __________ a gift a month before her birthday. **(she, her)**
2. Carly and __________ have become good friends this year. **(he, him)**
3. __________ haven't gone on a vacation in years. **(They, Them)**
4. Mrs. Wallace never gives __________ homework on weekends or holidays. **(we, us)**
5. Cory thanked __________ for helping him find the lost puppy. **(they, them)**
6. The letter was addressed to __________. **(I, me)**
7. The science award was presented to Cheryl and __________. **(he, him)**
8. Serena and __________ are going to the movies on Saturday. **(I, me)**
9. Fallon, Teri, and __________ are distant cousins. **(he, him)**
10. The first person to realize the mistake was __________. **(she, her)**
11. Billy and __________ are going bowling tomorrow night. **(we, us)**
12. __________ and she are researching the causes of the Spanish–American War for their group. **(He, Him)**

© 2002 by John Wiley & Sons, Inc.

Name ______________________________ Date ________________

5-15

Understanding Pronouns and Antecedents

Part A. Directions: Complete the sentences by writing the pronoun that agrees with its antecedent.

1. Shawna searched everywhere for __________ missing literature book.

2. The students in Mrs. Hernandez's class are expected to write the science formulas in __________ notebooks.

3. It was suggested that each person going on the trip bring __________ own lunch.

4. Kim, along with all of her friends, felt that __________ should have gotten the lead role in the play.

5. When Jonathan went shopping to buy his sister a birthday present, __________ bought __________ a CD.

6. Although the players tried __________ best, __________ were no match for __________ more experienced opponents.

© 2002 by John Wiley & Sons, Inc.

Name ______________________________ Date ________________

5-15

Understanding Pronouns and Antecedents *(continued)*

Part B. Directions: Rewrite the sentences so that the pronouns agree with their antecedents.

1. When Darlene left for college, her younger brother got his room.

____

____

2. Scott did the best they could on the test.

____

____

3. The members of the dance team did his or her best at the dance contest.

____

____

4. Gwen's sister Karen is taller than her.

____

____

5. The student who lost their keys should report to the office.

____

____

6. Phil and Zak think they're science project is the most original in the class.

____

____

© 2002 by John Wiley & Sons, Inc.

Name ______________________________ Date ________________

5-16

Understanding Indefinite Pronouns and Agreement with Verbs

Directions: Complete each sentence by writing the correct verb from the pair of verbs in parentheses.

1. Even though the students had visited the Liberty Science Center last year, everybody __________ willing to go again. **(is, are)**
2. Someone __________ left a coat in the auditorium. **(has, have)**
3. Of all the students who expressed interest in the advanced history class, most __________ highly qualified. **(is, are)**
4. Nobody __________ Mrs. Anderson's health class. **(fail, fails)**
5. Something __________ me it is going to rain on the day of our hike. **(tell, tells)**
6. Each of the penpal letters __________ addressed to a student in a different grade. **(was, were)**
7. Although it has been three months since he left, no one __________ heard from Bill. **(has, have)**
8. All of the students __________ about the upcoming dance. **(know, knows)**
9. Many in the class __________ there is too much homework. **(believe, believes)**
10. Everyone __________ school quickly on the day before spring break. **(leave, leaves)**
11. Each of the students __________ responsible for choosing his or her electives for next year. **(is, are)**
12. Every time Mr. Williams asks his students a question, several __________ their hands. **(raise, raises)**

© 2002 by John Wiley & Sons, Inc.

Name ______________________________ Date ________________

5-17

Using *Who*, *Whom*, *Whose*, and *Who's* Correctly

Directions: Complete each sentence by writing *who, whom, whose,* or *who's* in the blank.

1. __________ did Mr. Walker select to be keynote speaker at the Scholars' Luncheon?
2. __________ designed the bulletin board in the hallway by the cafeteria?
3. __________ most likely to win the election for class president?
4. __________ library privileges have been revoked until further notice?
5. __________ will receive the award at the assembly for best athlete?
6. __________ books were left on the bench outside the front door?
7. __________ were you talking to on the phone?
8. Mrs. Norton, __________ was the new teacher in eighth grade, quickly became a favorite of the students.
9. The volunteers for the charity drive must be individuals on __________ we can rely.
10. During the discussion of electronics, Marcus wondered __________ had invented the TV.
11. Kyle, __________ father is an officer in the army, lived in Germany for six years.
12. The teacher asked the party committee, "__________ responsible for the refreshments?"

© 2002 by John Wiley & Sons, Inc.

Name ______________________________ Date ________________

5-18

Using Comparisons of Modifiers Correctly

Directions: Complete each sentence by choosing the correct modifier from the pair of words in parentheses.

1. Winter is the ________________ season in the north. **(harsher, harshest)**
2. April did a ______________ job on her science lab. **(good, well)**
3. Even though they lived about the same distance from school and left about the same time, Juan arrived ________________ than Ted. **(earlier, more early)**
4. Many people consider New York City to be the world's ____________ financial center. **(greater, greatest)**
5. While vacationing with her family in the Bahamas, Rachel witnessed the ______________________ sunrise she had ever seen. **(spectacularest, most spectacular)**
6. The juggler was ______________________ than the magician at the community variety show. **(more entertaining, most entertaining)**
7. After being in bed an entire week with the flu, Leslie feels ______________ again. **(good, well)**
8. Moving the furniture out of the living room was a ______________________ task than Reilly had thought. **(strenuouser, more strenuous)**
9. Last week's thunderstorm was the ______________ anyone could recall. **(baddest, worst)**
10. Deanna seems ________________ than Sara. **(more sensible, most sensible)**
11. The brown puppy appeared to be stronger and ______________ than his brother. **(healthier, more healthy)**
12. Everyone felt that Jimmy was the ______________________ person in his family. **(friendliest, most friendly)**

© 2002 by John Wiley & Sons, Inc.

Name ______________________ Date ______________

5-19

Correcting Fragments and Run-ons

Part A. Directions: Correct each fragment by rewriting it as a complete sentence.

1. the towering mountains. ______________________

____

2. the thrills of white-water rafting. ______________________

____

3. Janet's Uncle Mike. ______________________

____

4. at the museum. ______________________

____

5. the launch of the spacecraft. ______________________

____

6. lost child in the park. ______________________

____

Part B. Directions: Rewrite and correct the run-on sentences.

1. Blue whales are the largest animals on Earth, they can grow to be over 100 feet long and weigh up to 150 tons. ______________________

____

____

© 2002 by John Wiley & Sons, Inc.

Name ______________________________ Date ________________

5-19

Correcting Fragments and Run-ons *(continued)*

2. Jennifer had never seen such a big mall, she decided she could spend days shopping there. ________________________________

____

____

3. Rick's favorite sport is baseball, his father's favorite sport is football. ________

____

____

4. Dan has never flown before, he looked forward to takeoff. ______________

____

____

5. Maria enjoys ice-skating, she doesn't like roller-skating. ______________

____

____

6. Kara could watch a movie, she could listen to music. ______________

____

____

© 2002 by John Wiley & Sons, Inc.

Name ______________________ Date ____________

5-20

Correcting Double Negatives

Directions: Rewrite each sentence correctly, eliminating the double negative.

1. Because of the snowstorm, there wasn't no school today. ____________

2. None of the kids had no ideas for which music to play at the party. ____________

3. They did not have enough snow to build no snowman. ____________

4. There won't be no homework over the long weekend. ____________

5. With the computers down, no one in the school could send no e-mail. ____________

6. Suresh couldn't find his keys nowhere. ____________

© 2002 by John Wiley & Sons, Inc.

Name ______________________ Date ______________

5-20

Correcting Double Negatives *(continued)*

7. Despite having searched all day, the investigators hadn't found no clues. ________

8. None of the sources they checked provided no information. ________

9. In some areas of the river, no fish can't live because of the pollution. ________

10. No progress wasn't made until the group decided on an interesting topic. ________

11. After practicing her gymnastics routine for three hours, Liz couldn't practice no more. ________

12. Tom doesn't believe there's no career more important than being a doctor. ________

© 2002 by John Wiley & Sons, Inc.

Name ______________________ Date ______________

5-21

Using Quotation Marks and Underlining (Italics) Correctly

Directions: Rewrite each sentence, being sure to correct quotation marks and underlining (italics).

1. I received five phone calls from her today, said Jimmy.

2. His favorite book is "Something Wicked This Way Comes" by Ray Bradbury.

3. "We got lost, said Monica, and by the time we finally found her house, the party was half over."

4. "Did you get caught in the storm? asked Mr. Taylor."

5. Kate loved the poem <u>The Road Not Taken</u> by Robert Frost.

6. Meg's father reads the New York Times every morning at breakfast.

© 2002 by John Wiley & Sons, Inc.

Name ______________________________ Date ________________

5-21

Using Quotation Marks and Underlining (Italics) Correctly *(continued)*

7. Pat titled her article How to Take Care of Your Puppy. ________________

8. What do you want to do Friday night? Tyler asked. ________________

9. Many readers find "The Diary of Anne Frank" to be one of the most memorable books they have ever read. ________________

10. The coach said, "Do your best". ________________

11. It's already dinner time," said Tania into the phone to her friend and I still haven't started my homework." ________________

12. One of my mother's favorite magazines is Good Housekeeping. ________________

© 2002 by John Wiley & Sons, Inc.

Name ______________________________ Date ________________

5-22

Understanding Friendly Letters

Directions: Rewrite this friendly letter on the lines below and correct the mistakes. (You may continue the letter on the back of this sheet.)

203 Sunset st.
Riverville, PA 12435
January 15, 2003

Dear Mark

How are you doing. Everything is great here. Im looking forward to your visit next month over the winter break

My dad has offered to take us to Philadelphia to a basketball game, I can't wait.

Write back soon

You're Friend

Billy

____

____

____

____

____

____

____

____

© 2002 by John Wiley & Sons, Inc.

Name ______________________________ Date ______________

5-23

Understanding Business Letters

Directions: Rewrite this business letter on the lines below and correct the mistakes. (You may continue the letter on the back of this sheet.)

654 Main St.
Center city FL 98762
Nov 15, 2003

Bright Color Art, Inc.
139 Coast blvd.
Ocean Town, GA 89763

Dear sir,

I would like to order your Pro Oil Paint Set, catalog number 86029. The cost of the set is $39.95, which includes shipping and handling, I have enclosed payment

Thank you.

sincerely
Janet Williams
Janet Williams

© 2002 by John Wiley & Sons, Inc.

Name ______________________________ Date ________________

5-24

Proofreading I

Directions: Rewrite the paragraph, correcting mistakes in punctuation and capitalization.

The cause of the extinction of the dinosaurs some 65 million years ago has been debated for decades Although the disappearance of the dinosaurs is often thought of as having occurred in a great, momentary Catastrophe in fact, many of the dinosaur families became extinct one by one. Over the course of many years. Various theories have been offered to explain the extinction; including major climate change, the explosion of a nearby star that bathed the Earth in excessive lethal radiation, or a giant Asteroid impact, which would have resulted in mass destruction dark clouds blocking the sun's light and heat and a worldwide collapse of the food chain. Whatever caused the disappearance of the dinosaurs also made it possible for mammals to become Earth's dominant species?

____

____

____

____

____

____

____

____

____

____

____

____

____

____

____

© 2002 by John Wiley & Sons, Inc.

Name ________________________________ Date ________________

5-25

Proofreading II

Directions: Rewrite the paragraph, correcting mistakes in punctuation, capitalization, and usage.

The blue whale is the largest animal that has ever lived. An adult blue whale may attain a length of 100 feet and weigh 150 tons (300,000 pounds. Despite it's size the blue whale isn't no active predator that seeks and attacks prey. Instead of teeth, blue whales have baleen plates connected to their upper jaws. The plates have bristles on there inner edges, which are used to capture plankton, the main diet of the whales. When feeding the blue whale swims with its mouth open, gulping seawater and plankton. then the whale shuts its mouth and forces the water out through the bristles, trapping the plankton. Found in all oceans blue whales were once hunted extensively, now they are an endangered Species, protected by law.

____

____

____

____

____

____

____

____

____

____

____

____

____

____

____

© 2002 by John Wiley & Sons, Inc.

Name ______________________________ Date ________________

5-26

Proofreading III

Directions: Rewrite the paragraph, correcting mistakes in punctuation, capitalization, and usage.

The Internet is more than just a medium for e-mail shopping and electronic entertainment. It contains information on virtually every topic. A search for a common topic such as Abraham Lincoln may come up with over 250,000 hits, or websites with information about Lincoln. A search for a less familiar topic, for example, the Komodo dragon a lizard that lives on some small Indonesian islands in the Pacific ocean, can yield over 100,000 hits. While this grate abundance of material proves to be helpful to millions of people every day it can also be a source of confusion. Depending on the sponsor's of the website, this information may or may not be reliable, it is necessary for the researcher to make sure that the information is accurate. This can be done by: visiting websites sponsored by respected individuals and organizations and by checking information against other sources. The value of the Internet far outweighed any potential problems it might cause.

© 2002 by John Wiley & Sons, Inc.

EIGHTH-GRADE LEVEL

Language Mechanics and Word Usage

PRACTICE TESTS

© 2002 by John Wiley & Sons, Inc.

Language Mechanics and Word Usage Practice Test I

Part 1. Directions: Read each sentence and look for mistakes in capitalization and punctuation in each line. Use your Answer Sheet to darken the letter of the line that contains the error. If there is no mistake, darken answer space D.

1. A. The cold, cloudy winter
   B. day, made Amanda long for
   C. the warm weather of spring.
   D. (no mistakes)

2. A. Eric packed his boots,
   B. skis, and poles for
   C. the Class ski trip.
   D. (no mistakes)

3. A. The evidence indicated that
   B. the suspect was the thief:
   C. however, he had an alibi.
   D. (no mistakes)

4. A. "What times does the
   B. basketball game start?"
   C. Paul asked his brother.
   D. (no mistakes)

5. A. Charles keys were found
   B. on the floor in the
   C. hallway by his locker.
   D. (no mistakes)

Part 2. Directions: Read each sentence and study the underlined part. Use the Answer Sheet to darken the letter of the answer that shows the correct capitalization and punctuation. If the underlined part is correct, mark answer space D.

© 2002 by John Wiley & Sons, Inc.

Language Mechanics and Word Usage
Practice Test I *(continued)*

1. Tara's art teacher Miss Carter illustrates the school's literary magazine.

   A. teacher, Miss Carter

   B. teacher Miss Carter:

   C. teacher, Miss Carter,

   D. (correct as it is)

2. "If it doesn't stop raining by lunch time said Jimmy baseball practice will be held in the gym."

   A. time, said Jimmy, baseball

   B. time," said Jimmy, "baseball

   C. time." Said Jimmy. "Baseball

   D. (correct as it is)

3. Jen's favorite poem is *The Bells* by Edgar Allan Poe.

   A. *The Bells*, by

   B. "The Bells, by

   C. "The Bells" by

   D. (correct as it is)

4. Maria brought the following items for the party pretzels, chips, cookies, and juice.

   A. party: pretzels,

   B. party, pretzels

   C. party; pretzels,

   D. (correct as it is)

5. Peter likes learning about wildlife, and he hopes to become a biologist someday.

   A. wildlife and he

   B. wildlife: and he

   C. wildlife and, he

   D. (correct as it is)

© 2002 by John Wiley & Sons, Inc.

Part 3. Directions: Read each set of sentences and decide which sentence of each set shows correct capitalization and punctuation. Use the Answer Sheet to darken the letter of your answer. If none of the sentences are written correctly, mark answer space D.

1. A. Angie looked forward to her familys summer camping trip.
   B. “Please open the window,” said Mr Smith to Edwardo.
   C. After playing, for more than, an hour, the puppy slept through the rest of the afternoon.
   D. (none)

2. A. “Have you seen my blue sweatshirt Jill asked her mother?”
   B. Calvin enjoyed the movie immensely and hoped there would be a sequel.
   C. Rain, always, depressed Zoe, especially, when it came on her day off from work.
   D. (none)

3. A. Mr. Walters reads *Time* magazine every week.
   B. The severe storm caused power outages throughout the eastern half of the State.
   C. Although she knew spring cleaning had to be done Jess never enjoyed dusting and vacuuming the house.
   D. (none)

4. A. The fog, drizzle, and cold temperatures made friday the kind of day most people preferred to forget.
   B. “Oh, no.” Denise exclaimed when her computer crashed and she lost her science report.
   C. The Thompsons are planning to visit Yellowstone National Park, Death Valley, and Pike’s Peak next year.
   D. (none)

5. A. To keep in shape, Sam jogs two miles every day.
   B. Julie liked history: but she found the exhibits at the Colonial Museum to be disappointing.
   C. The Observatory’s powerful telescope enables Astronomers to see some of the most distant stars.
   D. (none)

© 2002 by John Wiley & Sons, Inc.

Language Mechanics and Word Usage Practice Test II

Part 1. Directions: Identify the simple subject of each of the following sentences. Use the Answer Sheet to darken the letter of your choice.

1. Dark storm clouds thickened over the valley.
   (A: storm; B: clouds; C: thickened; D: valley)

2. After playing with the children, the puppy fell asleep on his pillow.
   (A: playing; B: children; C: puppy; D: asleep)

3. The minor accident at the town's main intersection snarled traffic for a mile.
   (A: minor; B: accident; C: intersection; D: traffic)

© 2002 by John Wiley & Sons, Inc.

Part 2. Directions: Identify the simple predicate of each of the following sentences. Use the Answer Sheet to darken the letter of your choice.

1. Charlene relaxes by listening to music.
   (A: Charlene; B: relaxes; C: listening; D: music)

2. Two inches of rain fell in the first hour of the storm.
   (A: inches; B: rain; C: fell; D: hour)

3. After searching his room, James looked through the rest of the house for his keys.
   (A: searching; B: room; C: looked; D: through)

Part 3. Directions: Choose the correct pronoun to complete each sentence. Use the Answer Sheet to darken the letter of your choice.

1. Billy and _______ are class officers.
   A. she B. her C. him D. me

2. _______ left his or her coat in the lunch room?
   A. Whom B. Whomever C. Who D. Whose

3. Each member of the boys' ice hockey team had to pack _______ equipment.
   A. their B. his C. they're D. his or her

Library Resource Center
Renton Technical College
3000 N.E. 4th St.
Renton, WA 98056

4. Sara's Uncle Bill sent _______ a gift for her birthday.

   A. them B. she C. us D. her

5. Tara and Peter visited _______ grandmother in Florida during the spring break.

   A. their B. there C. they're D. theyre

Part 4. Directions: Read each set of sentences and look for mistakes in the use of pronouns. Use the Answer Sheet to darken the letter of the sentence with the mistake. If all three sentences are correct, mark answer space D.

1. A. Paul and him are at the library.
   B. The message was for her.
   C. No one got the last problem right.
   D. (no mistakes)

2. A. Whose book is that?
   B. Who's going to the game tonight?
   C. Whom were you speaking to on the phone?
   D. (no mistakes)

3. A. The cat couldn't find its toy mouse.
   B. Someone left their coat in the lunch room.
   C. Mom left a note for me to pick up Jennifer after school.
   D. (no mistakes)

4. A. Your cell phone is on the table.
   B. Were planning to arrive by four P.M.
   C. It's 10:30 now.
   D. (no mistakes)

5. A. They've come all the way from California.
   B. Lee Ann is a better soccer player than she.
   C. Tom and them are in the first group.
   D. (no mistakes)

© 2002 by John Wiley & Sons, Inc.

Language Mechanics and Word Usage Practice Test III

Part 1. Directions: Read each set of sentences and decide which sentence of each set is correct. Use the Answer Sheet to darken the letter of your choice. If none of the sentences are written correctly, mark answer space D.

1. A. It snows six inches last night.
   B. Kristen doesn't like no rain.
   C. Either Sandy or Dennis is a homeroom representative.
   D. (none)

2. A. History is Meg's best subject: math is her worst.
   B. They enjoy camping, they camp in the mountains.
   C. The girls had went to a concert Saturday.
   D. (none)

3. A. Megan didn't feel good because of her cold.
   B. The boys went hiking. In the state park last week.
   C. They had gone shopping before going to the movies.
   D. (none)

4. A. Elena works in her father's store on weekends.
   B. Sunset over the mountains was the magnificentest site Heather had ever seen.
   C. Tom has swimmed across the lake many times.
   D. (none)

5. A. They went to the play and sit in the front row.
   B. The cookies on the table is freshly baked.
   C. At the family reunion, everyone set on the big porch and shared stories.
   D. (none)

6. A. Only one of the books are missing.
   B. Tammy went to soccer practice, she had dinner, she did her homework.
   C. Mrs. Williams has taught eighth grade for many years.
   D. (none)

7. A. There's never enough time in the day.
   B. The storm was the worse experience I ever had.
   C. Where is you're locker?
   D. (none)

© 2002 by John Wiley & Sons, Inc.

8. A. That's the quickest way to the highway from here.
   B. Last night we watched the delightfulest movie of all.
   C. Her friends and Sue always has lunch at the same table in the cafeteria.
   D. (none)

9. A. Tomorrow we went sightseeing.
   B. They had ate a full meal before leaving for the airport.
   C. If his grades don't improve, he won't be able to play any sports this quarter.
   D. (none)

10. A. Their car broke down. On the way to school.
    B. Samantha and Kim have been best friends for years.
    C. Last year's vacation was the better of all.
    D. (none)

© 2002 by John Wiley & Sons, Inc.

Part 2. Directions: Proofread the parts of the business letter and look for mistakes in each line. Use the Answer Sheet to darken the letter of the line that contains a mistake. If there is no mistake, mark answer D.

1. A. 59 Winter st.
   B. Harper's Creek, PA 84926
   C. April 17, 2002
   D. (no mistakes)

2. A. Peterson Sporting Company
   B. 717 Forest Hill Rd.
   C. Center City, CA 07462
   D. (no mistakes)

3. A. Dear Sir,
   B. I would like to order your insulated Hiking
   C. Boots, catalog number HB47320. Thank you.
   D. (no mistakes)

4. A. Sincerely Yours,
   B. Jonathan Andrews
   C. Jonathan Andrews
   D. (no mistakes)

Name ________________________________ Date ________________

Language Mechanics and Word Usage

PRACTICE TEST I: ANSWER SHEET

Directions: Darken the circle above the letter that best answers the question.

Part 1

1. ○ A ○ B ○ C ○ D
2. ○ A ○ B ○ C ○ D
3. ○ A ○ B ○ C ○ D
4. ○ A ○ B ○ C ○ D
5. ○ A ○ B ○ C ○ D

Part 2

1. ○ A ○ B ○ C ○ D
2. ○ A ○ B ○ C ○ D
3. ○ A ○ B ○ C ○ D
4. ○ A ○ B ○ C ○ D
5. ○ A ○ B ○ C ○ D

Part 3

1. ○ A ○ B ○ C ○ D
2. ○ A ○ B ○ C ○ D
3. ○ A ○ B ○ C ○ D
4. ○ A ○ B ○ C ○ D
5. ○ A ○ B ○ C ○ D

© 2002 by John Wiley & Sons, Inc.

Name ________________________________ Date ________________

Language Mechanics and Word Usage

PRACTICE TEST II: ANSWER SHEET

Directions: Darken the circle above the letter that best answers the question.

Part 1

1. ○ A ○ B ○ C ○ D
2. ○ A ○ B ○ C ○ D
3. ○ A ○ B ○ C ○ D

Part 2

1. ○ A ○ B ○ C ○ D
2. ○ A ○ B ○ C ○ D
3. ○ A ○ B ○ C ○ D

Part 3

1. ○ A ○ B ○ C ○ D
2. ○ A ○ B ○ C ○ D
3. ○ A ○ B ○ C ○ D
4. ○ A ○ B ○ C ○ D
5. ○ A ○ B ○ C ○ D

Part 4

1. ○ A ○ B ○ C ○ D
2. ○ A ○ B ○ C ○ D
3. ○ A ○ B ○ C ○ D
4. ○ A ○ B ○ C ○ D
5. ○ A ○ B ○ C ○ D

© 2002 by John Wiley & Sons, Inc.

Name ______________________ Date ______________

Language Mechanics and Word Usage

PRACTICE TEST III: ANSWER SHEET

Directions: Darken the circle above the letter that best answers the question.

© 2002 by John Wiley & Sons, Inc.

Part 1

1.	○ A	○ B	○ C	○ D
2.	○ A	○ B	○ C	○ D
3.	○ A	○ B	○ C	○ D
4.	○ A	○ B	○ C	○ D
5.	○ A	○ B	○ C	○ D
6.	○ A	○ B	○ C	○ D
7.	○ A	○ B	○ C	○ D
8.	○ A	○ B	○ C	○ D
9.	○ A	○ B	○ C	○ D
10.	○ A	○ B	○ C	○ D

Part 2

1.	○ A	○ B	○ C	○ D
2.	○ A	○ B	○ C	○ D
3.	○ A	○ B	○ C	○ D
4.	○ A	○ B	○ C	○ D

Language Mechanics and Word Usage

KEY TO PRACTICE TEST I

Part 1

	A	B	C	D
1.	○	●	○	○
2.	○	○	●	○
3.	○	●	○	○
4.	○	○	○	●
5.	●	○	○	○

Part 2

	A	B	C	D
1.	○	○	●	○
2.	○	●	○	○
3.	○	○	●	○
4.	●	○	○	○
5.	○	○	○	●

Part 3

	A	B	C	D
1.	○	○	○	●
2.	○	●	○	○
3.	●	○	○	○
4.	○	○	●	○
5.	●	○	○	○

© 2002 by John Wiley & Sons, Inc.

Language Mechanics and Word Usage

KEY TO PRACTICE TEST II

Part 1

1. ○ A ● B ○ C ○ D
2. ○ A ○ B ● C ○ D
3. ○ A ● B ○ C ○ D

Part 2

1. ○ A ● B ○ C ○ D
2. ○ A ○ B ● C ○ D
3. ○ A ○ B ● C ○ D

Part 3

1. ● A ○ B ○ C ○ D
2. ○ A ○ B ● C ○ D
3. ○ A ● B ○ C ○ D
4. ○ A ○ B ○ C ● D
5. ● A ○ B ○ C ○ D

Part 4

1. ● A ○ B ○ C ○ D
2. ○ A ○ B ○ C ● D
3. ○ A ● B ○ C ○ D
4. ○ A ● B ○ C ○ D
5. ○ A ○ B ● C ○ D

© 2002 by John Wiley & Sons, Inc.

Language Mechanics and Word Usage

KEY TO PRACTICE TEST III

Part 1

	A	B	C	D
1.	○	○	●	○
2.	○	○	○	●
3.	○	○	●	○
4.	●	○	○	○
5.	○	○	○	●
6.	○	○	●	○
7.	●	○	○	○
8.	●	○	○	○
9.	○	○	●	○
10.	○	●	○	○

Part 2

	A	B	C	D
1.	●	○	○	○
2.	○	○	○	●
3.	●	○	○	○
4.	●	○	○	○

© 2002 by John Wiley & Sons, Inc.

Section 6

Language Expression

While it is often interwoven with mechanics and usage, language expression is a topic that receives considerable emphasis in the typical language arts curriculum, and it appears either directly or indirectly on most standardized tests. Students who receive practical instruction in language expression generally achieve higher scores on the language components of standardized tests than those whose language arts instruction concentrates primarily on mechanics.

To support your students in their study of language expression, distribute copies of the two study sheets that are included in this section:

- Study Sheet 6-A, "A Proofreading Guide for Language Expression"
- Study Sheet 6-B, "Steps to Clear Expression"

An effective time to hand out these study sheets is when you introduce and teach topics in language expression. Since language expression is a prominent part of writing, many teachers utilize these study sheets during writing activities. Suggest that your students keep the study sheets in their folders for future reference.

Study Sheet 6-A, "A Proofreading Guide for Language Expression," offers several steps for how your students can improve their expression of ideas. Review the information with your classes and discuss the suggestions. Encourage your students to refer to this sheet whenever they are proofreading written work.

While many teachers find it beneficial to hand out copies of Study Sheet 6-B, "Steps to Clear Expression," at the beginning of the year, this study sheet can be used whenever you are teaching organizational skills for writing or speaking. Discuss the information with your students and emphasize that clear expression starts with solid organization. Ideas that are focused and logically organized provide the foundation for effective communication.

You may also find it helpful to review previous study sheets, including Study Sheets 2-C, "Homographs," 2-D, "Homophones," and 2-E, "Easily Confused Words," which can help your students avoid misusing words that cause confusion for countless students and adults. Encourage your students to always strive for clarity in their written and spoken words; to do less is to risk miscommunication and uncertainty.

This section also includes 15 worksheets and two practice tests that focus on the clear expression of English. Based on the skills typically found in an eighth-grade curriculum, the worksheets and practice tests are designed to prepare your students for the language expression portions of standardized tests.

Teaching Suggestions for the Worksheets

6-1: Expressing Ideas with Clarity

Begin this activity by discussing with your students the importance of expressing their ideas with clarity and brevity. This is seldom as easy as it sounds, however. Explain that clear expression is dependent upon various factors, including: word usage, subject–verb agreement, consistency with tenses, correct grammatical forms, and even punctuation.

Consider the difference of what a mere comma can do:

Aunt Mary Anne lost her keys.

Aunt Mary, Anne lost her keys.

The comma changes the meaning of the sentence entirely from a statement about Aunt Mary Anne to a statement of direct address to Aunt Mary about Anne.

Explain that brevity is also important to expression. The clutter of unnecessary words and phrases obscures ideas and makes for tedious communication.

For this worksheet, instruct your students to select the word or phrase that best replaces the underlined word or phrase in each sentence and makes the sentence clear. Note that some sentences may already be expressed clearly. For these sentences, your students should mark "no mistake." When your students are done, go over the worksheets and discuss any sentences they found to be confusing.

6-2: Organizing Sentences Clearly I

Start this exercise by emphasizing the importance of clear expression to written and spoken communication. Without clear expression, ideas may become lost in a muddle of poorly organized constructions. Only through clear expression can ideas be shared effectively.

For this worksheet, your students are given sets of four sentences from which they are to select the sentence that expresses the idea most clearly. Caution them to pay close attention to word order and weak constructions. Upon completion of the activity, correct their work and discuss any sentences that proved to be troublesome.

6-3: Organizing Sentences Clearly II

This worksheet is similar to Worksheet 6-2 and provides more practice in recognizing well-constructed sentences. Note that students are given sets of four sentences from which they are to select the sentence that expresses the idea clearly. Remind them to read each sentence carefully before selecting their answer.

When they are finished with the exercise, correct their work and discuss any sentences that your students found confusing.

6-4: Rewriting Sentences Clearly I

Begin this activity by explaining that most sentences should be written (or spoken) in the active voice. Most also should be written in chronological progression—what happens first should come first, what happens next should come next, and so on. (There are exceptions to these suggestions, of course, but for most students they are practical guidelines.)

Offer these examples on an overhead projector or the board:

The letter was received by Tom. (passive voice)

Tom received the letter. (active voice)

Note that the second sentence uses the stronger verb "received," is more direct, and is more concise.

Next offer these examples.

We went to the movies after dinner, and did our homework before dinner. (out of order)

We did our homework, ate dinner, and went to the movies. (better order)

Note that although the first sentence expresses the idea, the second sentence does so more clearly.

Instruct your students to rewrite the sentences on the worksheet so that each expresses an idea clearly. When your students are finished, go over the sentences. Ask for volunteers to read their sentences to the class. Mention that some sentences may be rewritten clearly in more than one way.

6-5: Rewriting Sentences Clearly II

This activity is similar to Worksheet 6-4. Begin by reviewing the importance of clear expression. Without clear expression, ideas are unlikely to be communicated effectively. Note that the sentences on the worksheet are unclear because words and phrases are out of order.

For this activity, your students are to rewrite sentences so that each expresses an idea clearly. After they have finished the worksheet, go over their sentences and ask volunteers to read their rewritten sentences to the class. Mention that some sentences may be rewritten clearly in more than one way.

6-6: Combining Sentences and Expressing Ideas Clearly

Begin this exercise by explaining that sometimes two sentences can be combined to express ideas. The combined sentences may express ideas more smoothly than the separate sentences. Note that combining sentences may also eliminate words, making the expression of ideas more concise.

For this activity, your students are to combine pairs of sentences. Point out that for some pairs they may need to add or delete words to make the combined sentence smooth and clear. Upon completion of the worksheet, go over the rewritten sentences and ask volunteers to read examples of their sentences to the class.

6-7: Understanding Topic Sentences I

Start this activity by explaining that well-written paragraphs contain a topic sentence that introduces the subject of the paragraph. The rest of the paragraph adds details to and explains the idea expressed in the topic sentence.

For this worksheet, your students are to read each paragraph and select the best topic sentence. Caution them to read the paragraphs and choices carefully before selecting their answers. When your students have finished, correct their work and discuss any paragraphs they found confusing.

6-8: Understanding Topic Sentences II

This activity is similar to Worksheet 6-7 and provides more practice with topic sentences. Begin by reviewing that a topic sentence is essentially what a paragraph is about. The remainder of the material in the paragraph provides information that explains the idea contained in the topic sentence.

Instruct your students to read each paragraph and the possible topic sentences that follow. Caution them to choose the topic sentence that best leads into the details of the paragraph. Upon completion of the worksheet, correct their answers and discuss any paragraphs your students found difficult.

6-9: Understanding Paragraphs I

Begin this exercise by discussing that a well-constructed paragraph has a topic sentence, details that explain the topic, and a concluding sentence that makes a final point about the topic. Solid paragraphs demonstrate unity of topic and details.

For this worksheet, your students are to read the paragraph and answer the questions that follow. Note that the numbers before the sentences of the paragraph are necessary for the second question. Once your students have finished the worksheet, correct their answers and discuss any questions they may have.

6-10: Understanding Paragraphs II

This activity is similar to Worksheet 6-9 and provides students with more practice with paragraphs. Begin by reviewing that a well-written paragraph contains a topic sentence, sentences containing details that explain the topic, and a concluding sentence that offers a final point about the topic.

Instruct your students to read the paragraph and answer the questions that follow. Encourage them to read carefully and note how the details logically develop the topic. Upon completion, correct the worksheets and answer any questions your students may have.

6-11: Organizing Paragraphs I

Start this exercise by explaining that paragraphs must be organized logically if they are to communicate information clearly. You may find it helpful to review Study Sheet 6-B, "Steps to Clear Expression," with your students. Emphasize that well-organized information is easier to understand than information that is organized in an inconsistent or confusing manner.

For this worksheet, your students are given several sentences that, when organized properly, build into an organized paragraph that expresses information clearly. Suggest that your students write a draft of the paragraph first, which they can revise before writing a final copy. Upon completion of the worksheet, go over the paragraphs and answer any questions your students may have.

6-12: Organizing Paragraphs II

This worksheet is similar to Worksheet 6-11. Start the activity by discussing the importance of organizing paragraphs so that they express ideas clearly. You might review that a good paragraph contains a topic sentence, details, and a concluding sentence. You might also find it helpful to review Study Sheet 6-B.

Instruct your students to organize the sentences on the worksheet into a paragraph. Suggest that they write a draft first and revise until they construct a paragraph that expresses ideas clearly. When your students are done, go over the paragraphs and answer any questions they may have.

6-13: Completing Paragraphs I

Begin this exercise by explaining that supporting details are an essential part of paragraphs. Without clear details, ideas lose focus.

For this worksheet, your students are to read paragraphs, which are incomplete. They are then to select the sentence that fits in the blank and best completes the paragraph. After they have finished the worksheet, correct their answers and discuss any problems they might have had in completing the paragraph.

6-14: Completing Paragraphs II

This activity is similar to Worksheet 6-13. Start by discussing that every sentence in a paragraph should be needed. Each sentence should advance and express the ideas contained in the paragraph as a whole. Unnecessary words or phrases should be avoided.

Instruct your students to read the paragraphs carefully, concentrating on the idea or scene the paragraph describes. They are then to select the sentence that fits in the blank and best completes the paragraph. Upon completion of the worksheet, go over the answers with your students and discuss any paragraph with which they had trouble.

6-15: Understanding Supporting Details

Begin this exercise by explaining that the details of a paragraph must support the topic sentence of the paragraph. Emphasize that all parts of a paragraph must build to a whole.

For this worksheet, your students are to select the details that best support the topic sentence. Caution them to read the details closely and choose ones that best support the topic sentence and make a clear, effective paragraph. Upon completion of the activity, correct the work of your students and answer any questions they may have.

Language Expression Practice Tests I and II

You may assign either or both of these practice tests. Test I concentrates on expressing ideas clearly and combining sentences. Test II focuses on topic sentences, organization of paragraphs, and supporting details. Using the Answer Sheets with these tests will give your students practice in marking answers on the answer sheets of standardized tests.

Answer Key for Section 6

6-1. **1.** B **2.** A **3.** B **4.** C **5.** D **6.** C **7.** B **8.** A **9.** D **10.** B

6-2. **1.** D **2.** C **3.** A **4.** B **5.** A **6.** D **7.** C

6-3. **1.** C **2.** D **3.** A **4.** B **5.** A **6.** B **7.** C

6-4. Answers may vary; possible answers include the following. **1.** Last night my family went out to an Italian restaurant for dinner. **2.** Erin planned to do her biology homework first, then her algebra, and finally her history. **3.** The class concluded their study of Shakespeare by performing parts of his plays. **4.** Sitting on the back porch on pleasant summer evenings, Talia enjoyed listening to music. **5.** Hoping to get the best buy for his money, John compared the features and prices of several stereo systems. **6.** Melissa enjoyed giving presents more than receiving them. **7.** Tara searched the entire neighborhood in hopes of finding her lost dog. **8.** After school Kevin had band practice, a dentist appointment, and a volleyball game. **9.** At the first sound of thunder in the distance, the coach called the soccer team off the field. **10.** He misses his uncle and aunt who moved to Florida last year.

6-5. Answers may vary; possible answers include the following. **1.** Kathy met several of her friends at the roller rink on Friday night. **2.** Getting a squirrel out of an attic can be a daunting adventure. **3.** It was clear to the scientists that pollution was causing the deaths of trees in the forest. **4.** As her father handed her the puppy for her birthday, the little girl's face brightened with happiness. **5.** Cheryl decided that the best way to clean her room was to start at the door and work her way inside. **6.** Not feeling well after he came home from school, Casey went right to bed. **7.** The man looked at the flat tire on his car in dismay, because he did not have a spare. **8.** Looking at the traffic tie-up ahead, Lauren worried that they would not arrive at the concert on time. **9.** A man who traveled widely, Uncle Bill had interesting stories to tell. **10.** Nan watched the shooting star streaking overhead, knowing it was a meteor and not a star at all.

6-6. Answers may vary; possible answers include the following. **1.** The girls hoped that their soccer game would not be postponed, but the heavy rain and thunderstorms almost guaranteed postponement. **2.** Liz's favorite ways to relax are listening to music and watching classic movies on TV. **3.** Jeff enjoys surfing at the shore, while Peter enjoys surfing the Internet. **4.** The snowstorm made many roads impassable, and the governor called a state of emergency. **5.** Tired of the cold weather, Hailey was anxious for spring to arrive. **6.** Sandra loves playing the violin, and her ambition is to play the violin professionally someday. **7.** The hawk circled the field, his eyes searching for prey below. **8.** Mario reviewed the notes and decided that he needed to find more information before he began writing his report. **9.** Watching the rain, Mandy figured it was a good day to catch up on her reading and sleep. **10.** Rudy waited nervously for the mail, hoping his application to the state orchestra would be accepted.

6-7. **1.** C **2.** A **3.** D

6-8. **1.** A **2.** C **3.** D

6-9. **1.** B **2.** C **3.** D

6-10. **1.** C **2.** D **3.** A

6-11. Paragraphs may vary slightly; a possible paragraph follows.

Censorship is the attempt by a person, a group, or a governmental body to prevent others from reading, writing, speaking, seeing, or hearing ideas that the censors believe are dangerous in some way. Censorship takes many forms. The banning of books, speeches, TV shows, movies, or works of art are common examples of censorship. Every nation has groups that would censor ideas. Those who practice censorship usually feel that by their acts they are protecting others from information that can cause harm. Although most democracies have laws protecting free speech, ideas must always be protected from censorship.

6-12. Paragraphs may vary slightly; a possible paragraph follows.

Understanding how to prepare for a major test is an important factor in attaining high scores. Most important, you need to be familiar with the material on which you will be tested. This will probably require some study or review before the test. Being familiar with the material will help to boost your confidence and help you to avoid obvious mistakes. On the night before the test, you should get a full night's sleep. The next morning, a good breakfast is essential. Together, being rested and having eaten a good breakfast will help to ensure that you are mentally alert. People who prepare properly for tests usually achieve higher scores than those who take tests unprepared.

6-13. **1.** B **2.** A **3.** D

6-14. **1.** D **2.** B **3.** C

6-15. **1.** B **2.** D **3.** C

Study Sheet 6-A

A Proofreading Guide for Language Expression

Answering the following questions can help you express your ideas.

1. Does each sentence express an idea clearly?
2. Does each paragraph express my thoughts clearly?
3. Does each paragraph start with a topic sentence that leads smoothly into the information that follows?
4. Does each paragraph end with a concluding sentence that sums up the paragraph or adds an important final point?
5. Are my main ideas supported with details?
6. Have I used words correctly?
7. Have I eliminated unnecessary words and ideas?
8. Have I avoided using intensifiers such as “really,” “very,” and “so”?
9. Have I avoided using qualifiers such as “sort of,” “kind of,” and “a bit”?
10. Have I used active constructions *(I sent the letter.)* rather than passive constructions *(The letter was sent by me.)*?
11. Have I used smooth transitions?
12. Have I used strong similes and metaphors for comparisons?
13. Do my subjects and predicates agree?
14. Have I used consistent verb tenses?
15. Do my words say exactly what I want to say?

© 2002 by John Wiley & Sons, Inc.

Study Sheet 6-B

Steps to Clear Expression

The following steps can help you to organize your ideas and express your thoughts clearly.

1. Focus your topic. Make it clear in your mind.
2. Think about what you want to write or say. If you need information, do research.
   - Brainstorm and try to generate as many ideas as possible.
   - Consult with other people about your topic. Others may be able to suggest ideas that you haven't considered.
   - Create a list of questions about your topic. Use the 5 W's—*who, what, where, when,* and *why*—and *how* to guide you in your research.
   - Check a variety of resources for information, including books, magazines, and the Internet.
3. Consider your audience. For example, information designed for classmates will require a different presentation from information designed for adults.
4. Build your ideas in logical steps. There are several ways you can share your ideas.
   - List your ideas from the most important to the least important.
   - List your ideas from the least important to the most important.
   - List your ideas according to time. What happens first comes first, what happens second comes second, and so on.
   - List your ideas according to a special order, such as spatial relationships in which ideas are arranged from left to right or top to bottom.
5. Make a simple outline of your ideas.
6. Stick to your topic. Do not drift onto other topics.
7. Use examples, diagrams, and pictures whenever possible to help show what you want to express.
8. Review your ideas and make sure all of them are clear.

© 2002 by John Wiley & Sons, Inc.

Name ______________________________ Date ________________

6-1

Expressing Ideas with Clarity

Directions: Read each sentence and decide if the underlined word or phrase is used correctly. If the underlined word or phrase is used incorrectly, place a check before the word or phrase that best replaces it. If the underlined word or phrase is used correctly, place a check before "no mistake."

1. Mrs. Barnett has teached American history for many years.

   A. ____ had teached C. ____ teaches

   B. ____ has taught D. ____ (no mistake)

2. Everyone stood and applauded now that the concert ended.

   A. ____ as C. ____ but

   B. ____ during that time D. ____ (no mistake)

3. The moment Sarah stepped onto the ice she felt her skates slipped out from under her.

   A. ____ has slipping C. ____ now slip

   B. ____ slip D. ____ (no mistake)

4. The competition at the piano contest was the most intensest Cory had ever experienced.

   A. ____ more intense C. ____ most intense

   B. ____ intenser D. ____ (no mistake)

5. We are having a history test tomorrow.

   A. ____ had C. ____ will having

   B. ____ have had D. ____ (no mistake)

© 2002 by John Wiley & Sons, Inc.

Name ______________________________ Date ______________

6-1

Expressing Ideas with Clarity *(continued)*

6. Now that Dad returned from his trip to Europe, he had gifts for everyone in the family.

   A. ____ Soon when C. ____ When

   B. ____ In the time D. ____ (no mistake)

7. Maria likes dancing, and she likes singing better.

   A. ____ or C. ____ or, however

   B. ____ but D. ____ (no mistake)

8. As soon the storm passed, the sun's rays poked through the clouds.

   A. ____ After C. ____ Whenever

   B. ____ Now that D. ____ (no mistake)

9. Having never tried an "advanced" ski hill, Deanna looked down the slope with a mix of fear and excitement.

   A. ____ have looked C. ____ will looked

   B. ____ has been looking D. ____ (no mistake)

10. Sean has recovered from the flu and was feeling well.

    A. ____ had felt C. ____ felt

    B. ____ is feeling D. ____ (no mistake)

© 2002 by John Wiley & Sons, Inc.

Name ______________________________ Date ________________

6-2

Organizing Sentences Clearly I

Directions: For each group of four sentences, place a check before the sentence that expresses the idea most clearly.

1. A. ____ We plan visiting the countries of Western Europe to spend our vacation.
   B. ____ To spend our vacation we plan visiting the countries of Western Europe.
   C. ____ Visiting the countries of Western Europe, we plan to spend our vacation.
   D. ____ We plan to spend our vacation visiting the countries of Western Europe.

2. A. ____ The actors and actresses were amateurs, although they provided a great performance.
   B. ____ They provided a great performance, although the actors and actresses were amateurs.
   C. ____ Although the actors and actresses were amateurs, they provided a great performance.
   D. ____ They were amateurs, although the actors and actresses provided a great performance.

3. A. ____ Remodeling their house proved to be a bigger project than the Turners had estimated.
   B. ____ The Turners had estimated remodeling their house proved to be a bigger project.
   C. ____ Remodeling their house than the Turners had estimated proved to be a bigger project.
   D. ____ A bigger project than remodeling their house proved to be, the Turners had estimated.

4. A. ____ Gusting out of the north, Rachel convinced the cold wind that winter had arrived.
   B. ____ The cold wind gusting out of the north convinced Rachel that winter had arrived.
   C. ____ Rachel convinced that winter had arrived, the cold wind gusting out of the north.
   D. ____ Out of the north the cold gusting wind that convinced Rachel winter had arrived.

© 2002 by John Wiley & Sons, Inc.

Name ______________________________ Date ________________

6-2

Organizing Sentences Clearly I *(continued)*

5. A. ____ Using the powerful telescopes at the observatory, astronomers could study distant stars.
   B. ____ At the observatory, astronomers, using powerful telescopes, could study distant stars.
   C. ____ Using the observatory, astronomers at powerful telescopes could study distant stars.
   D. ____ Astronomers could study distant stars at the observatory using powerful telescopes.

6. A. ____ A balanced diet, according to many doctors, and good health are the keys to regular exercise.
   B. ____ The keys are, to good health, according to many doctors, a balanced diet and regular exercise.
   C. ____ According to many doctors, good health, the keys are a balanced diet and regular exercise.
   D. ____ According to many doctors, a balanced diet and regular exercise are the keys to good health.

7. A. ____ She began studying, as soon as Melissa got home from school, for her history test.
   B. ____ As soon as Melissa began studying for her history test, she got home from school.
   C. ____ As soon as Melissa got home from school, she began studying for her history test.
   D. ____ Melissa got home from school as soon as she began studying for her history test.

© 2002 by John Wiley & Sons, Inc.

Name ______________________________ Date ________________

6-3

Organizing Sentences Clearly II

Directions: For each group of four sentences, place a check before the sentence that expresses the idea most clearly.

1. A. ____ Alan's ankle is fully healed, but now it took six weeks nearly.
   B. ____ Alan's ankle took nearly six weeks, but it is fully healed now.
   C. ____ It took nearly six weeks, but now Alan's ankle is fully healed.
   D. ____ Fully healed now, but it took Alan's ankle nearly six weeks.

2. A. ____ Because she could swim in her pool almost every day, Jamie liked summer, of all the seasons, best.
   B. ____ Jamie, of all the seasons, because almost every day she could swim in her pool, liked summer best.
   C. ____ Almost every day Jamie could swim in her pool because in summer, the seasons of all she liked best.
   D. ____ Of all the seasons, Jamie liked summer best because she could swim in her pool almost every day.

3. A. ____ Afraid of missing his morning bus, Dan dashed out of his house without having breakfast.
   B. ____ Dan dashed out of his house, afraid of missing his morning bus, without having breakfast.
   C. ____ Without having breakfast, Dan, afraid of missing his morning bus, dashed out of his house.
   D. ____ Missing his morning bus, Dan dashed out of his house afraid, without having breakfast.

4. A. ____ Tina sighed and sat down, looking at the pile of books on her desk to start her homework.
   B. ____ Looking at the pile of books on her desk, Tina sighed and sat down to start her homework.
   C. ____ Tina sighed, looking at the pile of books on her desk, and sat down to start her homework.
   D. ____ The pile of books on her desk, Tina, looking, sighed and sat down to start her homework.

© 2002 by John Wiley & Sons, Inc.

Name ______________________________ Date ______________

6-3

Organizing Sentences Clearly II *(continued)*

5. A. ____ In the weeks leading up to the dance recital, Jennifer practiced every day.

   B. ____ Leading up to the dance recital, Jennifer practiced every day in the weeks.

   C. ____ In the weeks, Jennifer practiced every day, leading up to the dance recital.

   D. ____ In the weeks leading up to the dance recital, Jennifer, every day, practiced.

6. A. ____ To think of an introduction for his report, after reviewing his notes one last time, Derek tried.

   B. ____ After reviewing his notes one last time, Derek tried to think of an introduction for his report.

   C. ____ Derek tried to think, after reviewing his notes one last time, of an introduction for his report.

   D. ____ After Derek, reviewing his notes one last time, tried to think of an introduction for his report.

7. A. ____ In the class, everyone looked forward to the annual spring dance, which was only two weeks away.

   B. ____ Everyone looked forward to the annual spring dance, in the class, which was only two weeks away.

   C. ____ Everyone in the class looked forward to the annual spring dance, which was only two weeks away.

   D. ____ Only two weeks away, everyone which was in the class looked forward to the annual spring dance.

© 2002 by John Wiley & Sons, Inc.

Name ______________________________ Date ________________

6-4

Rewriting Sentences Clearly I

Directions: Rewrite each sentence so that it expresses an idea clearly.

1. To an Italian restaurant last night, my family went out for dinner. ______________

2. Erin planned her biology homework to do first, finally her history, and then her algebra. ______________

3. By performing parts of his plays, the class, their study of Shakespeare concluded.

4. Sitting on the back porch, Talia, on pleasant summer evenings, enjoyed listening to music. ______________

5. For his money, John, hoping to get the best buy, compared the features and prices of several stereo systems. ______________

© 2002 by John Wiley & Sons, Inc.

Name ______________________________ Date ______________

6-4

Rewriting Sentences Clearly I *(continued)*

6. Melissa enjoyed presents, giving them more than receiving. ______________

7. In hopes, Tara, of finding her lost dog, searched the entire neighborhood. ______________

8. Band practice, a dentist appointment, and a volleyball game, Kevin had after school. ______________

9. In the distance, off the field, at the first sound of thunder, the coach called the soccer team. ______________

10. Last year he misses his uncle and aunt who moved to Florida. ______________

© 2002 by John Wiley & Sons, Inc.

Name ______________________________ Date ______________

6-5

Rewriting Sentences Clearly II

Directions: Rewrite each sentence so that it expresses an idea clearly.

1. At the roller rink, Kathy, on Friday night, met several of her friends. ______________________________

2. A daunting adventure getting a squirrel out of an attic can be. ______________________________

3. In the forest, that pollution was causing the deaths of trees, it was clear to the scientists. ______________________________

4. For her birthday, the little girl's face, as her father handed her the puppy, brightened with happiness. ______________________________

5. That to start at the door, Cheryl decided, and work her way inside was the best way to clean her room. ______________________________

© 2002 by John Wiley & Sons, Inc.

Name ________________________ Date ______________

6-5

Rewriting Sentences Clearly II *(continued)*

6. Casey, not feeling well, right after he came home from school, went to bed. ______

____

____

7. In dismay, the man, because he did not have a spare, looked at the flat tire on his car. ______

____

____

8. That they would not arrive at the concert on time, Lauren worried, looking at the traffic tie-up ahead. ______

____

____

9. Uncle Bill had interesting stories to tell, a man who traveled widely. ______

____

____

10. Not a star at all, Nan watched the shooting star streaking overhead, and knowing it was a meteor. ______

____

____

© 2002 by John Wiley & Sons, Inc.

Name ________________________________ Date ____________________

6-6

Combining Sentences and Expressing Ideas Clearly

Directions: Use another sheet of paper to combine and rewrite each pair of sentences. Make sure each new sentence expresses an idea clearly. (You may need to add or delete words for some sentences.)

1. The girls hoped that their soccer game would not be postponed.
   The heavy rain and thunderstorms almost guaranteed postponement.

2. One of Liz's favorite ways to relax is listening to music.
   Another one of Liz's favorite ways to relax is watching classic movies on TV.

3. Jeff enjoys surfing at the shore.
   Peter enjoys surfing the Internet.

4. The snowstorm made many roads impassable.
   The governor called a state of emergency.

5. Hailey was anxious for spring to arrive.
   Hailey was tired of the cold weather.

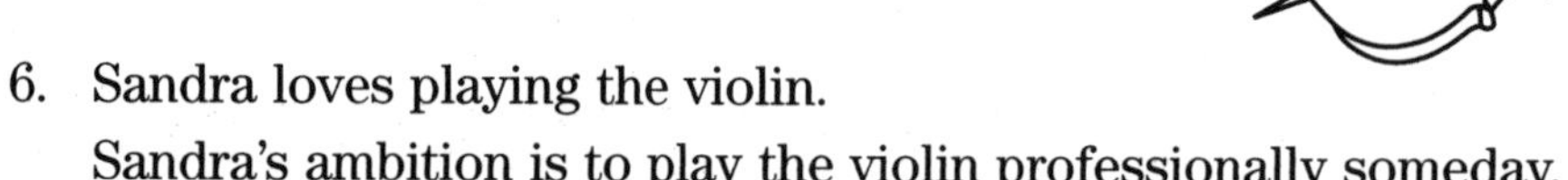

6. Sandra loves playing the violin.
   Sandra's ambition is to play the violin professionally someday.

7. The hawk circled the field.
   The hawk's eyes searched for prey below.

8. Mario reviewed the notes for his report.
   Mario decided that he needed to find more information before he began writing his report.

9. Watching the rain, Mandy figured it was a good day to catch up on her reading.
   Mandy decided to catch up on her sleep, too.

10. Rudy waited nervously for the mail.
    Rudy hoped his application to the state orchestra would be accepted.

© 2002 by John Wiley & Sons, Inc.

Name ______________________________ Date ________________

6-7

Understanding Topic Sentences I

Directions: Place a check before the best topic sentence for each paragraph.

1. ________________. It is believed that British soldiers stationed in Canada were among the first to play the game. In 1879, students at McGill University in Montreal established rules for the game, which had already achieved widespread popularity. By the late 1880s, Canada was home to several amateur hockey clubs and leagues.

   A. ☐ Ice hockey is a great game filled with action.
   B. ☐ Today ice hockey is popular in many countries in North America and Europe.
   C. ☐ The beginnings of modern ice hockey can be traced to the mid 19th century.
   D. ☐ Wayne Gretzky is considered to be one of the finest hockey players of all time.

2. ________________. During cold weather, when rain falls through a layer of very cold air close to the ground, the raindrops will begin to freeze. Since most of the raindrops do not freeze completely, sleet is usually accompanied by snow or rain. Like snow and freezing rain, sleet can make travel slow and hazardous.

   A. ☐ Sleet is a form of precipitation best described as partially frozen rain.
   B. ☐ Nobody likes sleet, which consists of partially frozen rain that falls to the ground.
   C. ☐ Sleet occurs in cold weather.
   D. ☐ Sleet can result in slippery road conditions, and drivers must proceed with caution.

3. ________________. According to the report, a line of severe thunderstorms was heading straight for them. Some of the storms could spawn tornadoes. Although she could not see any tornadoes heading their way when she looked out the window, Sara ordered her younger brother and sister into the basement. It was better to be safe than sorry.

   A. ☐ Sara was baby-sitting her younger brother and sister until their mother returned from shopping.
   B. ☐ Sara was alarmed at the weather bulletin and began to panic.
   C. ☐ Sara was worried because she knew that tornadoes could cause great destruction.
   D. ☐ Listening to the weather bulletin, Sara became instantly alert.

© 2002 by John Wiley & Sons, Inc.

Name ______________________________ Date ________________

6-8

Understanding Topic Sentences II

Directions: Place a check before the best topic sentence for each paragraph.

1. ______________. As Meg looked out her window that morning at the blanket of snow, she felt a rush of excitement. So far this winter had offered only flurries, and she had not even bothered to wax her skis. But now the whole valley was covered with fine powder. She could hardly wait to hit the slopes.

   A. ☐ It had snowed all night.

   B. ☐ Meg liked winter sports, especially ice-skating and skiing.

   C. ☐ Meg knew there would be no school today.

   D. ☐ It was a cold, wintry day.

© 2002 by John Wiley & Sons, Inc.

2. ______________. Although most puppies like to please their new masters, they also are playful, curious, and have a mind of their own. Some can be downright stubborn. A gentle, but steady hand is needed throughout the training period. A puppy that is given the proper training will grow up to be a well-mannered dog.

   A. ☐ Owning a puppy is a major responsibility.

   B. ☐ Puppies are a lot of fun and also a lot of work.

   C. ☐ Training a puppy requires patience and firmness.

   D. ☐ Most people who like animals will like owning a puppy.

3. ______________. Many people feel that there is not enough time in the day for them to do all of the things they must do. For these people, planning their day can enable them to manage time better. Even a simple schedule that lists events and their times can be helpful.

   A. ☐ Some people wake up too late in the morning, and then they don't have enough time.

   B. ☐ Most people are always in a rush.

   C. ☐ Most people find it beneficial to have a wristwatch.

   D. ☐ Time management is an important life skill.

Name ______________________________ Date ________________

6-9

Understanding Paragraphs I

Directions: Read the paragraph. Place a check before the answer of each question that follows.

[1]This process is commonly referred to as *global warming.* [2]To understand global warming, think of the Earth as being a giant greenhouse. [3]Just as the glass of a greenhouse traps the heat of the sun, making the interior warm, the Earth's atmosphere also traps the sun's heat. [4]Global warming can have disastrous effects on weather patterns, leading to crop damage. [5]Normally enough heat is trapped to keep the Earth's average temperature at around 58° F. [6]The burning of fossil fuels, however, releases gases such as carbon dioxide, which accumulate in the atmosphere and trap more of the sun's heat. [7]This raises the overall temperature of the Earth.

© 2002 by John Wiley & Sons, Inc.

1. What is the best first sentence for this paragraph?

   A. ☐ Many scientists are worried about what is happening to the temperature of the Earth.

   B. ☐ Many scientists believe that the Earth is getting warmer, and that the burning of fossil fuels is a major cause.

   C. ☐ The Earth is like a greenhouse that is out of control.

   D. ☐ It is getting hotter outside, and everyone needs to be concerned.

2. Which sentence does not belong in the paragraph?

   A. ☐ Sentence 2

   B. ☐ Sentence 3

   C. ☐ Sentence 4

   D. ☐ Sentence 5

3. Which sentence is the best concluding sentence for the paragraph?

   A. ☐ All nations of the world must unite in their efforts to stop global warming, which, if it becomes out of control, is likely to lead to major environmental changes.

   B. ☐ Global warming should be of concern to everyone, because it affects everyone.

   C. ☐ No one can predict the future of the Earth.

   D. ☐ Scientists continue to study global warming, hoping to gain a better understanding of the factors that affect the temperature of the Earth.

Name ______________________________ Date ________________

6-10

Understanding Paragraphs II

Directions: Read the paragraph. Place a check before the answer to each question that follows.

> [1] Although dreaming has been the subject of significant scientific study, the reason people dream has not been fully explained. [2] Still, much has been learned about dreaming. [3] Studies show that most dreaming occurs during REM sleep (rapid-eye-movement sleep). [4] This type of sleep is characterized by eye movement under closed lids and an increase in brain activity. [5] The typical individual has three or four periods of REM sleep each night in which dreams may occur, though he or she may not remember the dreams. [6] Nightmares are frightening dreams. [7] Dreams often include sharp images and may be accompanied by sensations of sound, smell, touch, and taste. [8] Most dreams contain emotion, which can be intense.

1. Which is the best first sentence for the paragraph?

   A. ☐ Dreams that occur when a person is awake are called daydreams.
   B. ☐ It is believed that most mammals dream.
   C. ☐ Dreaming is a form of mental activity that occurs during sleep.
   D. ☐ Nightmares can be so terrifying that they wake a person from a deep sleep.

2. Which sentence does not belong in the paragraph?

   A. ☐ Sentence 3
   B. ☐ Sentence 4
   C. ☐ Sentence 5
   D. ☐ Sentence 6

3. Which sentence is the best concluding sentence for the paragraph?

   A. ☐ Many researchers believe that dreams express the thoughts, fears, and worries of the dreamer.
   B. ☐ Dreams can be confusing.
   C. ☐ In ancient times, many people believed that dreams could foretell the future and they would plan their lives according to their dreams.
   D. ☐ Some people claim to remember all of their dreams in great detail.

© 2002 by John Wiley & Sons, Inc.

Name ______________________________ Date ________________

6-11

Organizing Paragraphs I

Directions: The sentences below belong to a paragraph. The sentences are out of order. Organize the sentences and write the paragraph so that it expresses ideas clearly.

The banning of books, speeches, TV shows, movies, or works of art are common examples of censorship.

Censorship takes many forms.

Censorship is the attempt by a person, a group, or a governmental body to prevent others from reading, writing, speaking, seeing, or hearing ideas that the censors believe are dangerous in some way.

Every nation has groups that would censor ideas.

Although most democracies have laws protecting free speech, ideas must always be protected from censorship.

Those who practice censorship usually feel that by their acts they are protecting others from information that can cause harm.

© 2002 by John Wiley & Sons, Inc.

____

____

____

____

____

____

____

____

____

Continue on the back of this sheet.

Name ______________________ Date ______________

6-12

Organizing Paragraphs II

Directions: The sentences below belong to a paragraph. The sentences are out of order. Organize the sentences and write the paragraph so that it expresses ideas clearly.

On the night before the test you should get a full night's sleep.

Most important, you need to be familiar with the material on which you will be tested.

The next morning, a good breakfast is essential.

Understanding how to prepare for a major test is an important factor in attaining high scores.

People who prepare properly for tests usually achieve higher scores than those who take tests unprepared.

This will probably require some study or review before the test.

Together, being rested and having eaten a good breakfast will help to ensure that you are mentally alert.

Being familiar with the material will help to boost your confidence and help you to avoid obvious mistakes.

____

____

____

____

____

____

Continue on the back of this sheet.

© 2002 by John Wiley & Sons, Inc.

Name ______________________________ Date ________________

6-13

Completing Paragraphs I

Directions: Place a check before the sentence that best completes the blank in the paragraph.

1. Shawna loves animals and her goal is to become a veterinarian someday. As a means of gaining experience, each Saturday she works in a local animal hospital. ______________. Since she has been working at the animal hospital, she has become more convinced than ever before that she would like to be a veterinarian.

   A. ☐ The work has turned out to be much harder than she thought it would be.

   B. ☐ She finds the work to be important and satisfying.

   C. ☐ She has to report to work at 9 A.M.

   D. ☐ Somedays Shawna does not feel like going to work, but she realizes she has made an important commitment.

2. George sighed, frowned, and shook his head. He had misplaced his car keys again. He did not have time to look, because he was already late for school. Suddenly, he smiled. ______________. Relief washed over him until he opened the drawer where the duplicate keys were supposed to be and found them to be missing, too.

   A. ☐ He would take the duplicate set of keys.

   B. ☐ He would call a friend for a ride.

   C. ☐ He would ask to borrow his mother's car.

   D. ☐ He would ask his mother what to do.

3. Herman looked down the slope. He considered himself to be a good skier, but he had never tried an expert hill like this one. Its steep angle, dips, and turns were scary. But there was always a first time for everything. ______________. Bending his knees and tucking his ski poles under his arms, Herman felt a rush of exhilaration as he sped downward.

   A. ☐ He stood there, paralyzed with fear.

   B. ☐ He hesitated, wondering if he should walk back down the hill.

   C. ☐ He saw himself in a hospital bed with several broken bones.

   D. ☐ He took a deep breath and pushed off.

© 2002 by John Wiley & Sons, Inc.

Name ______________________________ Date ________________

6-14

Completing Paragraphs II

Directions: Place a check before the sentence that best completes the blank in the paragraph.

1. Kelly always became nervous when speaking in front of others. As she waited to present her part of her group's project on the Civil War, she felt her palms getting sweaty. She remembered the sound advice her father had given her. ______________. When Kelly's turn came, she took a deep breath and stepped forward confidently.

   A. ☐ If you feel uncomfortable, let someone else present your part of the project.

   B. ☐ Don't go to school on the day of the presentation.

   C. ☐ Tell your teacher you are nervous and that you won't do the presentation.

   D. ☐ Take a deep breath, focus on your material, and speak to the audience.

2. The playful puppy did not realize that the old cat was in a disagreeable mood. As the cat was sunning himself on the floor of the porch, the pup pranced up to him. Stopping a few inches away, the pup crouched down and let out the meanest growl he could muster. ______________. Realizing that the cat did not want to play, the pup wisely backed up and turned his attention to safer amusements.

   A. ☐ The cat purred leisurely.

   B. ☐ The cat's sudden hiss, spit, and arched back surprised him.

   C. ☐ Not wanting to play, the cat rose and walked away.

   D. ☐ The cat ignored the pup, who continued to growl in his puppy's voice.

3. When Rodney agreed to clean out Mr. Taylor's garage, he thought his neighbor was being generous with the pay he offered. It was more than Rodney could earn cutting lawns and doing other odd jobs around his neighborhood for the next three months. Rodney figured he would need a day or two to clean the garage. ______________. The garage was filled with so much stuff that Rodney couldn't even step inside.

   A. ☐ Rodney couldn't even open the garage door.

   B. ☐ Rodney figured this would be one of the easiest jobs he ever had.

   C. ☐ That was until he opened the door.

   D. ☐ Rodney liked cleaning garages.

© 2002 by John Wiley & Sons, Inc.

Name ______________________________ Date ________________

6-15

Understanding Supporting Details

Directions: Place a check before the details that best develop each topic sentence.

1. Water is essential to life.

   A. _____ Water covers about 70% of the Earth's surface. Vast amounts of water are contained in the Earth's oceans, of which the Pacific is the largest. The world would not be the same without water.

   B. _____ It makes up 50% to 90% of the weight of plants and animals. Living cells consist mostly of fats, carbohydrates, proteins, salts, and similar substances in a solution of water. Blood in animals and sap in plants also are made up mostly of water.

   C. _____ Just about everyone knows that water is necessary for washing, cooking, and drinking, but not everyone realizes that our bodies are made up mostly of water. Thirst is your body's signal that it needs more water. Drinking plenty of water, eating a balanced diet, and exercising regularly are important factors to good health.

   D. _____ Without water, life as we know it would be impossible on Earth. Scientists believe that the Earth is the only planet in the solar system that has flowing water on its surface. Water is necessary for the functioning of every cell in our bodies.

© 2002 by John Wiley & Sons, Inc.

2. Mt. Everest is the highest mountain in the world.

   A. _____ It is just one of the mountains that make up the Himalayan Mountain range. It is higher than Mt. McKinley in North America, Mt. Aconcagua in South America, or any other mountain. Its peak remains snow-covered throughout the year.

   B. _____ Its summit is so high and the air so thin up there that climbers require oxygen masks. Several people have lost their lives trying to climb Mt. Everest, but others are still drawn by the challenge to scale the highest mountain in the world.

   C. _____ The mountain is named after Sir George Everest, who was the surveyor general of India from 1830–1843. It was in 1841 that Everest recorded the location and height of the mountain that now bears his name. Mt. Everest is a part of the Himalayan Mountain range.

   D. _____ Located in the Himalayan Mountain range in south-central Asia, Everest's peak rises 29,035 feet above sea level. That is nearly six miles above sea level. Everest reaches up through nearly two-thirds of the Earth's atmosphere.

Name ______________________________ Date ________________

6-15

Understanding Supporting Details *(continued)*

3. The size of our galaxy, the Milky Way, is difficult to comprehend.

   A. _____ The Milky Way is our home in space. It is but one of billions of galaxies throughout the universe, which many astronomers consider to be infinite. These astronomers believe that the universe has no end. Over 200 billion stars are located in the Milky Way.

   B. _____ The Milky Way is a spiral galaxy, much like a whirlpool in space. Our sun is but one of an estimated 200 billion stars in the Milky Way. It is located near the edge of one of the spiral arms, quite far from the center. Our sun is an ordinary star, one of the many in the galaxy.

   C. _____ A spiral-shaped galaxy, the Milky Way has a dense central region and several arms that trail off its center. Astronomers estimate that the Milky Way contains about 200 billion stars. The galaxy is about 10,000 light-years in thickness at its center and about 100,000 light-years in diameter. When a person considers that one light-year is about 6 trillion miles, the great size of the Milky Way can be understood.

   D. _____ A spiral-shaped galaxy, the Milky Way contains about 200 billion stars. Some scientists speculate that at least some of these stars harbor conditions necessary for life. It is possible, according to these scientists, that life exists elsewhere in our galaxy. But discovering that life will take a long time, because the Milky Way is so vast and stars (other than our sun) are so far away.

© 2002 by John Wiley & Sons, Inc.

EIGHTH-GRADE LEVEL

Language Expression

PRACTICE TESTS

© 2002 by John Wiley & Sons, Inc.

Language Expression Practice Test I

Part 1. Directions: Choose the best way to write the underlined part of each sentence. Use the Answer Sheet to darken the letter of your choice. If the underlined part of the sentence is correct, mark answer space D, "no mistake."

1. During the time Carl waited for the bus to arrive, he read a chapter of the mystery novel.

   A. In the time
   C. Since
   B. As
   D. (no mistake)

2. Holly likes to ice-skate, and she doesn't like in-line skating.

   A. or
   C. but
   B. despite the fact
   D. (no mistake)

3. The storm dumped several inches of rain on the town, and there is flooding on Main Street yesterday.

   A. had been flooded
   C. has been flooding
   B. was flooding
   D. (no mistake)

4. Having driven through the night, we reached Florida by dawn.

   A. We drove
   C. We were driving
   B. Having had driven
   D. (no mistake)

5. In spite of the fact she searched everywhere, Miranda could not find her history homework.

   A. Although
   C. However
   B. While
   D. (no mistake)

Part 2. Directions: Choose the sentence that expresses an idea most clearly. Use the Answer Sheet to darken the letter of your choice.

© 2002 by John Wiley & Sons, Inc.

Language Expression Practice Test I *(continued)*

1. A. To an area that was still covered with snow from the previous storm, the snowstorm brought several more inches of snow.

   B. The snowstorm brought, to an area that was still covered with snow from the previous storm, several more inches of snow.

   C. The snowstorm brought several more inches of snow to an area that was still covered with snow from the previous storm.

   D. Was still covered with snow from the previous storm, the snowstorm that brought several more inches of snow to an area.

2. A. In the collision with an opposing player, Jason limped off the court, having sprained his ankle.

   B. Having sprained his ankle in the collision with an opposing player, Jason limped off the court.

   C. Jason limped off the court in the collision with an opposing player, having sprained his ankle.

   D. Having sprained his ankle, Jason limped off the court, in the collision with an opposing player.

© 2002 by John Wiley & Sons, Inc.

3. A. That the algebra exam was the hardest test she had ever taken, Kirsten was convinced, and she hoped she passed.

   B. She hoped that she passed, Kirsten was convinced that the algebra exam was the hardest test she had ever taken.

   C. Convinced, Kirsten was, that the algebra exam was the hardest test she had ever taken, and she hoped she passed.

   D. Kirsten was convinced that the algebra exam was the hardest test she had ever taken, and she hoped she passed.

4. A. Since he is a vegetarian, George carefully plans his meals to make sure his diet is balanced.

   B. To make sure his diet is balanced, George carefully plans his meals, since he is a vegetarian.

   C. George carefully plans his meals, since he is a vegetarian, to make sure his diet is balanced.

   D. Carefully George plans his meals to make sure his diet is balanced, since he is a vegetarian.

5. A. Working Saturday and Sunday afternoons in her father's store, and between school, Grace did not have much time for her friends.

   B. Between school and in her father's store, working Saturday and Sunday afternoons Grace did not have much time for her friends.

   C. Between school and working in her father's store Saturday and Sunday afternoons, Grace did not have much time for her friends.

   D. Grace did not have much time for her friends, between school and, Saturday and Sunday afternoons, working in her father's store.

Part 3. Directions: Choose the sentence that combines the two sentences and expresses the idea most clearly. Use the Answer Sheet to darken the letter of your choice.

1. Having gotten home late from soccer practice, Teresa had dinner.
   After dinner Teresa started her homework.

   A. Teresa had dinner and started her homework, after having gotten home late from soccer practice.

   B. Teresa, having gotten home late from soccer practice, started her homework after dinner.

   C. Having gotten home late from soccer practice, Teresa had dinner and started her homework.

   D. After soccer practice, having gotten home late, Teresa had dinner and started her homework.

2. Sara wanted to go to the movies with her friends on Friday night.
   She promised the Carters she would baby-sit for them on Friday night.

   A. Sara wanted to go to the movies with her friends on Friday night, but she promised the Carters she would baby-sit for them.

   B. On Friday night Sara wanted to go to the movies with her friends, but she promised the Carters she would baby-sit for them on Friday night.

   C. Sara, on Friday night, promised the Carters she would baby-sit for them, but she wanted to go to the movies with her friends.

   D. Sara wanted to go, on Friday night, to the movies with her friends, but she promised the Carters she would baby-sit for them.

© 2002 by John Wiley & Sons, Inc.

3. Jimmy missed his old home in Florida.
He disliked the long, cold winters of Maine.

A. Jimmy disliked the long, cold winters of Maine, and Jimmy missed his old home in Florida.

B. Jimmy disliked the long, cold winters of Maine and missed his old home in Florida.

C. Jimmy disliked the long, cold winters of Maine, but he missed his old home in Florida.

D. In Florida, Jimmy missed his old home, and he disliked the long, cold winters of Maine.

4. Each night Mia's cat sleeps at the foot of her bed.
Her dog sleeps at the foot of her bed, too.

A. Each night Mia's cat sleeps at the foot of her bed, and her dog sleeps there, too.

B. Mia's cat and dog, each night, sleep at the foot of her bed.

C. At the foot of her bed, each night Mia's cat and dog sleep.

D. Each night Mia's cat and dog sleep at the foot of her bed.

5. Gillian didn't understand why she had lost ten points on the essay question.
Gillian's teacher explained that she had not answered the question fully.

A. Why she had lost ten points on the essay question, Gillian didn't understand, but her teacher explained that she had not answered the question fully.

B. Gillian didn't understand why she had lost ten points on the essay question until her teacher explained that she had not answered the question fully.

C. Not understanding why she had lost ten points on the essay question, Gillian's teacher explained that she had not answered the question fully.

D. Gillian's teacher explained that she had not answered the question fully, but Gillian didn't understand why she had lost ten points on the essay question.

© 2002 by John Wiley & Sons, Inc.

Language Expression Practice Test II

Part 1. Directions: Choose the best topic sentence for each paragraph. Use the Answer Sheet to darken the letter of your choice.

1. ________________. The president must schedule meetings, call the meetings to order, and see that the operations of the student council are carried out effectively. The president also is responsible for organizing the committees that set up fundraisers, sponsor student council dances, and plan special activities. Most student council presidents quickly realize that being president is a demanding job.

   A. Campaigning to be elected student council president requires time and effort.

   B. Being president of the student council is a major responsibility.

   C. Although many people might like to be a student council president, not everyone is qualified to be.

   D. Becoming a student council president is an excellent achievement.

2. ________________. It is thought that the game originated in India in the 6th century A.D. From there merchants and travelers carried the game along the trade routes to Asia, Persia, and eventually Europe. For many years chess remained a game of royalty and the aristocracy, but by the 18th century the game was played by the general public.

   A. Chess tournaments are found throughout the world.

   B. Chess is a game that relies on strategy, not chance.

   C. Chess can be an extremely competitive and intense game, requiring the utmost of concentration.

   D. Chess is among the oldest and most popular games in the world.

3. ________________. The first fossil evidence of coelacanths appears about 350 million years ago. Because there are few fossils of this fish in later time periods, paleontologists prior to 1938 believed that the coelacanth had been extinct for some 70 million years. In December of 1938, however, a fishing boat off the eastern coast of Africa pulled in a living coelacanth. Since then, other coelacanths have been caught.

   A. Paleontologists are scientists who study fossils and ancient forms of life.

   B. In 1938, fishermen were surprised when they caught a coelacanth.

   C. Scientists can study life of the past through fossils.

   D. The coelacanth is called a living fossil.

© 2002 by John Wiley & Sons, Inc.

4. ________________. The geographic North Pole is located in the central Arctic Ocean, in an area covered by drifting pack ice about 450 miles north of Greenland. Its location experiences six months of complete sunlight followed by six months of complete darkness. The geographic North Pole is about 850 miles from the magnetic North Pole, which is located in the Queen Elizabeth Islands of extreme northern Canada. A compass needle points to the magnetic North Pole.

   A. The Earth's geographic North Pole is not in the same location as the magnetic North Pole.

   B. Understanding the North Poles of the Earth is confusing.

   C. The North Pole of the Earth is in a frozen wasteland, which is difficult to reach.

   D. A compass can help you find the magnetic North Pole.

Part 2. Directions: Read the paragraph and answer the questions. Use the Answer Sheet to darken the letter of your answer.

© 2002 by John Wiley & Sons, Inc.

> [1]Major undersea earthquakes, landslides, or volcanic eruptions can cause tsunamis. [2]A tsunami may travel hundreds or thousands of miles across the ocean at speeds of up to 500 miles per hour. [3]In deep water a tsunami may only be a foot or two high. [4]Tsunamis are sometimes called tidal waves, but they have nothing to do with the tides. [5]When the wave reaches shallow coastal waters, it begins to build and may reach 50 feet or more in height.

1. Which is the best first sentence for the paragraph?

   A. The oceans can spawn dangerous waves.

   B. Tsunamis are powerful and can destroy vast areas of coastline.

   C. A tsunami is a large ocean wave caused by an undersea disturbance.

   D. Some tsunamis are small and are barely noticed.

2. Which sentence does not belong in the paragraph?

   A. Sentence 1

   B. Sentence 2

   C. Sentence 3

   D. Sentence 4

3. Which is the best concluding sentence for the paragraph?

   A. Such tsunamis can cause mass destruction.

   B. When at the shore, a person should always pay attention to the height of the waves.

   C. Once a tsunami has formed, it is impossible to stop.

   D. The only way to survive a tsunami is to reach high ground.

Part 3. Directions: Choose the details that best develop each topic sentence. Use the Answer Sheet to darken the letter of your choice.

1. Next summer the Smiths plan to travel out west.
   A. They will drive from their home in St. Louis to Death Valley. From there they intend to visit Yellowstone National Park, Pike's Peak, and Mount Rushmore. Although they have not worked out a schedule yet, they estimate they will need about a month to complete the trip.
   B. They have never visited the western states, and they are looking forward to their trip. Last year they went to New England, where a highlight of their stay was whale watching. That was the first time they had visited New England.
   C. The Smiths like to visit different parts of the country each year. They have never been out west before. Fortunately, being retired, they can travel whenever they wish.
   D. Mr. Smith has always wanted to see Death Valley, while Mrs. Smith would like to visit Yellowstone National Park. When they were planning their trip, they almost decided to go to Europe instead. They both would like to visit London, Paris, and Rome.

2. Amy's schedule was full for Saturday.
   A. On her way to dance practice, she wondered how she would get everything done. At practice, though, she became involved with her routine and forgot about all she had to do. By the time practice was finished, Amy was tired and figured that what she did not finish today she would do tomorrow.
   B. She did not mind, though. Amy was the kind of person who had a lot of energy and liked to keep busy. She did not like to sit around and be bored.
   C. She had dance practice from 9 to 11 A.M. On the way back from practice, she had to stop at the library to check out books for her science report. After lunch she had to watch her little brother, and after dinner she had to baby-sit for her neighbor. Hopefully, she would have a little time to relax.
   D. One of the first things she had to do was check out books from the library for her science report. The report was due in two weeks, and Amy wanted to start now so that she had a lot of time to finish. She always liked to finish projects in advance.

3. Dan took his position and waited for the sound of the starter's gun to start the race.
   A. He liked running. He ran each day to keep in shape. He also played soccer and basketball. Of all his friends, Dan was the most physically fit.
   B. He was ready. His muscles were tense, waiting. He knew that his competition was tough, and that he would have to run hard throughout the entire race. At the sound of the gun, Dan propelled himself forward, only one thought now on his mind—the finish line.

© 2002 by John Wiley & Sons, Inc.

C. He had worked hard to make the track team. Each morning for the past six months he woke up early and ran three miles before most people were even awake. Over those long months he had built up his stamina. He was now one of the school's top track athletes. He was proud of his accomplishments.

D. He was nervous. This is how he felt when he had to take a test for which he did not study. He wondered if his opponents were nervous. Glancing at them, he decided that they weren't. That only made Dan more uneasy.

Part 4. Directions: Read each paragraph. Choose the sentence that best fits in the blank. Use your Answer Sheet to darken the space of your choice.

1. When Vickie's math teacher, Mrs. Linden, asked her if she would like to tutor younger students in math, Vickie hesitated. She was not sure how much she would be able to help them. Mrs. Linden assured Vickie she would be a big help, and Vickie finally agreed. ________________. Only when she actually began tutoring fifth graders and saw how much they appreciated her help and how much they learned from her did Vickie know she had made the right decision.

   A. Vickie now was excited to help and felt certain that she would do a good job.

   B. After a few days, Vickie decided she did not want to help after all, and she told Mrs. Linden.

   C. Even with her teacher's assurance, though, Vickie was still nervous.

   D. Mrs. Linden was glad that Vickie decided to help.

© 2002 by John Wiley & Sons, Inc.

2. Ben stared at what had been his Aunt Janet's computer. The panel was open and several parts were scattered across the table. His Uncle Bill, who liked to tinker with things, had tried to install a new memory chip. ________________________. Ben sighed and picked up the new memory chip. This was as good a place to start as any.

   A. His uncle finally gave up, muttering that computers were too complicated for any man.

   B. When Aunt Janet realized that her husband could not figure out how to install the chip, she wondered what they would do next.

   C. Only when his uncle realized that he could not put the computer back together did he call Ben, who was the family computer whiz.

   D. Stumped, Uncle Bill called the computer company's customer support line for help.

Name ______________________________ Date ________________

Language Expression

PRACTICE TEST I: ANSWER SHEET

Directions: Darken the circle above the letter that best answers the question.

Part 1

1. ○ A ○ B ○ C ○ D
2. ○ A ○ B ○ C ○ D
3. ○ A ○ B ○ C ○ D
4. ○ A ○ B ○ C ○ D
5. ○ A ○ B ○ C ○ D

Part 2

1. ○ A ○ B ○ C ○ D
2. ○ A ○ B ○ C ○ D
3. ○ A ○ B ○ C ○ D
4. ○ A ○ B ○ C ○ D
5. ○ A ○ B ○ C ○ D

Part 3

1. ○ A ○ B ○ C ○ D
2. ○ A ○ B ○ C ○ D
3. ○ A ○ B ○ C ○ D
4. ○ A ○ B ○ C ○ D
5. ○ A ○ B ○ C ○ D

© 2002 by John Wiley & Sons, Inc.

Name ________________________________ Date ________________

Language Expression

PRACTICE TEST II: ANSWER SHEET

Directions: Darken the circle above the letter that best answers the question.

Part 1

1. ◯ A ◯ B ◯ C ◯ D

2. ◯ A ◯ B ◯ C ◯ D

3. ◯ A ◯ B ◯ C ◯ D

4. ◯ A ◯ B ◯ C ◯ D

Part 2

1. ◯ A ◯ B ◯ C ◯ D

2. ◯ A ◯ B ◯ C ◯ D

3. ◯ A ◯ B ◯ C ◯ D

Part 3

1. ◯ A ◯ B ◯ C ◯ D

2. ◯ A ◯ B ◯ C ◯ D

3. ◯ A ◯ B ◯ C ◯ D

Part 4

1. ◯ A ◯ B ◯ C ◯ D

2. ◯ A ◯ B ◯ C ◯ D

© 2002 by John Wiley & Sons, Inc.

Language Expression

KEY TO PRACTICE TEST I

Part 1

	A	B	C	D
1.	○	●	○	○
2.	○	○	●	○
3.	○	●	○	○
4.	○	○	○	●
5.	●	○	○	○

Part 2

	A	B	C	D
1.	○	○	●	○
2.	○	●	○	○
3.	○	○	○	●
4.	●	○	○	○
5.	○	○	●	○

Part 3

	A	B	C	D
1.	○	○	●	○
2.	●	○	○	○
3.	○	●	○	○
4.	○	○	○	●
5.	○	●	○	○

© 2002 by John Wiley & Sons, Inc.

Language Expression

KEY TO PRACTICE TEST II

Part 1

	A	B	C	D
1.	○	●	○	○
2.	○	○	○	●
3.	○	○	○	●
4.	●	○	○	○

Part 2

	A	B	C	D
1.	○	○	●	○
2.	○	○	○	●
3.	●	○	○	○

Part 3

	A	B	C	D
1.	●	○	○	○
2.	○	○	●	○
3.	○	●	○	○

Part 4

	A	B	C	D
1.	○	○	●	○
2.	○	○	●	○

© 2002 by John Wiley & Sons, Inc.

Appendix

Preparing Your Students for Standardized Proficiency Tests

Even as the debate over the value and fairness of standardized tests continues, standardized tests are an annual event for millions of students. In most school districts the results of the tests are vitally important. Scores may be used to determine if students are meeting district or state guidelines, they may be used as a means of comparing the scores of the district's students to local or national norms, or they may be used to decide a student's placement in advanced or remedial classes. No matter how individual scores are used in your school, students deserve the chance to do well. They deserve to be prepared.

By providing students with practice in answering the kinds of questions they will face on a standardized test, an effective program of preparation can familiarize students with testing formats, refresh skills, build confidence, and reduce anxiety, all critical factors that can affect scores as much as basic knowledge. Just like the members of an orchestra rehearse to get ready for a concert, the dancer trains for the big show, and the pianist practices for weeks before the grand recital, preparing students for standardized tests is essential.

To be most effective, a test-preparation program should be comprehensive, based on skills your students need to know, and enlist the support of parents. Because students often assume the attitudes of their parents regarding tests—for example, nervous parents frequently make their children anxious—you should seek as much parental involvement in your test preparations as possible. Students who are encouraged by their parents and prepared for tests by their teachers invariably do better than those who come to the testing session with little preparation and support.

What Parents Need to Know About Standardized Tests

While most parents will agree that it is important for their children to do well on standardized tests, many feel there is little they can do to help the outcome. Consequently, aside from encouraging their children to "try your best," they feel there is nothing more for them to do. Much of this feeling arises from parents not fully understanding the testing process.

To provide the parents of your students with information about testing, consider sending home copies of the following reproducibles:

- The Uses of Standardized Tests
- Test Terms
- Common Types of Standardized Tests
- Preparing Your Child for Standardized Tests

You may wish to send these home in a packet with a cover letter (a sample of which is included) announcing the upcoming standardized tests.

The Uses of Standardized Tests

Schools administer standardized tests for a variety of purposes. It is likely that your child's school utilizes the scores of standardized tests in at least some of the following ways.

- Identify strengths and weaknesses in academic skills.
- Identify areas of high interest, ability, or aptitude. Likewise identify areas of average or low ability or aptitude.
- Compare the scores of students within the district to each other as well as to students of other districts. This can be done class to class, school to school, or district to district. Such comparisons help school systems to evaluate their curriculums and plan instruction and programs.
- Provide a basis for comparison of report card grades to national standards.
- Identify students who might benefit from advanced or remedial classes.
- Certify student achievement, for example, in regard to receiving awards.
- Provide reports on student progress.

Test Terms

Although standardized tests come in different forms and may be designed to measure different skills, most share many common terms. Understanding these "test terms" is the first step to understanding the tests.

- *Achievement tests* measure how much students have learned in a particular subject area. They concentrate on knowledge of subject matter.
- *Aptitude tests* are designed to predict how well students will do in learning new subject matter in the future. They generally measure a broad range of skills associated with success. Note that the line between aptitude and achievement tests is often indistinct.
- *Battery* refers to a group of tests that are administered during the same testing session. For example, separate tests for vocabulary, language, reading, spelling, and mathematics that comprise an achievement test are known as the test battery.
- *Correlation coefficient* is a measure of the strength and direction of the relationship between two items. It can be a positive or negative number.

© 2002 by John Wiley & Sons, Inc.

- *Diagnostic tests* are designed to identify the strengths and weaknesses of students in specific subject areas. They are usually given only to students who show exceptional ability or serious weakness in an area.
- *Grade equivalent scores* are a translation of the score attained on the test to an approximate grade level. Thus, a student whose score translates to a grade level of 4.5 is working at roughly the midyear point of fourth grade. One whose score equals a grade level of 8.0 is able to successfully complete work typically given at the beginning of eighth grade.
- *Individual student profiles* (also referred to as reports) display detailed test results for a particular student. Some of these can be so precise that the answer to every question is shown.
- *Item* is a specific question on a test.
- *Mean* is the average of a group of scores.
- *Median* is the middle score in a group of scores.
- *Mode* is the score achieved most by a specific group of test takers.
- *Normal distribution* is a distribution of test scores in which the scores are distributed around the mean and where the mean, median, and mode are the same. A normal distribution, when displayed, appears bell-shaped.
- *Norming population* is the group of students (usually quite large) to whom the test was given and on whose results performance standards for various age or grade levels are based. *Local norms* refer to distributions based on a particular school or school district. *National norms* refer to distributions based on students from around the country.
- *Norm-referenced tests* are tests in which the results of the test may be compared with other norming populations.
- *Percentile rank* is a comparison of a student's raw score with the raw scores of others who took the test. The comparison is most often made with members of the norming population. Percentile rank enables a test taker to see where his or her scores rank among others who take the same test. A percentile rank of 90, for example, means that the test taker scored better than 90% of those who took the test. A percentile rank of 60 means that the test taker scored better than 60% of those who took the test. A percentile rank of 30 means that he or she scored better than only 30% of those who took the test and that 70% of the test takers had higher scores.
- *Raw score* is the score of a test based on the number correct. On some tests the raw score may include a correction for guessing.

© 2002 by John Wiley & Sons, Inc.

- *Reliability* is a measure of the degree to which a test measures what it is designed to measure. A test's reliability may be expressed as a reliability coefficient that typically ranges from 0 to 1. Highly reliable tests have reliability coefficients of 0.90 or higher. Reliability coefficients may take several forms. For example, parallel-form reliability correlates the performance on two different forms of a test; split-half reliability correlates two halves of the same test; and test-retest reliability correlates test scores of the same test given at two different times. The producers of standardized tests strive to make them as reliable as possible. Although there are always cases of bright students not doing well on a standardized test and some students who do surprisingly well, most tests are quite reliable and provide accurate results.
- *Score* is the number of correct answers displayed in some form. Sometimes the score is expressed as a scaled score, which means that the score provided by the test is derived from the number of correct answers.
- *Standard deviation* is a measure of the variability of test scores. If most scores are near the mean score, the standard deviation will be small; if scores vary widely from the mean, the standard deviation will be large.
- *Standard error of measurement* is an estimate of the amount of possible measurement error in a test. It provides an estimate of how much a student's true test score may vary from the actual score he or she obtained on the test. Tests that have a large standard error of measurement may not accurately reflect a student's true ability. The standard error of measurement is usually small for well-designed tests.
- *Standardized tests* are tests that have been given to students under the same conditions. They are designed to measure the same skills and abilities for everyone who takes them.
- *Stanine scores* are scores expressed between the numbers 1 and 9 with 9 being high.
- *Validity* is the degree to which a test measures what it is supposed to measure. There are different kinds of validity. One, content validity, for example, refers to the degree to which the content of the test is valid for the purpose of the test. Another, predictive validity, refers to the extent to which predictions based on the test are later proven accurate by other evidence.

© 2002 by John Wiley & Sons, Inc.

Common Types of Standardized Tests

Most standardized tests are broken down into major sections that focus on specific subjects. Together these sections are referred to as a battery. The materials and skills tested are based on grade level. The following tests are common throughout the country; however, not all schools administer every test.

- *Analogy tests* measure a student's ability to understand relationships between words (ideas). Here is an example: Boy is to man as girl is to woman. The relationship, of course, is that a boy becomes a man and a girl becomes a woman. Not only does an analogy test the ability to recognize relationships, it tests vocabulary as well.
- *Vocabulary tests* determine whether students understand the meaning of certain words. They are most often based on the student's projected grade-level reading, comprehension, and spelling skills.
- *Reading comprehension tests* show how well students can understand reading passages. These tests appear in many different formats. In most, students are required to read a passage and then answer questions designed to measure reading ability.
- *Spelling tests* show spelling competence, based on grade-level appropriate words. The tests may require students to select a correctly spelled word from among misspelled words, or may require students to find the misspelled word among correctly spelled words.
- *Language mechanics tests* concentrate on capitalization and punctuation. Students may be required to find examples of incorrect capitalization and punctuation as well as examples of correct capitalization and punctuation in sentences and short paragraphs.
- *Language expression tests* focus on the ability of students to use words correctly according to the standards of conventional English. In many "expression" tests, effective structuring of ideas is also tested.
- *Writing tests* determine how effectively students write and can express their ideas. Usually a topic is given and students must express their ideas on the topic.

© 2002 by John Wiley & Sons, Inc.

Common Types of Standardized Tests *(Continued)*

- *Mathematics problem-solving tests* are based on concepts and applications, and assess the ability of students to solve math problems. These tests often include sections on number theory, interpretation of data and graphs, and logical analysis.
- *Mathematics computation tests* measure how well students can add, subtract, multiply, and divide. While the difficulty of the material depends on grade level, these tests generally cover whole numbers, fractions, decimals, percents, and geometry.
- *Science tests* measure students' understanding of basic science facts.
- *Social studies tests* measure students' understanding of basic facts in social studies.

© 2002 by John Wiley & Sons, Inc.

Preparing Your Child for Standardized Tests

As a parent, there is much you can do to help your son or daughter get ready for taking a standardized test.

During the weeks leading up to the test . . .

- Attend parent-teacher conferences and find out how you can help your child succeed in school.
- Assume an active role in school. Seeing your commitment to his or her school enhances the image of school in your child's eyes.
- Find out when standardized tests are given and plan accordingly. For example, avoid scheduling doctor or dentist appointments for your child during the testing dates. Students who take standardized tests with their class usually do better than students who make up tests because of absences.
- Monitor your child's progress in school. Make sure your child completes his or her homework and projects. Support good study habits and encourage your child to always do his or her best.
- Encourage your child's creativity and interests. Provide plenty of books, magazines, and educational opportunities.
- Whenever you speak of standardized tests, speak of them in a positive manner. Emphasize that while these tests are important, it is not the final score that counts but that your child tries his or her best.

© 2002 by John Wiley & Sons, Inc.

During the days immediately preceding the test . . .

- Once the test has been announced, discuss the test with your child to relieve apprehension. Encourage your son or daughter to take the test seriously, but avoid being overly anxious. (Sometimes parents are more nervous about their children's tests than the kids are.)
- Help your child with any materials his or her teacher sends home in preparation for the test.
- Make sure your child gets a good night's sleep each night before a testing day.
- On the morning of the test, make sure your child wakes up on time, eats a solid breakfast, and arrives at school on time.
- Remind your child to listen to the directions of the teacher carefully and to read directions carefully.
- Encourage your child to do his or her best.

Cover Letter to Parents Announcing Standardized Tests

Use the following letter to inform the parents of your students about upcoming standardized tests in your school. Feel free to adjust the letter according to your needs.

Dear Parents/Guardians,

On ________(dates)________, our class will be taking the ________(name of test)________.

During the next few weeks students will work on various practice tests to help prepare for the actual test.

You can help, too. Please read the attached materials and discuss the importance of the tests with your child. By supporting your child's efforts in preparation, you can help him or her attain the best possible scores.

Thank you.

Sincerely,

(Name)

What Students Need to Know About Standardized Tests

The mere thought of taking a standardized test frightens many students, causing a wide range of symptoms from mild apprehension to upset stomachs and panic attacks. Since even low levels of anxiety can distract students and undermine their achievement, you should attempt to lessen their concerns.

Apprehension, anxiety, and fear are common responses to situations that we perceive as being out of our control. When students are faced with a test on which they don't know what to expect, they may worry excessively that they won't do well. Such emotions, especially when intense, almost guarantee that they will make careless mistakes. When students are prepared properly for a test, they are more likely to know "what to expect." This reduces negative emotions and students are able to enter the testing situation with confidence, which almost always results in better scores.

The first step to preparing your students for standardized tests is to mention the upcoming tests well in advance—at least a few weeks ahead of time—and explain that in the days leading up to the test, the class will be preparing. Explain that while they will not be working with the actual test, the work they will be doing is designed to help them get ready. You may wish to use the analogy of a sports team practicing during the pre-season. Practices help players sharpen their skills, anticipate game situations, and build confidence. Practicing during the pre-season helps athletes perform better during the regular season.

You might find it useful to distribute copies of the following reproducibles:

- Test-taking Tips for Students
- Test Words You Should Know

Hand these out a few days before the testing session. Go over them with your students and suggest that they take them home and ask their parents to review the sheets with them on the night before the test.

Name ______________________________ Date ________________

Test-taking Tips for Students

1. Try your best.
2. Be confident and think positively. People who believe they will do well usually do better than those who are not confident.
3. Fill out the answer sheet correctly. Be careful that you darken all "circles." Be sure to use a number 2 pencil unless your teacher tells you otherwise.
4. Listen carefully to all directions and follow them exactly. If you don't understand something, ask your teacher.
5. Read all questions and their possible answers carefully. Sometimes an answer may at first seem right, but it isn't. Always read all answers before picking one.
6. Try to answer the questions in order, but don't waste too much time on hard questions. Go on to easier ones and then go back to the hard ones.
7. Don't be discouraged by hard questions. On most tests for every hard question there are many easy ones.
8. Try not to make careless mistakes.
9. Budget your time and work quickly.
10. Be sure to fill in the correct answer spaces on your answer sheet. Use a finger of your non-writing hand to keep your place on the answer space.
11. Look for clues and key words when answering questions.
12. If you become "stuck" on a question, eliminate any answers you know are wrong and then make your best guess of the remaining answers. (Do this only if there is no penalty for guessing. Check with your teacher about this.)
13. Don't leave any blanks. Guess if you are running out of time. (Only do this if unanswered questions are counted wrong. Check with your teacher.)
14. Double-check your work if time permits.
15. Erase completely any unnecessary marks on your answer sheet.

© 2002 by John Wiley & Sons, Inc.

Name ________________________________ Date ________________

Test Words You Should Know

The words below are used in standardized tests. Understanding what each one means will help you when you take your test.

all	double-check	opposite
always	end	order
answer sheet	error	oval
best	example	part
blank	fill in	passage
booklet	finish	pick
bubble	following	punctuation
capitalization	go on	question
check	item	read
choose	language expression	reread
circle	language mechanics	right
column	mark	row
complete	match	same as
comprehension	missing	sample
continue	mistake	section
correct	name	select
definition	never	stop
details	none	topic
directions	not true	true
does not belong	number 2 pencil	vocabulary

© 2002 by John Wiley & Sons, Inc.

Creating a Positive Test-taking Environment

Little things really do matter when students take standardized tests. Students who are consistently encouraged to do their best throughout the year in the regular classroom generally achieve higher scores on standardized tests than students who maintain a careless attitude regarding their studies. Of course, motivating students to do their best is an easy thing to suggest but not such an easy goal to accomplish.

There are, fortunately, some steps you can take to foster positive attitudes on the parts of your students in regard to standardized tests. Start by discussing the test students will take and explain how the results of standardized tests are used. When students understand the purpose of testing, they are more likely to take the tests seriously. Never speak of tests in a negative manner, for example, saying that students must work hard or they will do poorly. Instead, speak in positive terms: by working hard and trying their best they will achieve the best results.

To reduce students' concerns, assure them that the use of practice tests will improve their scores. Set up a thorough test-preparation schedule well in advance of the tests, based upon the needs and abilities of your students. Avoid cramming preparation into the last few days before the test. Cramming only burdens students with an increased workload and leads to anxiety and worry. A regular, methodical approach to preparation is best, because this enables you to check for weaknesses in skills and offer remediation.

The value of preparation for standardized tests cannot be understated. When your students feel that they are prepared for the tests, and that you have confidence in them, they will feel more confident and approach the tests with a positive frame of mind. Along with effective instruction throughout the year, a focused program of test preparation will help ensure that your students will have the chance to achieve their best scores on standardized tests.